RENEWAL**DATE DUE** 574

GAYLORD			PRINTED IN U.S.A.

ENDURING SUCCESS

Enduring Success
What Top Companies Do Differently

Franz Bailom, Kurt Matzler

and

Dieter Tschemernjak

Translated by
Matthew Stevenson and Annette Joyce,
Language by Design

© Franz Bailom, Kurt Matzler and Dieter Tschemernjak 2007

First published in Austria in 2006 by Linde as *Was Top-Unternehmen
anders machen*
First published in English 2007 by
PALGRAVE MACMILLAN
Houndmills, Basingstoke, Hampshire RG21 6XS and
175 Fifth Avenue, New York, N.Y. 10010
Companies and representatives throughout the world

PALGRAVE MACMILLAN is the global academic imprint of the Palgrave
Macmillan division of St. Martin's Press, LLC and of Palgrave Macmillan Ltd.
Macmillan® is a registered trademark in the United States, United Kingdom
and other countries. Palgrave is a registered trademark in the European
Union and other countries.

ISBN-13: 978–0–230–55064–3
ISBN-10: 0–230–55064–9

This book is printed on paper suitable for recycling and made from fully
managed and sustained forest sources. Logging, pulping and manufacturing
processes are expected to conform to the environmental regulations of the
country of origin.

A catalogue record for this book is available from the British Library.

A catalog record for this book is available from the Library of Congress.

10   9   8   7   6   5   4   3   2   1
16   15   14   13   12   11   10   09   08   07

Printed and bound in China

For our "master teacher," Professor Hans H Hinterhuber, who always taught us to separate what is important from what is unimportant, to see the larger picture, rather than small details, to find enthusiasm for new ideas and to develop a feeling for vision and strategy. We dedicate this book to him.

Contents

Foreword

This book is written for people who want to make a difference. People who want to make a difference need "the serenity to accept the things they cannot change, the courage to change the things they can, and the wisdom to know the difference" (Friedrich Christoph Oetinger).

This book is intended to provide food for thought and give you the impetus to bring about those changes that are necessary to maintain or increase the competitiveness of the companies you run or the companies in which you work. It should help increase your awareness of what is essential and direct your attention towards those levers that have a decisive influence on the success of the company. "What Top Companies do Differently" is the result of a 4-year research project. It is a synthesis of our scientific studies, our experience in practice, and of numerous conversations with successful entrepreneurs and senior executives. Our objective was to find out the secret of top companies' success. With the help of numerous individuals and institutions, we were able to move a little further towards that goal.

We would like to thank the 1100 senior executives and companies who participated in our studies and made their valuable time and knowledge available to us for our analysis work. Particular thanks are due to Peter Brabeck-Letmathe, Nestlé; Markus Langes-Swarovski, Swarovski; Peter Lorange, IMD; Michael Mirow, Technische Universität Berlin; René Obermann, Deutsche Telekom; Stefan Pierer, KTM; Michael Popp and Uwe Baumann, Bionorica; and Hans-Joachim Reck, Heidrick & Struggles, who, in the course of intensive discussions, provided critical reflection on our research findings. They gave us an insight into their views on leadership and strategy, and their ways of thinking.

This research project was only possible thanks to the commitment of our enthusiastic colleagues at IMP. In particular, our thanks are due to Alexander Kausl and Andreas Staudacher for their considerable support in planning and carrying out the empirical studies: their contributions formed the central pillar of the entire research project. We also thank Johann Wiespointner, Markus Anschober, Josef Storf, and Werner Müller, who engaged us in thought-provoking discussion and whose valuable comments gave us much to think about.

Our thanks go to Artur Bobovnicky, Wolfgang Braitsch, Elisabeth Klapsch, and Monika Miller for their support during the entire research project. Thanks are also due to our co-operation partner, the Institute for International Research (IIR), Austria, Germany, Poland, Hungary, and the Czech Republic, and in particular to Manfred Hämmerle for his support during the empirical research.

We also owe our special thanks to Matthew Stevenson and Annette Joyce of Language by Design for the translation of the book.

In the course of our work we came to the realisation that ideas take time to develop, but that, if the direction is right, it is worth making mistakes, correcting them, learning from them, and taking detours. We hope readers will find just as much pleasure in reading this book as we have found in writing it.

And what did Nasreddin have to say on the matter? A furious author challenged: "How dare you describe my book as bad when you have never written a single book yourself?" Nasreddin replied: "I have never laid an egg in my life either. But I know how good a boiled egg tastes better than the hen does!"

For the sake of readability we have, for the most part, used the masculine form throughout this book; naturally the feminine form is also implied.

Franz Bailom, Kurt Matzler, Dieter Tschemernjak
Innsbruck and Linz (Austria), St Gallen (Switzerland), January 2007

1 In search of the secrets of success

Over 10 years ago, against a background of ever-increasing customer demands, Jack Welch, the former CEO of General Electric, predicted a development that companies in virtually all branches of industry would come to know: "It's going to be brutal. When I said a while back that the 1980s were going to be a white-knuckle decade and the 1990s would be even tougher, I may have understated how hard it's going to get." The results of our many years of research bear out Jack Welch's statement. Customers want the highest quality at the lowest prices. At the same time, many industries are suffering from over-capacity. Increasing market transparency is turning customers into well-informed, merciless buyers and it is becoming harder for companies to differentiate their offerings from those of competitors, which results in fierce competition on price and quality. It is only through continuous innovation and improvement of their products and services or clear price advantages that companies are able to maintain their competitive positions over the long term at all. Practice shows that, despite what are in some cases significant improvements in quality, very few companies manage to maintain their position in the market, let alone increase their prices.

Our analyses of over 1100 companies over a period of 4 years confirm that many companies find themselves in a difficult situation – torn between quality and price. The market demands a continuous increase in quality while allowing very little scope for increasing prices. Around a third of the companies were forced to improve the quality of their products and services without being able to increase their prices. Almost a third even had to accept price reductions despite improved quality.

Furthermore, there is much to suggest that the majority of companies have all but exhausted their potential to reduce costs in their European locations. Many companies work on the assumption that there is little scope to optimize processes further. Senior executives are searching for a way out by taking what are in some cases drastic outsourcing measures, and increasingly switching to low-wage countries.

1

In this context it is striking that, despite these difficult conditions, there are still companies who manage to achieve lasting success and above-average results.

Against this background we set ourselves the objective of discovering the reasons for sustained competitive advantage. That is, we attempted to find answers as to why there are companies who are constantly ahead of their competitors, and to establish which elements within a company must be managed in a certain way due to the relationships between them to bring about lasting success.

This is of course a most ambitious goal, especially since success and failure depend on a myriad of factors. Academics in management theory have been attempting to edge closer to this challenging goal since the 1980s.

In 1982, two McKinsey consultants, Peters and Waterman,[1] triggered a veritable flood of research activities with their book *In Search of Excellence*. The countless studies that have appeared since then have reached vastly differing conclusions according to the method used, the sample surveyed, or the period over which the research took place (Table 1.1). Many of these studies only examined a small number of large successful companies;[2] others focused on small companies who were world market leaders.[3] Some of these studies used large samples of companies as their basis,[4] while others restricted themselves to interviews with the CEOs of visionary companies with proven long-term success and compared them to a control group of less successful companies.[5]

Without doubt, most of these studies have helped us to better understand why certain companies are more successful than others. They have drawn our attention to central issues such as vision and leadership, core competencies, market orientation, corporate culture, and market share, to name but a few.

As convincing as the individual studies are, they differ greatly in the conclusions they reach. There are several reasons for this: first, we believe that the success factors of large American companies cannot readily be applied to medium-sized European companies – the economic, cultural and social environments are too different. Secondly, not all of the studies on success factors were carried out with sufficient scientific rigor, with Peters and Waterman being criticized for not having approached the subject using "reliable research methods,"[6] for example. Many of the companies Peters and Waterman identified as successful were no longer in existence a few years later or ran into serious difficulties. Many of the studies which have appeared up to now identify success factors which are more or less independent of one another. We believe, however, that it is entirely possible that individual success factors can influence one another, making complex models which take such interdependencies and interaction into account necessary if sound conclusions are to be reached.

For many reasons, some scientists are of the opinion that it is not at all possible to find general success factors which apply regardless of industry and size of company.[7] Methodological problems are the primary reason for this.

Table 1.1 The most significant studies on success factors

Authors/book title	Method	Findings
Peters and Waterman: *In Search of Excellence*, New York 1982	Analysis of 43 successful companies	Eight success dimensions: proactiveness; close customer relationships; entrepreneurial freedom; productivity on the part of employees; a system of values the company is seen to live by; focusing on the core business; flexible, uncomplicated organizational structure; freedom and control within company management
Buzzel and Gale: *The PIMS Principles*, New York 1987	Evaluation of a database containing key figures for over 3500 strategic business units	Eight main strategic factors: market share; productivity; intensity of investment; relative customer value; rate of innovation; growth rate of the market; vertical integration; relative costs
Simon: *Hidden Champions: Lessons from over 500 of the world's best unknown companies*, Boston 1999	Analysis of over 500 "unknown" world market leaders	Several common characteristics of unknown world market leaders: they place value on "psychological" market leadership (market leadership is more than just market share); they create market niches and develop unique products; narrow specialization is combined with global marketing; close customer relationships are the lynchpin; innovation provides the foundations for market leadership; they operate in markets with intense competition and gain competitive advantage through differentiation rather than cost; performance and team-oriented corporate culture; strong and dynamic senior executives
Collins and Porras: *Built to Last*, London 1998	Analysis of 20 companies with "cult status," which are visionary and have been successful over the long term	Three formal principles as regards strategy: it is not the supplying of goods and services, but rather creating a stable system for supplying them that is of primary importance (it is not the product, but the business model that counts); the focal point is the duality of "and," and not "either/or" assumptions (e.g. high quality and low costs); organizations need fundamental core values
Nohria, Joyce and Roberson: *What Really Works*, New York 2003	Analysis of 60 companies from 40 industries	The 4+2 formula: companies who excel in the four primary management disciplines (strategy, execution, culture and structure) and in two of four optional secondary disciplines (talent, innovation, leadership, and mergers and partnerships) are more successful than their competitors and increase shareholder value

For instance, if one analyses successful companies only, it could be easy to misinterpret the findings. In his essay on Best Practice studies in the *Harvard Business Review*, Jerker Denrell[8] quotes a lecture on the characteristics of successful companies. Based on an analysis of successful cases, the lecturer came to the conclusion that good leaders had two decisive characteristics in particular: they are able to hold on firmly to an idea despite initial failures, and they can persuade other people about it and sweep them along. This would sound plausible and convincing enough if it were not for the fact that exactly the same characteristics can also be found in senior executives who failed spectacularly having convinced others to throw their money away on a pointless idea too.

The second problem lies in the sample and is known by the term "survival bias." Since, as a rule, particularly unsuccessful companies soon disappear from the market, they are not usually the subject of scientific studies and the reasons for their failure can only be examined with difficulty.

Finally, a phenomenon known in psychology as "causal attribution" arises, particularly in those studies which fall back on interviews with successful and unsuccessful entrepreneurs or senior executives. There is a tendency to attribute success to oneself and failure to other people or to circumstances.

In order to counter such problems in the most effective way possible, we chose a very complex research design which consisted of four main phases and entailed over 4 years' intensive research work in total:

1. As a starting point for our research work we took Richard D'Aveni's[9] idea of hypercompetition, according to which competitive advantages are compensated for by competitors increasingly quickly. According to D'Aveni, a price-quality competition develops which leads to companies constantly having to innovate and increase quality – often whilst under pressure to reduce prices at the same time. Our experiences in practice showed that many companies are indeed subject to this competitive dynamic. But we also observed time and time again that some companies manage to swim against the current: they innovate without coming under pressure to reduce prices. In order to find out how this is possible, we carried out a cross-industry survey involving 371 managers in the first and second tiers of management in companies from Austria, Germany, and Switzerland. We were indeed able to find such companies: around 14 percent of the sample in total. They were not only innovative and able to defend themselves against price deterioration, but were also considerably more successful than all the other companies in financial terms. When we compared these top companies with the rest, we found marked differences in strategic orientation, above all with regard to building on employees' potential, innovation orientation, core competences, market orientation, and cost reductions. We will discuss this in detail in the next chapter.

2. In the second phase of our research project we compared our findings with those of other studies and carried out extensive literature research. We also talked in depth to people in industry and discussed the findings of the study with hundreds of senior executives who were attending lectures at various events or the MBA programs at which we were teaching. A complex cause-and-effect model emerged from this, which we tested empirically in a major international study.

3. For this we developed a sophisticated research instrument which formed the basis of a study involving over 700 senior executives from a representative cross-section of industries and companies of different sizes in 10 European countries. In order to meet the highest scientific standards, the relationships between innovation orientation of top management, competence-based management, market orientation, entrepreneurship culture, strength of corporate culture, innovative ability, market position and the success of the company were estimated using structural equation modeling with Partial Least Squares (PLS), a statistics program which makes it possible to simultaneously test the effects of numerous variables in a complex model. The result was a model which explained a considerable part of the overall success of a company.

4. Albert Einstein once said: "Not everything that counts can be measured and not everything that can be measured counts." This of course applies to empirical management research too. We therefore supplemented our wide-ranging quantitative studies with qualitative interviews with the most successful managers in the German-speaking countries. Their main views are presented in Chapter 11 of this book.

Every year, thousands of articles on management appear in hundreds of academic journals. Around 30,000 different management books are already available and thousands more come on the market every year.[10] Most of them are concerned with single, isolated parts of the puzzle and do not provide the complete picture. This book is also concerned with individual methods and instruments, but that is not our focus. The view of the whole is to the fore. We would like to identify those few key levers that are decisive for the success of a company and to increase top executives' awareness of the things that are strategically significant and therefore require their full attention. We hope we have succeeded in this aim and that, with this book, we are able to make a contribution to increasing the competitiveness of European companies.

2 The customer-value competition is pushing many companies to the limit of their possibilities

The starting point for the first analysis of over 370 companies from Austria, Germany, and Switzerland was Richard D'Aveni's[1] ideas on the topic of "hypercompetition." Essentially, we wanted to find out whether and to what extent the "hypercompetition" predicted by Richard D'Aveni had already become a reality and how companies generally react to it.

Essentially, D'Aveni assumes that globalization, deregulation, and privatization will dramatically change competitive dynamics. The more intense the competition, the more transparent the markets and the lower the switching barriers for customers, the more important it is to persuade customers of the value of a product or service – of the customer value, in other words. The value attributed to a product or service by the customer is the result of two factors: the perceived quality and the price.[2] This can be represented by a two-dimensional matrix (Figure 2.1). Here, there are zones of different customer value: the straight line represents an equilibrium, where the price–performance ratio is balanced. To the right of the straight line, a product or service offers high quality at a relatively low price; to the left of the straight line the price is too high in relation to the quality. If a company wishes to win market share (company A, on the right in Figure 2.1), it can achieve this by improving quality or reducing prices. The competitor positioned immediately next to it (company B) will be forced to react and must follow suit, triggering a chain reaction in the entire market. The equilibrium line shifts to the right: quality increases while the price level remains the same or even falls.

Against this background, we focused on examining companies with regard to the following central questions:

- What is the top executives' assessment of the current and future market and competitive situation?
- What do they consider to be the key challenges with regard to successfully confronting the market dynamics of the future?
- How successful are the companies studied at facing these challenges today and which strategic thought patterns guide them in this task?

7

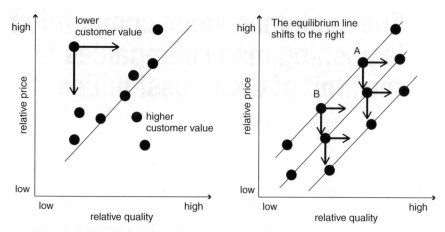

Figure 2.1 Customer-value competition[3]

CHANGING MARKET DYNAMICS – THE PROFITABILITY OF MANY COMPANIES IS INCREASINGLY AT RISK

The results of this first phase of analysis confirm that, aside from the difficult overall economic situation in the last few years, competition has intensified dramatically.

Any advantages gained through quality or innovative advances are counter-acted increasingly quickly by competitors' aggressive competitive behavior. At the same time, price competition has intensified dramatically. Most companies see themselves confronted with an extremely difficult situation which resembles a downward spiral. The constantly increasing quality demands of customers and enormous pressure on prices threaten the profitability of many companies. In the opinion of over 80 percent of the senior executives interviewed, customers' bargaining power has increased significantly in the last 3 years.

These developments have been primarily brought about by over-capacity, fewer differentiation opportunities, and growing market transparency. These factors have turned customers into well-informed, merciless buyers. In the view of the top managers interviewed, at present few companies are still succeeding in differentiating themselves from the competition with lasting effect.

In order to find out what repercussions these competitive dynamics have on companies, we asked the senior executives in our sample a simple question: we asked them to tell us how the quality of their products and their prices had changed in the last 3 years. The results were sobering: they fully corroborated our hypotheses regarding the shifting of the equilibrium line (Figure 2.2):

Increased prices/ lower quality level **1.6%**	Increased prices/ quality level unchanged **4.8%**	Increased prices/ higher quality level **14.3%**
Prices unchanged/ lower quality level **1.6%**	Prices unchanged/ quality level unchanged **8.3%**	Prices unchanged/ higher quality level **27.0%**
Lower prices/ lower quality level **1.9%**	Lower prices/ quality level unchanged **8.3%**	Lower prices/ higher quality level **32.4%**

(left axis label: Price development; bottom axis label: Quality level development)

Figure 2.2 Price and quality development in the last 3 years

- For over 70 percent of the companies interviewed, the quality level demanded by the market had been raised significantly. The companies anticipated a further increase in quality demands in the future.
- Almost 60 percent of the companies were not able to set higher prices despite continual product improvements and a higher quality level.
- Over 30 percent of the companies even had to accept price decreases for their products or services despite a higher quality level.

As a result, companies in almost all industries have to accept a dramatic shift of the equilibrium line to the right of the price–quality matrix. For individual suppliers this means that continuously improving customer value will become a prerequisite for succeeding in this competitive environment.

Consequently, we considered it important to find out which strategic challenges decision-makers consider it necessary to overcome in order to be able to hold their own within this competitive dynamic over the long term.

Key strategic challenges as seen by decision-makers

Evidently only around 14 percent of companies manage to swim against the current; that is, to innovate and command higher prices in the market (see Figure 2.2). In order to check whether these companies are also more financially successful we compared their profitability with that of the rest of the companies: over 56 percent of these companies were more profitable than the industry average, almost 40 percent were averagely profitable, and the rest of the companies ranked lower. Therefore, these companies not only did better with regard to quality improvements and price increases, but were also considerably more profitable. From this point on, we will term these companies "innovators" and the rest of the companies "optimizers."

Enduring success

The greatest strategic challenges

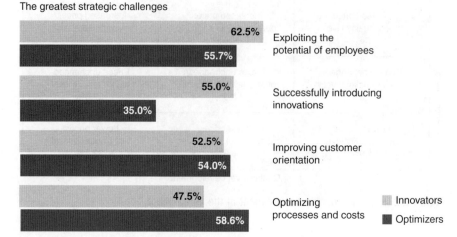

Figure 2.3 Strategic challenges as seen by senior executives

In the view of most of the senior executives interviewed, the future success of a company fundamentally depends on (Figure 2.3):

• the extent to which it can manage to change its cost structures so as to be up to the considerable challenges presented by price competition;
• the extent to which it can manage to increase the commitment of its employees and thereby exploit their real potential in order to make the organization flexible, innovative, and powerful in the international competitive environment;
• the extent to which it can manage to continue to increase customer orientation in spite of enormous pressure on prices; and
• the extent to which it can manage to successfully introduce innovations to the market.

Analyzing these statements enabled us to gain an initial, deeper insight into the strategic thought patterns of the decision-makers, since it revealed that over 80 percent of the companies – the optimizers – seek their salvation in improving existing processes. In doing this, the senior executives allow themselves to be heavily influenced by the paradigm of cost-reduction. This involves making processes even more efficient and better, exploiting the potential of employees in order to realize further cost savings, developing products with as little investment as possible, and making business processes yet more efficient by means of new IT solutions. This group attaches significantly less importance to strategically realigning the company through radical process changes and successfully introducing innovations. In many cases, companies in this group do not really believe it is possible to successfully differentiate themselves from the competition through unique products and services.

Only 14 percent of the companies interviewed – the innovators – put their faith in the development of what are sometimes "radical," market-changing innovations in products and processes. These companies are fundamentally driven by the paradigm of differentiation. Cost-optimization is still a consideration in these companies, but it is not the driving force behind the strategy.

Consequently, the question arose as to how successful the activities of these two groups – the optimizers and the innovators – really are in this highly competitive market environment.

SUCCESS OF THE OPTIMIZERS IN THE CUSTOMER-VALUE COMPETITION

How successful are the optimizers in terms of their cost management?

The results of the study illustrate that, when compared internationally, most of the optimizers have not succeeded in improving their cost structures with lasting effect. This is all the more remarkable considering that 75 percent of all the managers interviewed indicated that they had carried out what were most probably extensive cost-reduction programs in the last few years.[4] These programs primarily focused on well-known courses of action, such as overhead-value analysis and process-cost analysis based on the value-chain concept.

Within the last 3 years, the cost situation of the optimizer group has developed as follows:

- Only 34 percent of the companies managed to achieve a sustained reduction in relative costs.
- 30 percent of the companies indicated that they had held costs at approximately the same level.
- Costs had continued to rise at 26 percent of the companies.

The situation within the companies demonstrates that operational excellence and cost-optimization continue to be key issues. At the same time, however, it is clear that, when viewed overall, measures whose scope is limited to optimizing processes and costs do not go nearly far enough to ensure success in today's competitive environment. This is also borne out by the findings of our study. At almost 65 percent of the companies interviewed, the cost-reduction programs they carried out have brought about no improvement or only short-term improvements in their competitive position.

To what extent do the optimizers succeed in exploiting the potential of their employees?

There is no question that exploiting the potential of employees also plays a key role in helping companies to cope with the challenges they face. This is also shown by the high strategic significance the senior executives interviewed placed on employee commitment. In their view, employee commitment has a decisive influence on the success of both innovations and cost-reduction programs. Eighty percent of the decision-makers see employees' commitment to company objectives as the central success factor with regard to achieving sustained cost-reduction. However, at the same time, the senior executives in the group of optimizers work on the assumption that on average around 60 percent of employees are fully committed to the company; in the case of the innovators, the figure is over 70 percent.

In this context, the findings show that, despite the right level of awareness on the part of the decision-makers, companies are seemingly still failing to implement concepts which increase employee commitment over the long term. In our opinion, a major reason for this is that in many cases employees cannot identify with "their" company in terms of what it does (products/services) or on an emotional level (relationships with colleagues/managers). Often, employees seem to have lost sight of the "purpose" of their company and what it does, and therefore also their "inner motivation." This makes them feel as though they are unable to make an adequate contribution. Accordingly, these employees also have difficulties with regard to their personal development within the context of their working environment – that is, their company – hardly a situation which is conducive to increasing motivation and commitment.

How is customer orientation developing in the optimizer group?

Although the companies interviewed have had a rethink on customer orientation within the last few years and some of them have made large investments, this has in many cases only led to modest successes in this area. Many of the companies were able to increase neither customer loyalty rates nor the number of new customers. A very large number of companies still fail to systematically strengthen customer and market orientation in their organizations. It is not by chance that almost 50 percent of the senior executives interviewed pinpoint improving customer orientation as the key strategic challenge their company faces.

Particularly in the last few years, managers have had to learn from bitter experience that the much-praised customer-relationship management (CRM) systems have made the way the company attends to customers neither more effective nor more efficient. Experience shows that most of these companies neglected to develop innovative strategies for CRM and market development before pressing ahead with the implementation of appropriate CRM systems. Knowledge of the criteria which drive customers' purchasing decisions is a central, basic prerequisite for developing successful customer-relationship strategies. Our many years of research on this topic and our consulting experience support the view that many companies' lack of knowledge about purchase decision-making criteria can be attributed to the fact that they did not use adequate methods in their customer analysis. Often, customers' real problems are not adequately identified and transferred into product–service bundles which deliver value. Furthermore, in our experience, there are also deficiencies as regards the use of permanent systems which continually provide suitable performance measures on which companies can base sound strategic decisions regarding CRM and market development.

What role do product innovation efforts play for the optimizers?

The study shows that, at present, evidently only a few managers in the optimizer group are prepared to make larger-than-average investments in the innovative strength of their company. The innovation management practices of these senior executives are focused primarily on improving existing products and on building relationships with new customers and developing new markets. At the same time, almost 70 percent of the decision-makers interviewed are of the opinion that only very few companies succeed in differentiating themselves from competitors through product innovation.

Hence, in many industries, gearing the innovation process toward the improvement of existing products leads to homogenization. Companies' room for maneuver becomes smaller and smaller. As a consequence, senior executives and employees often spend more time grappling with the competitive situation than with the question of how they could create real added value for customers and other business partners by means of innovations. As a result, true innovations frequently fail to materialize or innovations do not meet market requirements or customer needs.

THE INNOVATORS' SUCCESS IN THE CUSTOMER-VALUE COMPETITION

The analysis of the "innovator" group essentially led us to the following key conclusions: unlike the "optimizer" group, this group has succeeded significantly more often in radically changing the industry. In many cases they actually managed to achieve higher prices in the market by introducing new products or to carve out clear advantages for themselves in terms of value creation and competitive advantage through radically changed business models (Figure 2.4).

Fundamentally, the cause of this is that these companies actively want to change the market. They place particular emphasis on making sure they understand the market and their customers' expectations, as they want to develop

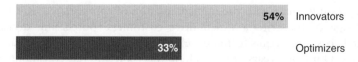

54% Innovators

33% Optimizers

Figure 2.4 Differentiation through innovation

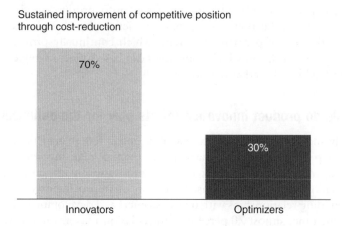

Sustained improvement of competitive position
through cost-reduction

70%

30%

Innovators   Optimizers

Figure 2.5 Effects of cost reduction on optimizers and innovators

the solutions of tomorrow for existing and potential customers. They are considerably more successful than the optimizers at exploiting the potential of their employees. Indeed, the decision-makers of the companies in the innovator group state that over 70 percent of their employees are fully committed to the company.

However, perhaps the most impressive finding is that often these companies not only possess advantages in terms of their products, but that they have also dramatically improved their cost structures over the years. The reason for this is that on the one hand they are far more radical when it comes to critically assessing and changing existing processes and do not merely optimize them; on the other hand they already start thinking about how the processes behind new products and services can be made efficient at the development stage, thereby often securing a favorable cost position for themselves in the process (Figure 2.5).

SUMMARY CONCLUSIONS TO PHASE 1

If one follows Schumpeters'[5] conclusions, a prerequisite for the emergence of value is essentially "creative destruction." This insight is not entirely new, although the growing awareness that, in many industries and companies, changing systems is more important than merely improving them arguably is. The results of our study clearly show that significantly more importance is placed on maintaining existing processes than on creatively developing new ones.

Most companies strive for continuous improvement and optimization and still concentrate very heavily on process and cost optimization. Increasing efficiency becomes the highest goal. But in choosing this goal, companies generally have to accept price-reductions, although they are continually increasing the quality of their products and services. Furthermore, these are mostly purely defensive measures. Numerous empirical studies show that there is hardly any correlation between measures such as downsizing and outsourcing and sustained corporate success.[6] Historically there are few examples of companies which became great through shrinking.

As has always been the case with entrepreneurial activities, visionary thinking, the courage to make radical innovations, as well as systematic customer and market orientation are necessary for building sustained competitive advantage. In addition, the potential of employees should be put to the best use and an environment should be created in which employees can further develop their skills whilst feeling committed and enthusiastic with regard to the company's goals and their own personal goals.

Consequently, we asked ourselves why in today's management practice so little importance is attached to the creative destruction theory put forward by Schumpeter.

In principle, we assume that there are various causes for this. Nevertheless, at this point we wish to critically assess what are in our opinion two very important drivers which are to some extent mutually dependent:

1. How decision-makers view their role; and
2. Growing pressure from the capital markets.

How decision-makers view their role

When it comes to the question of how senior executives view leadership, it is perhaps Jack Welch who most aptly got to the heart of the matter. He pointed out over and over again that "The world of the 90s and beyond will not belong to managers or those who can make the numbers dance. The world will belong to passionate, driven leaders – people who not only have enormous amounts of energy but who can energize those whom they lead."[7] Nicolas G. Hayek, the founder of Swatch and a legend in watchmaking, takes the same line when considering the situation in many companies: "We need the return of entrepreneurs with pioneer spirit and not just managers who manage into the ground what is already there."

These opinions join seamlessly with the work of Hans Hinterhuber. In his book *Leadership*, he notes aptly that "The attractiveness and the profit

and growth perspectives in a market are important, but only partly explain
the success of a company. The attractiveness of the market is like the wind
that blows into the sails: anyone can sail in favorable conditions; in adverse
conditions, however, experienced captains, that is, leadership and strategy, are
decisive when it comes to reaching the destination. Leadership means finding
out which way the wind is blowing, reckoning with calms, and becoming even
stronger in a calm through pro-active behavior. It is not the wind, but the
sails that determine the course. The sails are leadership and strategy."[8]

In this context Hinterhuber also brings out the differences between leadership and management. He essentially points out that leaders always try to
create new paradigms and thereby possess the ability to stimulate and inspire
employees and to enable them to discover and implement new possibilities, as
well to voluntarily and enthusiastically lend their support to the realization of
common goals.[9] In contrast, managers tend far more to work within existing
paradigms and try to do everything to realize the optimal solutions within
these paradigms.

If one followed this line of thinking, one could conclude that most senior
executives carry out their responsible tasks within the company without the
requisite vision or willingness to change or take risks. If one asks why this
"leadership paradigm" has spread so far within the last few years, then the
answer probably lies in the increasing pressure from the capital market, which
forces senior executives to prioritize short-term efficiency and performance
rather than long-term success potential and investments. The idea of shareholder value has gained broad acceptance in Europe too.[10] The international
controls on movement of capital were relaxed as far back as the 1970s, the
European Single Market program was started in the mid-1980s, the Euro
was introduced as an internal currency, and European-competition policies
demand extensive capital market reforms – all of which promoted transparency
in the international capital markets and facilitated the movement of capital. The
pressure to produce high returns for investors grew. At the same time changes
emerged on the management floors of European companies. The introduction
of stock options, more frequent changes in management within companies,
and an increasing number of corporate finance managers and graduates from
elite business schools reinforced this gearing toward shareholder value and
accelerated the introduction of value-oriented management concepts.[11] Since
we consider the shareholder-value approach to be one of the most dangerous
management errors of the last few decades, we would like to discuss it in more
depth at this point.

The influence of increased pressure from the capital markets

With the essay "Selecting Strategies that Create Shareholder Value," which
appeared in the *Harvard Business Review*, and his book, which was published
5 years later, Alfred Rappaport,[12] the father of the shareholder-value approach,

set something in motion which changed management practice with lasting effect and went well beyond most management trends in terms of its intensity and duration.[13] The belief that companies should be run with investors' interests in mind gained wide acceptance. Based on developments in American corporate practice, corporate value increasingly became a primary objective and maximizing it a focus for managerial activity. Senior executives find themselves forced to systematically judge all the business units of the company, its strategies, and its concepts, in terms of whether they raise the value of the company or destroy it. Increasing value became a measure of managerial effectiveness. There is no question that the shareholder-value approach has come in for heavy criticism[14] – its fiercest critics arguably include Fredmund Malik in the German-speaking world and Henry Mintzberg in international management literature – and serious doubts have been raised as to its effectiveness and also to some extent its justifiability. Regardless of one's views on the shareholder-value approach, the fact is that companies – particularly if they are quoted on the stock exchange – are coming under increasing pressure to increase their value. Often, it is hardly possible to manage companies on this basis and there is a great risk that "finance fundamentalists" – as Nestlé CEO Peter Brabeck-Letmathe terms them – will dictate courses of action. The causes of this are the increasing level of finance raised through the capital markets, high capital mobility, and the increasing "majority" of investors. Fredmund Malik, head of the Malik Management Centre in St Gallen, Switzerland, also sees shareholder value as one of the greatest errors in management literature of the last few years:

"The idea that a company's objective must be to increase its value is wrong... The company's purpose must be to be competitive in its chosen area. That is something very different to value. A company is competitive if it can do whatever the customer is paying for better than other companies. For this very reason, one could also logically say that a company's purpose was the same thing as satisfying customers... Creating jobs can be neither a company's aim nor that of shareholder value. A company's purpose is to aim for customer value."[15]

The shareholder value trap

Along with the shareholder-value approach, management practices which put investors' interests first have also taken hold in Europe in the last few years and German-speaking countries have not escaped them. Of course, initially it was above all large public limited companies such as VEBA, Mannesmann, and Siemens who started using value-oriented ratios in their corporate management back in the 1990s, but now unlisted companies are also taking an interest in value-oriented corporate management.[16] As long ago as 1999, two-thirds of DAX 100 companies in Germany stated that they used a value-oriented ratio system in their financial controlling.[17]

However, aiming only at share price increases or maximizing owners' returns holds great danger for companies and society as a whole. According to Henry Mintzberg,[18] one of the leading management thinkers, the shareholder-value approach is driving a wedge into our society. In this context, the practice of tying senior executives' salaries to share prices has also been heavily criticized. Around 95 percent of S&P 500 companies in the USA now grant share options to their senior executives; for DAX 30 companies the figure is way over 80 percent.[19] The problem with this is that remuneration systems become unbalanced. For example, in 1997 Michael Eisner received share options in the amount of $565m as CEO of Walt Disney – that is more than the combined salaries of the top 500 CEOs in Great Britain in the same year. During the 1990s, the average salary of a CEO in the US rose by 570 percent; company profits, on the other hand, only grew by 114 percent. The average wages of workers remained at the level they were at in the 1970s. No society can sustain this situation over the long term. There is a great risk that focusing only on shareholder interests could undermine the foundations of society. Milton Friedman's statement is often quoted: "The only social responsibility a company has is to make profits." Developments in the US, where there are more millionaires than ever, but also more people living under the poverty line than ever, demonstrate that this "flood of affluence" should not only be viewed as positive. In an interview with the journal *Academy of Management Executive*, Mintzberg even said: "We are certainly seeing some of the trend toward shareholder value in Europe. I don't know whether they'll wake up and realize what nonsense shareholder value really is, or whether they will keep pursuing it until people are out in the streets protesting. It is a philosophy of greed, not a philosophy of large institutions serving society as well as their own particular needs. It's antisocietal, and the only advantage to it sweeping through Europe and Japan is that it will decrease the damage of our own nonsense in North America. So if others are stupid enough to do it, that will only help North American business."[20]

From a management point of view, there are primarily two important issues in the shareholder value discussion: (1) the risk of short-term thinking and decision-making and (2) the necessity for growth.

Although the proponents of the shareholder-value approach claim that a management strategy which is rigidly geared toward net present value is in essence a long-term one since unaccrued interest has to be deducted from all cashflows expected in the near and distant future and decisions must be made in such a way that the net present value is maximized taking into consideration risks, practice shows very clearly that short-term share price increases or positive quarterly reports are given precedence. Particularly in the US, where institutional investors, primarily insurance companies and pension funds, hold substantially larger blocks of shares, there is enormous pressure as regards short-term performance.[21] Pension funds in particular have hardly any long-term strategic interest in the companies whose shares they buy, looking instead for investments and returns, that is short-term increases in earnings,[22] which they owe to millions of investors. The situation in Germany is somewhat different. There too large institutional investors – above all banks – hold large blocks of shares. However, it was always the case that these investors had a strategic interest and hardly exerted any pressure with regard to short-term performance. Over the medium and long term, however, the question arises as to what effects changing the state pension system over from the traditional pay-as-you-go system to a fully funded system will have. If in future – similar to in the US – a large proportion of the population wish to secure their pensions through shares, share funds, or pension funds, then substantial shares in companies will be held by owners who will tend to be short-term speculators who invest their money not in companies, but in shares, which they will sell just as quickly as they acquired them if they will make a profit by doing so.[23] Wherever one stands on the shareholder-value approach, the fact is that companies will be increasingly obliged to cover the cost of capital and achieve an increase in value, the main prerequisite for which is securing market position through clearly focusing on customer value.

The second problem raised by the shareholder-value approach is the growth trap. Companies who are committed to shareholder value have to grow – whether they want to or not. A glance at the statistics clearly shows one thing: there can be no lasting increase in value without growth.[24] Figure 2.6 shows that during the period under review, from 1992 to 2001, those American companies who increased their share price or total shareholder return by the most were also the ones who achieved above-average growth.

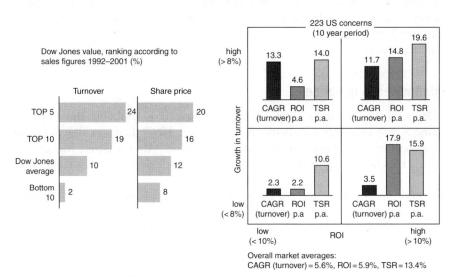

Figure 2.6 Increase in value and growth[25]

Even high and profitable growth is not sufficient to achieve further increases in value, since with highly valued growth companies the growth has generally already been taken into account in the share price.

This can present a dilemma, particularly for large companies. Companies must show growth rates that exceed expectations in order to prevent their share price from falling – regardless of how high the expected growth rates actually were.[26] This leads to a situation where large companies often react too slowly to new or changing markets. Clayton Christensen, a Professor at Harvard University, sees the situation as follows: companies have to grow. The larger the companies are, the more difficult it becomes for them to enter small, newly emerging markets because they – at least in the first phase – do not offer enough growth potential.

We believe that it is not only listed companies that have been heavily influenced by the work of Alfred Rappaport, but small and medium-sized companies also feel increasingly obliged to think in terms of short-term efficiency. In our view, this also results, aside from the market conditions, from the fact that the management thinkers' great "pitches" are heavily marketed. Many senior executives are confronted with this knowledge via books and lectures in an interesting but often unconsidered way. In addition, many consultancy firms present these "new" management approaches and the methods that have been developed for them as all-encompassing solutions, which no company can do without.

At the same time, it should not be overlooked that pressure from the capital markets has also increased considerably for smaller companies. The Basel II rating process and the resulting interest rate policy of the banks have also helped to ensure that a short-term, risk-averse approach is rewarded. In many cases, the readiness to take the risks which are invariably connected with investing in forward-looking innovations is sorely put to the test by increased interest rates.

Unanswered questions

Citius, altius, fortius – faster, higher, further. It is probably the Olympic motto that Pierre de Coubertin formulated in 1897 that best describes the competitive situation of many companies today: "Always faster, higher and further." Or one might also say: "Pressure from all sides." By this we mean:

1. *growing pressure from the customer*, that is, supplying higher and higher quality at lower and lower prices;
2. *growing pressure from the capital markets*, that is, safeguarding the interests of shareholders and guaranteeing adequate returns; and
3. *growing pressure to create value for employees*, that is, bringing on and keeping highly qualified, committed employees in order to exploit their potential.

We are convinced that the long-term success of a company is more dependent than ever on the ability to create value for these three key stakeholders: the customers, the employees, and the shareholders. It is of decisive importance not to lose sight of any of these interest groups. We consider a balanced "increase in value" to be of fundamental importance.

The findings of this first phase of analysis clearly illustrate that under these conditions only a few companies manage to actively develop in a self-determined manner. The cause essentially seems to lie in the management paradigm that prevails today. However, in order to be able to reach sound conclusions regarding the factors which have an influence on sustained corporate success, we dealt intensively with the following questions in Phase two of the research project:

- Where do the decisive differences between successful and less successful companies lie in relation to the success drivers under investigation?
- How is it possible for senior executives to establish the necessary success mechanisms in their companies in order to manage the success factors?

We will attempt to provide answers to these questions in the following chapters.

3 The IMP Model: The strategies of winners

In this chapter we describe the statistical model and the key findings of our study. It provides an understanding of how we defined and measured the success factors and – in simple terms – how we statistically derived our conclusions. Readers who are less interested in these details can skip this chapter and move directly to Chapter 4 in which we proceed with a more practice-oriented discussion of our findings.

The key objective of the whole research project was to identify the driving factors behind corporate success. To this end, in the first step it was essential to define exactly what is understood by sustained corporate success. Defining success purely according to financial ratios seemed to us to be unsatisfactory. Financial ratios are based on past performance; they register changes inside and outside the company too late. If developments have been negatively reflected in financial ratios, it is usually already too late to react. Managing purely according to financial ratios would be like attempting to steer a car at 100km/hr whilst only looking in the rear-view mirror. Therefore, it was important to us to also take other criteria relating to the future into account besides financial ratios. In order to be successful in the short and medium term it is necessary to achieve sufficient return on investment. In order to be successful over the long term, a company must set its course for the future today. Therefore, for the purposes of our study, we defined success according to four dimensions:

1. profitability;
2. growth;
3. advantageous market position with regard to quality, brands, and so on; and
4. subjective assessment by the most senior executives as to how well the company is prepared for the competitive conditions and challenges of the future.

Based on our findings from the first study, we developed a multi-stage research design and passed it through a total of five major phases:

1. In the first step we carried out extensive literature research and went through all the important scientific and practice-related publications of the last 25 years in the area of strategic management and marketing. On this basis, we developed a complex hypotheses model (Figure 3.1) with the objective of investigating cause-and-effect linkages between the success factors we had identified.
2. The next step involved operationalizing the individual factors and thereby making it possible to measure them in order to obtain a basis for the questionnaire in the quantitative study. While doing this we attached particular importance to using scientifically tested question batteries on the individual success factors in order to ensure the highest possible data reliability and validity.
3. In the third step, we defined the sample. The questionnaire was sent to 3000 senior executives in the first and second tiers of management at companies from the widest possible cross-section of industries in more than 10 European countries. Over 700 senior executives, who each represented a strategic business unit, returned the questionnaire.
4. In order to examine the relationships between the success factors we used complex statistical methods, including structural equation modeling, which

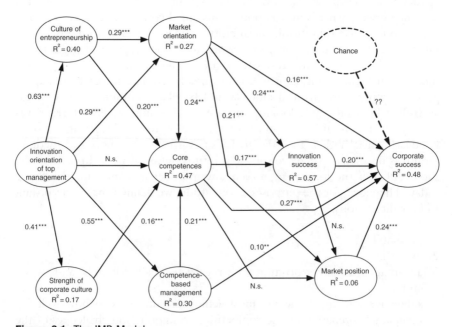

Figure 3.1 The IMP Model

have found strong resonance in management and particularly marketing science in the last few years. In our work we employed the PLS approach.[1] For this we used the software SmartPLS 2.0.[2] This approach enabled us to identify the relationships between the individual factors, which were each measured by a whole range of statements in the questionnaire.[3] As a result we obtained information about whether the statements used in the questionnaire measure in a reliable and valid way (indicator reliability, internal consistency, average variance extracted, and discriminant validity), whether the presumed relationships are also statistically significant, and how strongly the individual factors influence other factors (significance of the relationships and proportion of explained variance, R^2). The results of our statistical analyses meet the highest requirements[4] according to all established criteria and the model also effectively explains a considerable part of corporate success (see Figure 3.1).

5. In the fifth step the more than 700 strategic business units were clustered into three groups based on their performance: top performers, average performers, and underperformers. The criteria used for this were profitability, growth, and market position compared with the industry average, as well as the assessment of future success potential. Subsequently, the companies in each cluster were examined as to their level of performance in the individual success factors so as to better illustrate the specific differences between the groups.

Based on the findings from our study, we were then in a position to develop an evaluation model which enables the individual companies to compare themselves with the top performers in their own industry, as well as in other industries (benchmarking). This will enable individual companies to draw their own strategic conclusions from the study findings.

THE IMP MODEL

In this section we will give a brief description of the model we developed from our research using the PLS approach. It shows the way the success factors work and how they influence each other. From this we derive our core theses, which we will discuss in depth in the following chapters.

We also examined whether and to what extent the (potential) success factors contribute to corporate success (measured in terms of profitability, growth, advantageous market position as regards quality, brands, and so on, and the question of how well the company is "equipped for the future"), as well as how the success factors act in combination.

In this connection, we examined the following success factors:

1. *Market orientation*: By market orientation, we understand the extent to which information about the market (customers, competitors, changes

within the industry, and so on) is systematically generated, whether this knowledge is circulated and shared among the individual departments in the company, and whether it also actually forms the basis for decisions (regarding product development or strategies, for example).[5]

2. *Innovation in products and services*: Here, we measured whether the companies succeed in developing new products and services which give them an edge over competitors, and whether they also succeed in introducing these innovations to the market.[6]

3. *Competence-based management*: By this, we understand a company's efforts to build core competences, to protect them, and to use them to their advantage in the competitive environment.[7]

4. *Core competences*: We define core competences as skills, technologies, resources, processes, know-how, and so on, which (i) are of value in the market, since they offer the customer a particular benefit; (ii) are unique, that is, no other competitor has them; (iii) cannot be easily imitated; and (iv) cannot easily be substituted by other skills, technologies, and so on.[8]

5. *Culture of entrepreneurship*: This type of culture is measured in terms of the extent to which (i) the employees within a company are dynamic and entrepreneurial and also prepared to take risks; (ii) senior executives are entrepreneurs and innovators who are willing to take risks; (iii) values such as commitment to innovation and flexibility prevail; and (iv) strategic priorities are geared toward growth and innovation.[9]

6. *Intensity of culture*: By this, we understand the extent to which there is a strong corporate culture within an organization which finds expression in its own language and shared rituals. Strong corporate cultures are primarily found if (i) management positions are mainly filled internally and the focus is on internal development and (ii) errors tend to be tolerated as long as employees abide by the core values of the company.[10]

7. *Innovation orientation of top management*: We describe top management as innovation-oriented if (i) it continuously encourages employees to think about and implement original and new approaches; (ii) it makes sufficient resources available for innovations; (iii) it is prepared to take the necessary risks to exploit innovation and growth opportunities in the market; and (iv) the most senior executives constantly search for new and unusual solutions to problems.[11]

8. *Market position*: This is measured in terms of the market position the company holds (market share).

THE RESULT: EXPLAINING 50 PERCENT OF CORPORATE SUCCESS IS A LOT, BUT AT THE SAME TIME NOT MUCH

Figure 3.1 shows the model in which the relationships between the success factors can be seen. The numbers on the paths (arrows) indicate how strongly one factor influences the other and whether the relationship is statistically significant. A link labeled with ******* means that there is a very high probability (99 percent) that the relationship found between two factors is not coincidental; thus, for example, a high level of market orientation actually leads to a company's products and services being more innovative. The R^2 figure indicates how much of the variance of the dependent variables can be explained. The factors in the model explain 57 percent of innovation success and 48 percent of corporate success.

Using this research approach, we succeeded in developing a scientifically sound success model with which we can explain the almost 50 percent of corporate success which can be directly influenced. However, we are also aware that success and failure are dependent on a range of factors which cannot be influenced and whose impact could not be reliably evaluated here, such as, for example, oil price increases, wars, terrorist attacks, diseases, and so on.

The senior executives with whom we discussed our model "confirmed" it time and again; equally, they brought to our attention the fact that chance, or rather recognizing and exploiting opportunities, is also a parameter for explaining corporate success that should not be overlooked. We subsequently contacted a number of individuals who had been very successful over many years and asked them: "When you look back on your business successes, what role did chance, or rather recognizing and exploiting opportunities, play?" The answers of these individuals, who, due to their success, did not need to explain to us how well they had had everything under control, surprised us.

They reckoned that at least 20–30 percent of success was determined by chance and gut instinct. We subsequently took every opportunity to ask this question – whether in one-to-one conversations or at lectures. Chance was always confirmed as a success driver. This suddenly put our study findings in a completely different light: we were able to explain 50 percent of success using the factors we had identified which lay entirely within the management's sphere influence; at the same time, taking into account the experiences described above, we had to assume that a further, not inconsiderable part of success was determined by chance and intuition. However, it was no longer possible for us to incorporate the dimensions of chance and exploiting chance into the quantitative model design in this phase. We focus on this subject in a later chapter.

CORE FINDINGS

Our theoretical deliberations, the experiences we gained from working with many companies, numerous conversations with senior executives, and above all the empirical data from our study enable us to draw two key conclusions:

1. The success of a company is determined not so much in the market, but inside the company itself. This may sound somewhat provocative. Of course, it is ultimately the customer who decides a company's success and

competitors also play an important role. However, our opinion here is somewhat different: it is not so much the structure of the markets, the attractiveness of the industry, or the rules of the game within the industry which are the decisive factors; above-average success depends very significantly on factors inside the company. This is borne out by the fact that there are companies which achieve above-average success in completely unattractive industries and very unfavorable conditions. Companies which achieve above-average success, whether in attractive or less attractive industries, have some key common traits. These include, primarily, the ability to innovate, core competences, and market orientation. These factors lie entirely within the sphere of influence of a company's management, which has its hands on the controls through its innovation orientation and the way it shapes the corporate culture.

2. It is not individual management methods and tools, but ultimately the top management team's attitudes, values, thought patterns, and approach which form the basis for sustained success. Of course, methods and tools are necessary for the successful running of a company, but methods, processes, and tools are only of use when it comes to "doing things right," that is increasing efficiency. But being efficient is not sufficient for achieving sustained and long-term success – it is necessary to do "the right things."

Let us now look at the individual findings of our empirical study in detail.

We assumed that the success of a company fundamentally depended on the innovation orientation of its management, the kind of corporate culture it has and its intensity, core competences, competence-based management, innovation in products and services, market orientation and, not least, market position. In fact, the findings of the structural equation model calculated using the PLS approach show that these seven factors explain around 50 percent of corporate success.

For a more detailed explanation of the findings, we will first focus only on the right-hand side of our path model (Figure 3.2). It can be seen that the factors on this side of the model have a direct influence on corporate success. At the same time, the model shows that these factors are to some extent conditional or dependent upon each other to be able to deliver their "effect." For instance, innovation performance is enhanced when market orientation is sufficiently developed, core competences are present and are being exploited, and attention is being paid to developing new competences through competence-based management.

The core competences ($\beta = 0.27^{***}$) and the competence-based management, which to a significant extent determines them ($\beta = 0.10^{**}$), have the strongest direct influence on corporate success in this connection. Over a decade ago, Prahalad and Hamel wrote in an essay in the *Harvard Business Review* that "Only core competences ensure survival."[12] This view became prevalent in strategic management theory and practice. The findings

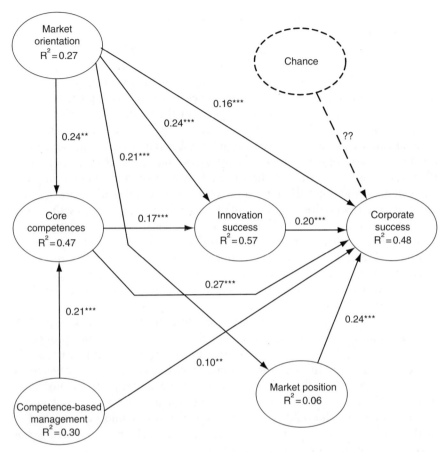

Figure 3.2 Success as a result of market orientation, innovation ability, market position, and core competences

of our study also provide firm evidence that developing, nurturing, and exploiting core competences bring about above-average success. Possessing and managing core competences means developing unique skills, resources, know-how, and/or processes. If these skills and resources are of value to customers, if they are rare and, at the same time, cannot be imitated or substituted, then we term them "core competences."

We speak of competence-based management when companies attempt to develop such core competences and align strategic decisions, such as focusing, innovation decisions, market entry, or outsourcing, with their core competences. The results of our study confirm this assertion: core competences have a strong influence on corporate success. However, we also examined the relationship between core competences and innovative ability and found a further, indirect correlation between core competences and success, which comes about through innovation.

Market position also plays an important role ($\beta = 0.24$***). A dominant market position not only brings about economies of scale and experience curve effects, which lead to cost advantages and therefore higher returns; sometimes a dominant market position makes it possible to influence, or even decisively determine, the rules of the game in the market. In particular, the PIMS studies[13] have shown how important market position is for success – especially where products and services are not differentiated. At the same time, our findings also illustrate that in many areas uniqueness is more important than size. We also examined the extent to which market orientation, core competences, and innovation in products and services influence market share. Only market orientation increases market share; in our study, neither core competences nor innovation in products and services had a significant influence on market share. At first glance this is counterintuitive, but it can be explained. Here, we must first remember that market position was measured in comparison with competitors. This means that we did not examine the relationship between these factors and growth, but the relationship between these factors and market leadership.

Core competences do not automatically lead to market leadership; they relate to unique resources and skills which either lead to inimitable products or services (behind which there is a differentiation or niche strategy), or to significant cost advantages through, for example, process or technology competences (behind which there is frequently a cost–leadership strategy). In the first case, it could be that low market share goes hand in hand with core competences; in the second case, it could be that core competences could generate higher market share. Therefore, although there may be a relationship, there is not necessarily one, and it may not be a direct one.

The finding that innovation in products and services does not automatically lead to higher market share is also counterintuitive, but this too can be explained. Being innovative means being first to the market. The question of whether innovators, that is pioneers, generally also have higher market shares has been tested in numerous studies. Although the findings were not always clear-cut, some studies indicated that this relationship does not always exist. For example, in a large-scale study within 50 product categories, Gerard Tellis and Peter Golder[14] found that innovators and market pioneers only held a dominant market position in 11 percent of cases; on average, market share was 10 percent. How can that be explained? Practical examples, in particular, seem to contradict this. For example, Procter & Gamble describes itself as the inventor of the nappy, which the company introduced to the market in 1961. However, the nappy had in fact been introduced back in 1935 under the name of Chux. Procter & Gamble was therefore not the innovator; in 1961, Chux was even named as the best brand of nappy by Consumer Reports and a few years later the brands were still rated as equal. Only over time, due to superior marketing by Procter & Gamble, did Pampers achieve a significantly higher market share than Chux.[15] In reality, Apple was not the pioneer of the personal computer, either. The PC from MITS (Micro Instrumentation and Telemetry System) was introduced as early as 1975 and was described by *Business Week* in 1976 as "the IBM of home computers."[16]

Frequently, innovations are connected with a differentiation or niche strategy; only follower companies aim for the mass market. Therefore, market-leading follower companies are often associated with the innovation and the real innovators remain unknown, often focusing only on small niches or the small group of "early adopters" and not on the mass market.

Innovation in products and services only leads to dominant market positions if companies also home in on the mass market, their management pursues the objective of market leadership with vigor, there is the necessary financial commitment, the product is continuously enhanced, and the relevant resources as well as brand awareness, distribution strengths, and so on can be exploited.[17] Therefore, there is not always a direct relationship between innovation in products and services and market position or between core competences and market position. It is also vital to recognize that there are different market phases. Only when companies succeed in developing strategies which correspond to these market lifecycles, will it be possible for them to change from pioneers into market leaders.

We mentioned at the start that competitiveness can only be safeguarded by continuous innovation – often with little or no scope for increasing prices. Therefore, it is not surprising that the ability to continually successfully improve or even redevelop products and services and thereby make them more innovative has a strong influence on corporate success ($\beta = 0.20$***). The company's ability to produce these innovations is in turn significantly determined by market orientation ($\beta = 0.24$***) and existent core competences ($\beta = 0.17$***).

Ultimately – and this belief has not only become prevalent in management and marketing theory – the market and in particular the customer decide the success of a company. Therefore, it is very significant whether companies effectively and efficiently pick up signals from the market, circulate and process them within the company as necessary, and respond to them with programs and strategies. We describe companies who master this as market-oriented and the results of our study show clearly that customer and market orientation have an influence on success ($\beta = 0.16$***).

The five factors explained previously – core competences, competence-based management, innovation in products and services, market orientation, and market position – are important drivers of success. If these factors are well developed in a company (it has strong core competence management, it successfully introduces innovative products onto the market, it is very market-oriented and currently holds a strong market position) it is highly likely that the company will be very successful. However, in our study we went a step further and asked ourselves the following question: if these are the five key drivers of corporate success, then what factors affect them; that is, how is it possible to influence the drivers? Let us now consider the left half of our path model (Figure 3.1).

Whilst market orientation, innovation in products and services, core competences, and competence-based management are closely connected with methods and processes, we will now address the soft factors, which are far more closely connected with attitudes, values, and orientation.

Working on the assumption that innovative performance determines the future viability of a company to a considerable degree, it appears from the data that innovative performance is in turn significantly determined by competence-based management, existent core competences, and market orientation. The question is, what influences these factors? The results show clearly that a company is in a position to build and manage core competences if high innovation orientation on the part of top management leads to competence-based management, and there is an entrepreneurial corporate culture ($\beta = 0.20***$), a strong corporate culture ($\beta = 0.16***$), and market orientation which extends beyond the here and now. Building and developing core competences requires the concentration of strengths, setting objectives for the long term, comprehensive and far-reaching understanding of the market, the willingness to invest, the courage to leave gaps – in the sense of jettisoning "ballast" – and also the willingness to take risks. Building a strong culture of entrepreneurship within the company requires that the most senior executives consistently bring in visionary thinking and constantly require it of employees, that employees are familiar with the company's strategic goals and can identify with them, that employees recognize what contribution they can and should make within the company and, above all, that core values exist within the company which are actually lived by and which directly or indirectly drive forward the whole company's willingness to innovate and change things.

Building market orientation which extends beyond the here and now requires:

- that the most senior executives look intensively at the company's markets and the developments outside the company's immediate market segments;
- that marketing departments are established which take on the challenge of really intending to identify new market opportunities before these become obvious;
- that platforms are established within the company in order that these opportunities can be collectively discussed; and
- that processes and structures are set up which ensure that the market knowledge that has been collectively gathered is exploited.

We were able to show with our study that the probability of success increases significantly if the above-mentioned elements are present and there is the necessary interplay between them. Finally, one can see from the model that the innovation orientation of top management has a decisive influence on these dimensions and their interplay, and one can deduce from this that, ultimately, a company's success is decisively determined by its strategic positioning and the ideals and values of senior executives that underpin it.

4 What makes top performers different

To enable us to generate sound information about the fundamental differences between successful and less successful companies, we compared data from over 700 companies using the path model we had developed. Using a number of indicators, we additionally measured how well defined the identified factors were in each company. For example, a high value for the "market orientation" factor means that the company should be regarded as very market-oriented, because:

- many activities are undertaken to generate information on the requirements of current and potential customers and competitors' activities, and so on;
- this information is communicated and discussed on a broad basis within the company; and
- this knowledge is an important basis for business decisions (for example, for the development of completely new products).

The results illustrate the significant differences between successful and less successful companies with regard to the identified success factors.

In the following section, we intend to explain these particular characteristics in more detail and to illustrate them by using concrete examples selected from the group of top performers (the best 15 percent). First of all, the following specific characteristics can be identified:

- Top performers never settle for today's success because they explicitly assume or "foresee" that, in principle, every market is subject to a lifecycle. They see their own role in this process as drivers of innovation in the corporate system who must keep initiating and driving forward radical strategic changes.
- The most senior executives themselves look intensively at today's market and the emerging opportunities in the entire market system. Based on this knowledge, they can recognize which of the company's competences need to be strengthened and they are prepared to invest in them.

- Top performers impress with an extensive understanding of innovation and they are conscious of the fact that they must also pay particular strategic attention to introducing their innovations to the market.
- In their competitive strategies, top performers rely more on being unique than on "just" winning market share.
- Top performers possess a particular kind of corporate culture which is actively shaped, demanded, and promoted by the most senior executives.

TOP PERFORMERS NEVER SETTLE FOR TODAY'S SUCCESS

Companies' success depends significantly on the most senior executives. This bold statement results from the insight that companies who achieve above-average success have something in common that starkly distinguishes them from less successful companies. Top companies and, in particular, the most senior executives never settle for today's success under any circumstances. The constant will to change both large and small things emerged from the analysis as perhaps the most significant cardinal characteristic of companies who achieve above-average success.

For example, when asked what he sees as the principal reason for Nestlé's success, Peter Brabeck-Letmathe, the CEO of Nestlé, answered: "It is not a question of thinking about what has made us successful in the past; the question is primarily what we must do so that we will be successful in the future. I'll think about the reasons for the success we've achieved when I'm retired. At first that sounds very simple, but it is perhaps the most difficult task for companies, particularly if they are already very successful, because if they are already successful the organization continually attempts to draw on past success patterns. This seems logical at first and above all gives those involved a feeling of efficiency and security. That is exactly what they must resist using all means available."

Michael Mirow, who has been head of strategic planning at Siemens for over 15 years, takes the same line: "In my experience, today's success represents one of the greatest dangers for companies. Companies should not allow themselves to become frozen in today's success and no longer agonize about what they need to do for tomorrow's success. I am convinced, and my experience tells me this, that tomorrow always works differently to today. But in order to master tomorrow, companies must do everything they can to prepare themselves today. By that I mean that the entire management team must also think radically now, for who can really guarantee that success will continue for the next 10–20 years with today's products and technologies. Unfortunately, it has often been the case that very successful business units have been the ones to miss radical leaps in technology. They were so enthusiastic about the here and now, that they could always produce reasons which argued against a change. But at some point the market and requirements did actually change and there was in fact no more time available to act in a meaningful way."

These two statements are representative of a wealth of statements from very successful senior executives with whom we had the opportunity to speak in depth about success and failure during the course of this research project.

There is no doubt that it is important to know that successful companies place the highest strategic importance on constant change or further strategic development. However, only when we understand why they do this so rigorously will we be able to grasp the necessity of this way of thinking.

Fundamentally, what lies behind it is the ability to free oneself from current day-to-day business matters and to view market activity from a "helicopter perspective," as Hans Hinterhuber[1] continually insisted in his works. Because if one enters this meta-level, it becomes immediately clear that every market passes through the different phases of a lifecycle. A market emerges, grows, becomes saturated, and must be revived by radical changes if it is not to disappear into insignificance. It is beyond dispute that nobody can estimate how long the individual phases will last and it is also possible that a phase will be missed out. However, it is crucial that companies realize that this market logic has always existed and that it will always be there in the future too. Continuous further development involves continually introducing new pioneer phases in the company in good time.

If we look at the less successful companies, it is noticeable that in many cases they find themselves in an advanced phase of market maturity with their products and services. They are battling on all fronts with increasing competition. At first the situation seems no more worrying than usual because they manage to survive in the short to medium term by improving existing processes and achieving the associated reductions in costs. In the medium to long term, though, many of these companies face an almost insoluble problem. On the one hand they are not in a position to create a "new" market or to bring about a change in the market; on the other hand they lack the know-how and necessary structures for developing markets that are in phases other than maturity. In many cases they do not have the knowledge, resources, or structures that would enable them to enter and develop a new market or to drive through a change in a market that is in a maturity phase.

The successful companies try to "anticipate" the markets of tomorrow. Sometimes their decisions in favor of a particular field appear highly risky and are also roundly condemned by analysts, who are driven by shareholder value. Analysts cannot deal with this way of thinking, which implies a willingness to invest in areas whose profitability can often not be assessed there and then – that is not where their interest lies. They are not interested in the fact that future viability can only be assured if there is very early investment in opportunities which are not yet 100 percent manifest.

Our conversation with Stefan Pierer, CEO and major shareholder of KTM, a large European manufacturer of motorcycles, clearly illustrates this strategic way of thinking. In 1992, Stefan Pierer bought parts of the company from the bankrupt's estate. Within a few short years, he and his team managed not only to develop KTM into a very profitable company, but also into one of the largest motorcycle manufacturers in Europe with the highest growth rates. When asked where he sees KTM's future, he answered: "We bought the motorcycle division of KTM. Behind it lay the know-how for manufacturing excellent off-road motorcycles. Initially, we focused on setting up the business anew and soon saw that we were already well on the way to achieving this. During this phase I reached the decision to enter the street-motorcycle business. This was a completely different business, and at the time we didn't really know how it actually worked. Almost everyone – both inside and outside the company – more or less said I was crazy. We lacked know-how, we had no access to the market, and so on, but it was clear to me that the growth potential that KTM needed could only lie in the street-motorcycle sector. We took a different path to our established competitors: we decided to build a new category of street motorcycles using unusual technology and with an unusual design, and it worked. Today, we face a new challenge. In the future the motorcycle market is unlikely to continue to experience the growth rates we would hope for. We need only observe that nowadays many 18-year-olds no longer take their motorcycle test because they're told from all sides – and rightly so, unfortunately – how dangerous riding motorcycles is, so we at KTM have to ask ourselves how we're going to deal with this. We're going to build a car. Again, it will be a completely new concept and, again, everyone is saying I'm crazy. I realize that it's risky too. Therefore, we must take all the necessary measures to minimize the risk, without letting that slow us down. But if I see at any point that we're not going to manage it, I'll stop the process before it destroys us. But from today's standpoint it would be at least as risky in the long term not to try it."

These examples clearly reflect what the empirical data we analyzed from over 700 companies brought to light. At the companies who achieve above-average success, the most senior executives are themselves the most important innovation drivers in the companies. As a next step, we were then interested in finding out about the fundamental similarities this group of senior executives share. At the same time, we were of course conscious of the fact that these successful senior executives differ greatly in their character, manner, and leadership style, but there was reasonable evidence to suggest that, on a fundamental level, there is something that makes this group stand out.

THE MOST SENIOR EXECUTIVES ARE THEMSELVES THE INNOVATION DRIVERS IN THE COMPANY

When we talk here of innovation drivers, we do not mean that the senior executives create the actual product innovations, although that also happens; what we understand by this term is that they drive the corporate system forward in such a way that the organization is "forced" to continually make radical (innovative) observations on a product, process, and business model level.

So what similarities were we able to identify when analyzing this group of top senior executives? For the purposes of the analysis, we first concentrated on leadership literature[2] and conversations with leading managers who have demonstrated above-average success with companies over a sustained period. Secondly, we also took the opportunity to talk in depth to Hans-Joachim Reck, a partner at Heidricks & Struggles, one of the leading headhunting companies worldwide, as well as to Peter Lorange, the President of IMD, one of the world's leading business schools, about their views on the common characteristics of the people at the very top.

- A particular characteristic that these leading managers share is that they are real visionaries. They want to create something with their companies that goes way beyond financial success. When talking to them it is noticeable that they say very little about current problems and that they far prefer to reflect on future opportunities. It is particularly striking that, as they do this, they do not give one the feeling that they are chasing illusions, but rather can very clearly explain why and for what reason they are confident about following a particular path. What impresses one is their practical, specialized market knowledge, as well as the knowledge from completely different fields and areas that they draw on and link up. Furthermore, they convey something which is very difficult to describe. It is this feeling, this emotion, that there is something very special and far-reaching about this or that path or, as Viktor Frankl would perhaps say: "That you yourself can sense a purpose in it."
- However, this visionary outlook does not prevent them from seeing that in order to be able to drive forward the necessary developments they need the best senior executives and employees.

Professor Popp, the CEO of Bionorica – one of the leading European phytopharmaceutical companies – put his finger on it when he said: "I always had a certain idea of the way we had to develop the company, but for a long time we only came closer to our goals with great difficulty. Although the management team always gave actions their nod of approval, they never really put their heart, soul, and commitment into actually implementing them. Only when I became fully aware of this and we replaced key members of the management crew did the success start to come. On the one hand, the new management crew had a considerably more critical approach during discussions than the managers I had replaced. They called far more into question and long discussions were necessary for a common agreement to be reached as to which opportunities we should concentrate on. I have to admit that there were also times when the team did not share my convictions and, in spite of this, I still held on to them. The remarkable thing was that my team did not leave me in the lurch following such 'radical' decisions, but instead used all their ability and put 100 percent commitment into actually setting these things in motion. The success that subsequently materialized was only possible due to the quality and commitment of these employees. Today, we are even more radical in our approach than we were back then and it works unbelievably well."

Although these senior executives know that the quality of their management team is crucial when it comes to implementing their ideas, they try to maintain contact with as many employees from as many different hierarchy levels within the company as possible. They themselves get involved in different training programs and question-and-answer sessions and they try to talk directly to employees as they do their rounds.

A former employee of GE said of his experience with Jack Welch: "In 1990, I moved to the European Headquarters of GE Plastics in Holland where I was responsible for logistics. After a short time, I was accepted into a group with 13 other employees who twice a year had the opportunity to speak face-to-face with Jack Welch, not only to listen to his views, but also to be asked for their personal opinions by him. In the group were people from different hierarchy levels and areas of responsibility. These sessions were the greatest thing I've had the opportunity to experience in my career up to now not only in terms of content but also, in particular, in terms of emotion. You can't put into words what these conversations triggered in us all. The great shining light discussed with us the core strategic issues that, in his view, GE should concentrate on, as well as things we only partly understood, could not categorize or were only peripherally involved with in our day-to-day business. He talked, asked, and really listened to us. I especially remember that at the beginning of these sessions he always reported on the core strategic issues. These 'sermons' were always tremendously electrifying because during them you could really experience this individual's authenticity and strength of will." This employee left GE 10 years ago, but when you speak to him about it today, you can tell he is still a GE man at heart. Jack Welch held this exchange of views throughout the entire concern with many groups of employees.

- However, it is not only these individuals' visionary approach and their desire to interest the best employees in their company; they are also impressive because, in their own individual way, all these individuals are very proud of their companies' products and services. If you have the opportunity to speak to them about it, you can sense that they know exactly what their products can do and where the benefit for the customer lies. An impressive example of this is the positive experience we had with Mr Brabeck-Letmathe, the CEO of Nestlé. During our visit to the group headquarters in Vevey, we did not only receive tremendously valuable tips and comments on our model; the CEO of a company that sells a billion products worldwide each day personally presented his products to us. During our conversation, Peter Brabeck-Letmathe pointed out that it is extremely important to him that the people in the headquarters never forget that Nestlé's success is primarily based on its products. The systems are merely tools for safeguarding the necessary processes. For this very reason he decided that the fifth and highest floor of the exclusive headquarters should not accommodate the top management. Instead, Nestlé's products should be displayed there, there should be the opportunity to taste them, and pleasant rest areas should be set up for employees so that they come into contact with the products every day. As we were leaving, Mr Brabeck-Letmathe said: "If you have a little more time, I would like to show you our fifth floor too." We went via a wide staircase directly from the main nerve centre of Nestlé Plc into the "Nestlé exhibition." The way he escorted us through the different product areas was fascinating.

- However, top senior executives do not only know and cherish the products and services, but, in particular, they also know and understand their markets and customers. The time and commitment that they invest in them are impressive. On average, they spend more than 50 percent of all their time moving around in the markets, either spending time directly with customers or at their respective branches. They are far less interested in reports and figures than in ensuring that, by holding direct conversations, they will not lose the feeling, as they often describe it, for the customers and the market logic. Doing this enables them to refocus on the question of what they must do in order that they will be successful tomorrow.

- They possess an extraordinary head for business which they themselves often describe as intuition, gut instinct, or exploiting chances. When they reflect on their successes, they point out that at least 30 percent of the really major strategic decisions were essentially "intuitive decisions" and that, often, exploiting chance or unplanned events played a significant role in them. According to Peter Lorange of IMD, what distinguishes these really successful senior executives is, among other things, a certain instinctive fine feeling that is extremely difficult to understand and explain. In his opinion, they recognize and exploit opportunities that others only begin to see much later on.

The findings of our research project presented so far show that top performers are driven by a massive will to change things. This will to make changes is fundamentally shaped by the most senior executives. However, it is also clear from looking at the common characteristics of leading individuals that we identified that these visionary individuals do not act in isolation. They know that they need the best senior executives and employees and act accordingly; they identify with the companies' products and services, they know and understand the markets and their customers because they take the time to find out about them through personal experience, and they possess an extraordinary head for business which enables them to quickly exploit chances as they arise.

TOP PERFORMERS SUCCEED IN COMBINING FORWARD-LOOKING MARKET KNOWLEDGE WITH SUSTAINED COMPETENCE MANAGEMENT

During the analysis, the question arose as to whether and to what extent orientation toward the market and the development of unique competences play a role at the successful and less successful companies.

It emerged that the top performers fundamentally geared themselves toward the basic principles of the resource-based view in their strategy development. They know their core competences very well and attempt to create new market opportunities with these competences. At the same time, however, creating and developing new core competences also plays a decisive role in their strategic planning, since these companies realize that, in order to safeguard their success over the long term, they must establish new core competences to be able to respond to the constantly changing challenges of the markets with new solutions. When developing new competences, the top performers continually concern themselves with the question of which direction the markets of tomorrow are developing in. However, for them, this means considerably more than customer orientation. They do not settle for identifying and fulfilling existing customer expectations; in their view, strategic success depends on the extent to which they can succeed in creating new customer expectations and new markets. A key prerequisite for this is continually sourcing market knowledge (customers, competitors, markets, technologies). This involves far more than just fulfilling customers' existing desires; it is about anticipating the problems customers will have tomorrow. At the same time, they know that they must anticipate the market systems, rules of the game, and technologies of the future in their entirety, since there is little point in developing products for the problems customers will face tomorrow if they do not know which technology to use to introduce them into the "new" market. During this process, they connect the market knowledge they have generated with the question of which competences they must build within the company and within the entire market system in order to actually establish sustained competitive advantage.

For example, thanks to the grinding technology which was developed by Daniel Swarovski back at the end of the 19th century and then constantly improved, Swarovski has created a skill set within the company that enables it to produce and cut crystals in a unique way. Up to now, no competitor has been able to imitate this skill set, which starts with materials sourcing and goes right through to production, cutting, and grinding. The core output are crystals that inspire customers, thanks to their variety, their shapes, their colors, and the way they play with the light.

The Tirol-based family business, which today has over 16,000 employees and turns over more than €2m, was essentially an anonymous supplier to fashion and light designers until the mid-1970s. Since then, Swarovski has not only accomplished the feat of turning a "cheap product," fashion jewellery, into a luxury product, but has also transformed itself into a global luxury brand.

In what was perhaps the most difficult phase in the company's history – the mid-1970s, when the oil crisis plunged the market for crystal chandeliers and haute couture into crisis – Swarovski decided to no longer only supply crystals to industry, but also to produce figures – initially it was only animal figures – by gluing together crystal pieces, and to sell them under its own name. These figures became real collector's pieces all over the world. Swarovski recognized customers' needs and founded its own club to accommodate them. Today, around 450,000 club members have the latest figures delivered to them annually.

In the midst of this success, Swarovski began to think seriously about other markets which might be interested in the crystal expertise from Wattens, Austria. It recognized the enormous potential of the "new" fashion market. At that time, crystal appliqué was not en vogue. Swarovski asked himself which additional competences the company would need in order to be able to exploit this potential. The company began to step up its contact with fashion designers and increasingly put its product development team onto looking into fashionable uses for crystal. It soon recognized that it would need its own trend experts to be able to develop this market really successfully. The company began setting up its own trend department, which has since worked exclusively on locating new trends way ahead of time and developing suitable stones and crystal applications in good time. Today, together with the world's most renowned trend researchers, designers and artists, this group continually publishes design magazines in which every conceivable creation is presented. The success that has resulted from this is impressive. Today, so many of the world's best-known fashion designers use Swarovski's products and know-how that the *Frankfurter Allgemeine Zeitung* has already written about the "Swarovskiization" of fashion.[3]

The group of less successful companies tends to rely on a significantly different approach to strategy development. On closer observation, it soon becomes apparent that, essentially, only a few managers really concern themselves with their customers' problems, let alone work on solutions to them. Many senior executives focus far more intensively on their competitors and try to outstrip them in one way or another, since they hope that by doing this they will be able to hold their companies on a successful course over the long term. Executives at board level frequently fall prey to a fatal error: they consider the fact that their company works "better," "faster," or "more cheaply" than its competitors as proof that their products also address the desires and needs of customers better. Orientation toward competitors is at the fore and these companies' prime concern is analyzing and observing them. The potential for innovations remains marginal with this approach, as the tools companies use do not enable them to identify customers' future problems either. In many cases, this leads to a situation where companies are always chasing the market and are never involved in shaping it.

TOP PERFORMERS SHOW AN IMPRESSIVE UNDERSTANDING OF INNOVATION

In his memoirs, Werner von Siemens wrote: "In my view, a significant reason that our factories flourished so quickly was that the products we were manufacturing were for the most part based on our own inventions. Although in most cases these were not protected by patent, they still always gave us a lead over our competitors which usually lasted long enough for us to gain another lead through new improvements."[4] What Werner von Siemens said over 50 years ago has lost absolutely none of its relevance today.

There is much to suggest that ever-increasing international competition on price and quality results in companies – especially those from high-wage countries – having to significantly improve their innovation performance to compensate for the disadvantages of their location. However, unlike in the past, it is necessary for companies to have an extensive understanding of innovation, which must take process as well as product innovations into account. At the same time, they must pay particular attention to the speed factor with respect to all aspects of innovation. According to Werner Steinecker, a director on the board of Upper Austrian Energie AG, the success formula is "imagination × speed," as nowadays the principle of "the big ones eat the small ones" applies less than the principle of "the fast ones eat the slow ones." Profits from investments must be invested in new developments as rapidly as possible if competitive leads are to be maintained.

Product innovations

With products that are successful today, companies must increasingly aim to introduce new product generations with clear benefits to the markets at considerably shorter intervals. Only by doing this will they open up the opportunity to command the higher market prices that are necessary for European locations. At the same time, European companies must be significantly more prepared to invest in radical, rather than incremental, innovations than in the past. Other studies also show this. There is a close correlation between the proportion of radical innovations and return on innovation.[5] Radical innovations, however, can only come about if a company sets itself the goal of developing new solutions for the markets of tomorrow.

In Peter Lorange's view, it is recognizing opportunities which are not obvious that is the starting point for radical innovations: "When it comes to developing real product innovations, companies must understand two things:

1. Marketing departments must take on the challenge of really intending to identify new market opportunities before they become obvious. This is the only way it will be possible for them to actively shape the market and to not always have to chase the market. This requires that marketing departments in particular are shaped by visionary thinking and are not just guided by a copycat mentality. However, today it is often the case that vast amounts of quantitative market research data are evaluated and processed in marketing departments by young and sometimes very inexperienced marketing people. There is no doubt that this is of considerable help to companies in identifying low-risk innovation strategies. Frequently, though, this conceals the danger that endless statistical analyses obscure one's view of what is really important, that is, the future. This makes it impossible for the marketing department to perform its proper role – that of an innovation driver.

2. The most senior decision-makers must be prepared to set up this kind of marketing department in their companies. In addition, it is particularly necessary that they insist that their marketing departments take a considerably broader and more open approach to market research activities. For example, this involves intensifying qualitative market research activities, carrying out active market observations on the ground, obtaining the opinions of internal decision-makers who actually operate within the market, or searching for information sources which lie completely outside the company's own market. At the same time, the most senior decision-makers must ensure that the information that has been gathered is not evaluated by the marketing department in isolation, but discussed and processed in conjunction with many different decision-makers within the company. The most senior executives must themselves assume a central role in these discussion sessions; only then will they be able to provide research and development departments with a clear development brief with regard to these opportunities. Elaborating and signing off such briefs is the task of top management. This is because strategies and their implementation in the market can only really work within the framework of concerted actions on the part of the whole company."

Process innovations

Companies must also dramatically increase their innovation performance on a business-processes level. It is necessary to take what may be radical approaches in order to significantly improve cost structures at an international level. Sometimes it will be necessary to align value-creation chains in a completely different way to the way they are aligned today.

T-Mobile International provides an impressive example of a cost-reduction program which has had lasting effect. René Obermann, Chairman of the Board of Deutsche Telekom, knew when he took on the role that the strategic focus for the next few years had to be on market as well as cost innovations. Along with his team, he initiated the "Save4Growth" program.

"Right in the phase when we were consolidating our market leadership in Germany, we had to ask ourselves how we would be able to safeguard this success over the long term. During the discussions regarding market developments that we had at the time, it became clear to us that we had to optimize our cost structures in the light of increasing innovation. Even back then we recognized that competition would dramatically increase and that improvements in quality would not enable us to increase our prices. We decided, among other things, to develop a program which would enable us to exploit all the cost-optimization potential in the company without reducing our level of innovation. During this process, it was particularly important to me that this potential was identified and exploited from our own ranks. We initiated a project under the title of 'Save4Growth,' in which the 40 most important senior executives of T-Mobile were to participate. We decided that these 40 top managers should work closely together every day from 8 o'clock in the morning until 4 o'clock in the afternoon for 6 weeks in order to share experiences on this subject, to analyze and discuss, and of course to formulate ideas and suggestions for meaningful cost savings. From 4 p.m. to 7 p.m. – and sometimes it was, of course, far later – each team member carried out his or her 'actual' management tasks. It was a radical project which helped us make tremendous progress on two levels in particular. After 6 weeks, we had formulated over 120 individual building blocks; many of these offered huge savings potential, others less so. On the whole, though, what was impressive were ideas the team had come up with for taking T-Mobile forward through innovation, including where costs were concerned. At the same time, something had come to life within this team which was of tremendous importance for realizing the more than 120 projects. We were all proud of the results and realized that we had to carry this very emotive topic into the company together, for it was clear to us that the workforce would not welcome us with open arms and that for this very reason we would have to do everything in our power to convince them of the benefits of the 'Save4Growth' path.

When we toured through the regions presenting our program, which entailed some radical changes, to employees and other stakeholders, things turned out as we thought they would. We sometimes faced resistance at or after the presentations but the team worked on doggedly using all their persuasive powers and we soon noticed that the employees were starting to come to terms with the program. However, this was not enough for us and we stepped up our personal commitment. After about a year, the success we had been striving for slowly started to come. An increasing number of employees recognized the opportunities behind the program and one could feel the growing emotional commitment. Then things moved quickly and today I venture to say that we in the company are, for the most part, proud that we are more effectively able to exploit new opportunities through our 'thrift.' We invested and continue to invest what we save in new developments and markets with a promising future. Today, I would venture to say that our cost structures are best in class, without us having put our innovation and quality leadership at risk."

If one considers the top performers as a whole in terms of the innovation logic demonstrated above, it is striking that they systematically endeavor to realize innovations at both levels. In this regard it is particularly striking that these companies frequently try to drive forward innovation in an integrated way. That is, many of them set themselves the objective of setting up and using radically changed procurement and production processes during the development of completely new products and services. By doing this they are on the one hand striving for innovation leadership, while aiming at optimizing their cost structures using what are sometimes radical approaches on the other. This also explains the results of our studies, which illustrate that top performers not only possess competitive advantages, thanks to their innovations on the product side, but that many of them also have better-cost structures than the other companies compared at an international level. Over two-thirds of the top companies have been able to make a sustained improvement in their competitive position during the last 3 years, thanks to the cost-reduction programs they have introduced. In comparison, less than 36 percent of the remaining companies in our studies succeeded in doing this, even though their main focus was on costs reduction.

The different importance that companies attach to innovation as a whole becomes evident when they are viewed in terms of how embedded innovation is within the organization. Every second top company has implemented systematic innovation processes, whilst this is the case with less than a third of the other companies.

TOP PERFORMERS RELY MORE ON UNIQUENESS THAN ON MARKET SHARE

In April 1981, Jack Welch took over the management of the heavily diversified General Electric group. When he retired in 2001 he was named "Manager of the Century" by Fortune magazine in recognition of his extraordinary achievements for GE during the course of his 20-year period in office. The group's profits had increased eightfold and the group's share price had risen by approximately 5000 percent.[6] One of Jack Welch's key principles immediately after assuming his post was the rule "#1 or #2: fix, sell or close."[7] Each business unit had to reach position one or two in the market. If this did not happen, it was sold. If it could not be sold, it was closed. Behind this lay a simple but effective principle: return on investment is heavily dependent on market position. This had primarily been shown by the PIMS studies.[8] There is no doubt that relative market share is an important driver of success.

Economies of scale and experience curve effects (learning effects) cause unit costs to decrease as volumes rise. This generally gives market leaders clear cost advantages. Jack Welch's principle of "#1 or #2: fix, sell or close" has been much copied and market share has been elevated to a key strategic objective.

There are of course numerous industries in which market position is the decisive factor. It is said that there is an experience curve effect of around 50 percent[9] in the production of computer hard drives; that is, each time the cumulative production volume is doubled, the unit costs are reduced by 50 percent. At one clothing manufacturer we were able to calculate an experience curve effect of 65 percent. Car manufacturers work on the assumption that the economies of scale which are necessary if they are to be competitive on a global level can only be achieved with an annual production of 100,000 units.[10] Market position is the decisive factor in all cases where volume has a significant effect on costs and where suppliers primarily operate a cost–leadership strategy in the overall market.

However, overall, it should never be forgotten that the strategic significance of experience curve effects should always be considered from two viewpoints. First, the experience curve concept should always be seen in the context of the industry in which the company is operating. Secondly, it is also necessary for companies to consider which market segments within the relevant industries they actually operate or intend to operate in. In the case of the niche manufacturer Porsche, currently one of the most successful car manufacturers, it is clear that experience curve effects play another role, than is the case for the Volkswagen Group. In particular, this differentiated view of experience curve effects and economies of scale affects the majority of small and medium-sized companies. They often operate in clearly defined niches and the basic strategy is usually differentiation.

The results of our study clearly show that although market position indisputably has an important influence on success ($\beta = 0.24***$), uniqueness in the form of core competences is of even more fundamental importance; it has a direct effect ($\beta = 0.27***$) and an indirect effect – through innovation success ($\beta = 0.17***$) – on corporate success (see Figure 4.1).

So uniqueness is, in many cases, more important than size. Fredmund Malik even said: "Size is increasingly unimportant ... the awkwardness of large companies, their bureaucracy, the lack of orientation in middle tiers of management, their slowness, and so on, paralyze their size advantages."[11]

Clayton Christensen, a professor at Harvard University, also points out the pitfalls of "unbridled" growth: companies must grow, due to shareholder-value thinking, among other things. The larger companies are, the more difficult it becomes for them to enter small, newly emerging markets, as these markets – at least in the first phase – do not offer sufficient growth potential. Whereas a €50m company needs an additional turnover of €10m to attain a growth rate of 20 percent, a €5m company needs a €1m market to attain the same growth rate. Therefore, large companies often assume a waiting position until

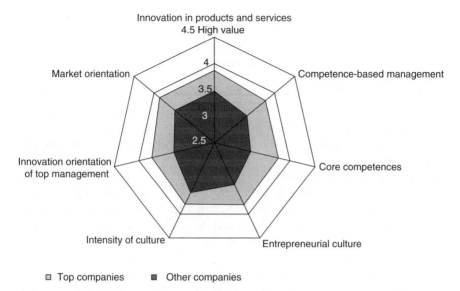

□ Top companies   ■ Other companies

Figure 4.1 The differnce between top companies and the rest

the new market is large enough to be interesting, but then it is often too late. Small companies have already entered the market with an innovation. This could be seen with digital photography, handhelds, and music downloads, as well as with the Minimill steel technology or hydraulic excavators. In all these cases, the established companies held on to tried-and-tested technology for too long, since the newly emerging markets were too small and offered too little growth potential – until what were mostly small innovators took over the market with completely new technology.[12]

A study by Thomas Hutzschenreuter,[13] who examined over 637 companies of different sizes over a period of at least 13 years, also shows that striving blindly for growth does not automatically lead to success. The findings of this study are sobering. Almost 90 percent of these companies were markedly growth-oriented. However, only around 20 percent of them managed to also increase their value; the remaining 80 percent destroyed value through growth. Of course, the reasons for this are manifold. The fact is, however, that it is extremely difficult for a company to remain profitable and increase its value whilst it is experiencing strong growth. So it seems that growth is not a magic bullet.

The reason for this is that the pressure to grow can put long-term competitiveness at high risk, since this way of thinking often leaves no scope for innovations.

At this point, one should once again keep in mind the entire dynamic that ultimately makes successful companies what they are. It seems obvious that this dynamic can only come into existence if the majority of employees are prepared to be a part of it. If one follows this line of thinking, the key significance of corporate culture becomes immediately obvious.

But what lies behind the term "corporate culture," and why is this type of culture so crucial for success?

Mary Douglas,[14] an anthropologist, provides some very enlightening answers to this question. In her opinion, culture is essentially the things that are important to a group. This is about significantly more than "values." Based on this, Frenzel, Müller, and Sottong[15] deduce that: "We direct our energies toward and concentrate our resources on what is important to us; what is important to us controls the way we think. We are prepared to overlook and ignore other things for it – and even to disregard orders and norms. Based on the dominant type of 'importance' within a company, a group does certain things over and over again, it adopts certain practices and rituals in order to prevent certain things from happening and to make it probable that certain other things will happen."

In this process, it is ultimately the top senior executives who decisively "determine" – through their decisions, their attitude, the things they communicate, and their rules – which things are important in and for the company. The type of culture that results from this consequently determines which chances, possibilities, and options a company recognizes in the first place and doggedly pursues, or whether it is blind to the opportunities that arise along the way.

TOP PERFORMERS PUT STRONG EMPHASIS ON CULTURE DEVELOPMENT

The results of our analysis clearly illustrate that a very particular type of culture is significantly better developed at the top performers than at the remaining companies. For the most part, top performers possess a type of culture that we would term an "entrepreneurship culture."

Corporate cultures can be differentiated according to two dimensions.[16] They can either be more oriented toward the market, competition, and customers, or place the emphasis on internal processes, integration, and harmonization of processes. The second dimension represents a continuum between the extremes of organic and mechanical processes. The emphasis is either on flexibility, continuity, and individuality, or control, stability, and order. We describe cultures which are outward-looking and which foster flexibility and spontaneity as entrepreneurship cultures. They possess the following characteristics:[17]

1. The dominant characteristics are entrepreneurship, dynamism, and the willingness to take risks, rather than standardization or formalization.

2. Senior executives assume the role of entrepreneurs and innovators who are prepared to take risks, rather than being coordinators or administrators.
3. The forces that hold the company together are a commitment to innovation, flexibility, and entrepreneurship, instead of rules, procedures, and guidelines.
4. The strategic priorities are innovation and growth and less so constancy, stability, and smooth-running procedures.

Furthermore, it is striking that the top performers attach considerably more importance to actively working on the company's culture than the other companies. They believe that dealing with the increasing market dynamic in a proactive way demands a new dimension from companies in terms of their will to change and their readiness to change. In our view, flexibility and speed are becoming the mainstays of ensuring a company's long-term survival in more and more sectors. For this reason, the top performers are convinced that everything must be done to counteract the latent risk of constant resistance to change in the companies. For this, they especially need to understand that working on the company's culture is a further fundamental factor in ensuring future success and is perhaps one of the most important tasks of top management.

The results of our analysis show that the following dimensions of culture development are at the fore of top performers' thinking:

- They try to involve their employees considerably more intensively in their own company's strategic work than the other companies do. In their view, only when as many employees as possible are familiar with and understand the real challenges in the market environment and their own company's strategic options can they gear their actions and sense of responsibility accordingly. For them, a culture of open information and intensive discussion are of key importance in this context.
- They try to drive forward innovative organizational and personnel-development concepts whose goal it is to break down mental barriers and to bring about an openness toward new things. Their aim in doing this is, in particular, that the senior executives and employees will once again begin to concern themselves, independently and in teams, and in a more creative and above all forward-looking way, with the company's challenges, in terms of the small and the big picture.
- They are striving to bring about a positive "we feeling" in the company which is based on "important points" which the company lives by and which speak to the employees on an emotional level. This is about developing a new kind of stability for employees – detached from processes and business models – since the necessary will and readiness to change can only be achieved if there is emotional security for employees, despite the constant "upheaval." In future, without this emotional "glue" of shared

"importance," it will not be possible to create a "community" of employees who will fight for their company with the necessary commitment.

- They put all their resources into ensuring that all their senior executives possess the necessary leadership qualities and are able to bring about this common sense of "importance." Only then is it possible to kindle the desired goal-oriented commitment in as many employees as possible. If the company succeeds in doing this, the employees will also be able to identify more strongly with "their" company and its products or services, as well as with "their" job. Furthermore, our experiences show that employees in top companies have the feeling of being integrated in terms of their relationships with both other colleagues and superiors. This helps employees identify with and feel more attached to the company, which in turn greatly helps to increase their commitment. Through this kind of culture development these companies manage better than others to arouse the willingness of their employees to actively make changes themselves, to home in on and foster the relevant skills of the employees, as well as to provide the opportunity for individual employees to get involved in the company's objectives. Employees from top companies also exhibit a higher degree of commitment than employees from the remaining companies in our study.

Markus Langes-Swarovski gave us an impressive example of kindling common "importance" in a genuine and dedicated way. He underlined the fundamental strategic importance of active culture development for Swarovski's corporate success:

"For us, the company's culture has always been an important key to our corporate success. About 3 years ago, when the new generation took over the management of the company, we initiated an integrated strategy process. It seemed only logical to me that culture development should be a key cornerstone in this process, since I was conscious of the fact that we could only remain successful if we constantly change and develop further. To this end, it was necessary to achieve and encourage a certain will to change within the company. This is tremendously difficult, especially in successful phases, as each change appears, at first glance, to lead to additional work and expense and to uncertainties which can negatively affect current performance. For this reason, I asked myself how I could succeed in systematically embedding this willingness to change in Swarovski. It was clear to me that this plan must involve giving the senior executives and employees really fundamental anchor points which would illustrate to them at all times that they should continually venture to think up and try something new. Swarovski's history was of great help to me in this task.

"The future always needs an origin."

When I intensively studied Swarovski's history, what I had always been told became crystal clear to me in the truest sense of the word. Daniel Swarovski, the founder of the company, was a progressive avant-gardist and a courageous entrepreneur who knew how to introduce new success phases using radical steps again and again. This spirit was also well developed in the following generations and it became clear that willingness to change and avant-gardism have always constituted the actual entrepreneurial core of the company.

"Constantly disturbing the core is the task of company management."

I set myself the objective of developing this core further and it became clear to me that my main task must be to constantly disturb the company with feeling and to challenge it. However, first it was important to develop really challenging objectives and ideals for the future of the company with which one could identify, particularly on an emotional level.

"A 111-year-old viewpoint reaching beyond the parameters of the moment."

We began – initially in a small group – to describe challenging ideals for the company. While doing this, we thought about the implementation process right from the start. As we did this it became clear that first the dialog and in particular the discourse about these ideals could create the momentum that could trigger change. Consequently, we created platforms in the company management on which it was possible to discuss the future whilst at times being completely detached from today's situation. This discourse, which is institutionalized today, continually breaks down established ways of thinking.

"Culture development as a core element of branding from the inside."

At the same time, it was also important to bring all our employees to the point where they continually reflect on the future of the company. In my view, this is the only way to trigger an emotional bond to the company which will make it possible to develop the corporate culture further. We decided to base this process around Swarovski's branding, since we were convinced that our brand was the "hook" for our identity and culture.

In order to stimulate this process of internal branding, we developed a series of tools, which, among other things, used "euphoric TV pictures" from staged events to show future opportunities for the company. For me, the success of this exercise can partly be seen in the fact that these pictures emotionally moved our employees to the point of being touched. This approach even resulted in a very special vocabulary developing within our company.

"Transporting our brand values by means of poetry and art."

In the center of this was always the "brand romance" we had developed in collaboration with artists, which was to transport our brand values by means of poetry and art (explosion of expression). Professionally designing these communication instruments is a key prerequisite for success. During brand-romance events at Swarovski, we had various pictures of the Swarovski company professionally filmed by directors from Los Angeles. That is, good realization of the ideas was always of great importance to us.

However, it is not sufficient to hire professional scriptwriters if these values and the possible future of the company are not shared honestly and emotionally. It is important to keep in mind that we only developed these very elaborate tools for the purposes of internal communication with our employees. But when content and form come together and 16,000 employees feel the Swarovski brand, you can save a great deal on traditional advertising. Nevertheless, crystal also represents the perfect medium for telling stories. Although the employee does not get a finished answer, he has a good basis on which to think about the future of the company. Of course, such activities must run parallel to the "classic" strategy process. Furthermore, it is important to create an open platform for discussion and discourse without changing all the main features of the brand. The brand should provide us with the direction for growth and thereby keep its validity, since collective ownership can come about through repetition."

During our conversation with Markus Langes-Swarovski, we were ourselves "electrified" by the intensity with which he conveyed to us the spirit he is striving for. In the last few years, he has himself spent around 50 percent of his time on developing and implementing this "culture program." He was himself heavily involved in the presentations and discussions on history, strategic objectives, brand romance, and so on, at all hierarchy levels right through to production.

In this chapter we have described the relevant success factors and their combined effect using the success model we developed as a basis. In performing this task, a particular concern of ours was to show the differences between the top performers and the remaining companies with regard to the model and to illustrate them using selected examples. However, it is important to us to give you some new ideas along the way which may enable you to give substance to the building blocks of success contained in the model within the context of your company. Therefore, in the following chapters we will study the individual building blocks of success in greater detail and attempt, through scientific insights and practical experience, to characterize the new challenges and provide new food for thought.

5 Market orientation: Understanding markets, shaping the future

As our model shows, market orientation is one of the key drivers of success. We describe as market-oriented those companies which (1) continuously generate knowledge about markets and stakeholders; (2) systematically distribute this knowledge within the company and make it accessible to the key decision-makers; and (3) base their innovations and strategies on this market knowledge. Formulating the market strategies which result from this process is a task for top management, and it is becoming increasingly important. Three trends account for this in particular: (1) the new sources of innovation; (2) increasingly complex market systems; and (3) the failure of classic, quantitative market research techniques where innovations are concerned.

SOURCING MARKET KNOWLEDGE: THE NEW SOURCES OF INNOVATION

Successful innovators distinguish themselves by systematically exploiting all the sources of knowledge outside of the company. They have an open innovation process and integrate external R&D results and innovations, they integrate key customers into development processes, and they exploit the potential of user innovations.

The R&D – including basic research – is a strategic asset for many large companies. However, giants of the industry, such as IBM, DuPont, or Siemens, are facing increasing competition from small start-ups which carry out little or no basic research of their own[1] and nevertheless successfully bring innovations onto the market with a fraction of the resources of their competitors. These companies have a different understanding of innovation and make their innovation processes completely open by systematically exploiting the knowledge of suppliers, customers, research institutions, or partner companies.

According to Henry Chesbrough from Harvard University a paradigm shift – from a closed to an open innovation model – lies behind these developments.

Table 5.1 The open versus the closed innovation model[2]

Principles of closed innovation	Principles of open innovation
"The best people work in our company"	"There are many good people outside the company whose potential we can exploit"
"We need our own R&D"	"External R&D can provide us with valuable help; internal R&D should help us to better exploit external R&D"
"We need our own R&D in order to be the firstmover"	"We do not have to invent everything ourselves to be the innovation leader"
"The winners will be those companies who can transform their own R&D into innovations on the market the fastest"	"A good business model is more important than being first on the market"
"We will win if we develop the best ideas and innovations ourselves"	"We will win if we are the best at exploiting internal and external ideas"
"We must protect our intellectual property so that we cannot be copied"	"We must benefit from the intellectual property of others and exploit it if it will be of benefit to us"

Whereas in the past innovations were, in the main, generated in the R&D departments of companies, in the future innovation will increasingly take place in innovation networks. This involves exploiting all sources of innovation inside and outside the company. Competitiveness will increasingly be a question of exploiting network resources. Companies which work according to the open innovation model adhere to a few characteristic principles (Table 5.1): (1) they cooperate with the best people inside *and* outside the company; (2) they exploit R&D outside of the company – their own R&D primarily serves to harness external expertise; (3) they believe that they do not have to carry out R&D in-house in order to benefit from it; (4) they believe that a superior business model is more important than being first on the market; (5) they believe that the companies who are the best at exploiting internal *and* external knowledge will win on the market; and (6) they benefit from the knowledge and know-how that they make available to others and from the knowledge and know-how of others with whom they cooperate.

Open innovation processes

The basic conditions for innovations have radically changed in the last few years.[3] Important innovations increasingly come from small and medium-sized companies, as well as start-ups, "knowledge workers" are increasingly mobile and want to sell or license their intellectual property, research establishments and universities see new sources of income in marketing their knowledge and are increasingly entering into partnerships with industry, and the Internet provides completely new ways of searching for the best experts for certain problems and their solutions anywhere in the world.

Successful companies have already reacted to these changed conditions, they systematically exploit all internal and external innovation sources and see opening the innovation process up to the outside world as a means of accessing ideas and marketable solutions more quickly and less expensively. The principle of "innovations emerge inside the company" has changed into the principle of "innovations emerge in networks" a long time ago. In many industries, more innovations come from the outside than from the inside. Even back in the 1980s, almost 80 percent of innovations in scientific instruments came from customers; in the manufacture of semiconductors and circuit boards, the most important innovations do not come from the developers of the relevant process technologies, but from the semiconductor manufacturers themselves. In the case of thermoplastic applications around a third of innovations came from suppliers.[4] A McKinsey study of the automotive industry shows that even today around 65 percent of a car is already being built by suppliers; by the year 2015, this proportion is predicted to have increased to 75 percent.[5] This is changing the competition between companies into a competition between networks. Only the companies with the best and most innovative network partners can achieve the highest level of innovative ability. Systematically and effectively exploiting external knowledge from partners will therefore increasingly become a matter of survival.

Exploiting external knowledge

The Bell Laboratories are arguably among the most well-known research centers in the world. The best researchers work there – up to now 11 Nobel Prize winners have contributed to Bell Labs' success. Lucent inherited Bell Labs from AT&T and was in the best position to be successful in the market for telecommunications equipment. Nevertheless, without having anything approaching the R&D resources of Lucent, Cisco Systems succeeded in keeping up with Lucent and to some extent even beating it on the market.[6] Lucent and Cisco are direct competitors in a market involving very complex technology; both competitors regularly bring innovations onto the market – with one major difference: the resources that are employed and the way innovations come about. Lucent invests large sums in researching new materials and developing components and systems which have been the basis of radical innovations in numerous products and services. Cisco, on the other hand, constantly exploits the knowledge that already exists outside the company. The company continuously and systematically keeps a lookout for start-ups which are bringing new products and services onto the market. Cisco invests in these start-ups – some of which have been founded by ex-Lucent employees – and enters into partnerships with them or acquires them. In this way – that is, through integrating external knowledge and the results of R&D efforts outside the company – Cisco manages to keep up with probably the best research institutions in the world without having to make large investments in its own R&D. This is not an isolated case: an increasing number of companies systematically search for innovations outside their own company boundaries and then integrate them.

In 2002, Procter & Gamble, a manufacturer of consumer goods which has a long and successful tradition of in-house research, set itself the objective of generating 50 percent of its innovations outside the company within 5 years. To achieve this, it created the role of "director of external innovation."[7] His task is to link the company with as many external R&D partners as possible, to change the innovation culture and above all to battle against the "not-invented-here" syndrome and redefine R&D within the company. This is not about outsourcing R&D; it is about searching for good ideas externally, assessing them with regard to their marketability, and integrating them in order that Procter & Gamble's researchers and developers can develop new products and bring them to market more efficiently and effectively. The idea is simple: there are around 8600 scientists within Procter & Gamble; there are around 1.5 million outside the company. The 15 most important suppliers to Procter & Gamble employ over 50,000 R&D staff, who offer enormous potential which can be exploited. Today, Procter & Gamble maintains fruitful networks with numerous R&D partners and suppliers. For example, YourEncore, an Internet platform which brings around 800 retired top scientists and engineers from 150 companies together with customers was founded as part of this networking strategy. This enables Procter & Gamble to bring an enormous wealth of experience and expertise from other companies and industries into its own company. Currently, over 35 percent of innovations at Procter & Gamble come from outside the company. In the year 2000, it was still 15 percent: the success rate of innovations has more than doubled.

Even Nestlé, the world's largest food company with over 240,000 employees, uses external innovation in the process of transforming itself into the world's leading food, nutrition, health, and wellness company. The company set up its own Corporate Wellness Unit at the highest level for this transformation process and equipped it with the necessary resources. Essentially, this unit must drive forward change in the internal and external mindset. This task involves, in particular, developing scientifically sound competitive advantages with regard to wellness and health in the product portfolio. In addition to carrying out research and development work internally, Nestlé has also founded two funds. One is a venture fund, in which a group of specialists pursues the objective of seeking out interesting developments in the areas of health and wellness from all over the world and participating in them. In particular, the specialists look into the development work of small research groups or small companies. Should something appear promising, they try to participate in it and to support the research and development work with resources. Those developments which actually produce interesting products are subsequently transferred into the second fund. This fund has the task of developing the product idea into a successful business. Those companies whose products realize a certain volume of business are then taken into the Nestlé organization. This enables Nestlé to first track down and test ideas in the market very quickly and flexibly and subsequently to market only those products with the best prospects of success in the most global rollout possible.

The Internet provides entirely new ways of accessing external knowledge and innovations. This presents many companies with major challenges. Some of them have neither the resources nor the expertise to open their innovation process in the way that Procter & Gamble has done, for example. Therefore, in the last few years, companies have emerged which specialize in making it easier to use the Internet "marketplace" for innovation and mediate between "innovation seekers" and solution providers; one might say they act as "innomediators."[8]

On average, developing a new medicine costs $500m and takes around 15 years up until the point when the medicine is patented. Therefore, pharmaceutical companies are continuously looking for new ways to improve the R&D process and make it less expensive. In 2001, Eli Lilly founded an Internet-based platform with the objective of bringing together experts from all over the world in order to solve complex problems. The site is open to everyone. The problem to be solved is put up for discussion until somebody finds an answer and receives a fee of up to $100,000 in return. Via this Internet platform, thousands of scientists work on problems for Eli Lilly without being employed there. This platform is so successful that intermediary services are now supplied on the open market to companies in the pharmaceutical, chemical, and biotechnological industries, as well as consumer goods companies.[9]

So, companies who work to the open innovation model systematically use knowledge and ideas not only from institutions outside the company, but also from suppliers, customers, competitors, and network partners. This openness comes from top management, which maintains close relationships with all the "innovation partners" and constantly scans the market for new developments. A further characteristic of these companies is that the knowledge generated in this way is not just handed to the R&D department and used there; everyone, from researchers and developers through to production and distribution managers, works closely together in the innovation process. The challenge lies in overcoming the "not-invented-here" syndrome and always viewing external ideas positively. This is the task of top management. In most companies, researchers and developers concern themselves more with subjects that they themselves find interesting and less with subjects that customers are interested in and for which there is a market.[10] Opening the innovation process not only makes it possible to better exploit external knowledge for innovations, but it also changes the culture of a company from that of a company which is concerned with itself to that of a company which systematically generates external knowledge and orientates itself strongly toward the outside world.

Procter & Gamble's experiences show that the model of open innovation works best if:

1. networking with research partners, institutions, suppliers, or individuals is driven forward by top management, which personally builds and maintains the relationships;
2. the model of open innovation is organizationally anchored in top management (at P&G a member of the top management of the group has been assigned this task);
3. the culture of innovation is changed and, most importantly, the "not-invented-here" syndrome is overcome – this requires a new approach to R&D tasks, away from thinking: "We make innovations," toward thinking: "We gather the best ideas from inside and outside the company and R&D has the task of exploiting these ideas." (P&G employees receive an incentive payment for innovations, regardless of whether the innovation came from inside or outside the company); and
4. the systematic search for new ideas is supplemented by a systematic assessment of these ideas' chances of success on the market.

Integrating key customers: Lead users and online communities

In the 1980s, Hilti began looking into flexible and easy-to-use fastening systems. Up until that point, there were no functionally efficient systems, but it could be seen that some customers had developed their own solutions. Therefore, Hilti tried to integrate these customers into a development project. Fourteen lead users were selected from a group of 150 users – lead users are particularly demanding clients whose requirements are months or even years ahead of the mass market; these customers have their own ideas for innovations and could significantly benefit from innovations themselves. In a workshop, these lead users then developed an innovative fastening system which formed the basis for a new business unit at Hilti.[11]

Johnson & Johnson Medical brought three world firsts onto the market which were not developed by the company itself, but by its customers. In this process, the company screened the market for lead users, selected them according to well-defined criteria and brought them together in a lead-user workshop, where the customers themselves developed a new film for covering robots used in surgery, an all-in-one solution for preventing particulate matter from becoming airborne during operations, and an integrated sterile system for supporting patients' legs during hip operations (Figure 5.1).

There are innovative customers who have found their own solutions to problems or developed them themselves in almost all product areas, not just in the business-to-business sector. Around 20 percent of mountain bikers work on their own mountain bikes and have ideas for solutions that they realize themselves; this figure is almost 40 percent for extreme sports and

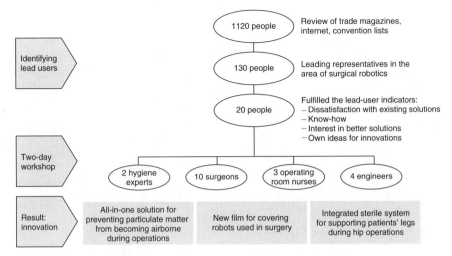

Figure 5.1 The lead-user model at Johnson & Johnson Medical[12]

almost 10 percent for outdoor consumer goods.[13] Companies do not only find new sources of innovation by using this unexploited knowledge of leading customers; lead users have a series of characteristics which companies can exploit (Figure 5.2):

1. Their needs are months or even years ahead of the mass market. Therefore, they can be put to good use anticipating new needs.
2. They are very demanding and have their own ideas for solutions. Solutions which are developed by lead users are generally very application- and customer-oriented and hit upon customers' true problems and needs.
3. They are often opinion leaders, use the product they developed themselves with conviction, and then make a significant contribution to quickly establishing the innovation on the market.

Not all customers are equally innovative. It can be said of almost all innovations that are introduced onto the market that initially a small group of customers immediately react to the innovation. Customers' adoption of an innovation usually resembles a bell curve (see Figure 5.2). This can be primarily attributed to the fact that there are customers who feel a need significantly earlier than others. Therefore, quantitative market research studies and product tests in the mass market do not always produce meaningful results. Customers who do not yet have a requirement for a product often reject an innovation in such studies. Therefore, they are not reliable study subjects. On the other hand, if it is possible to satisfy lead users, it can be assumed that the product will have good chances of success in the mass market months or years later.

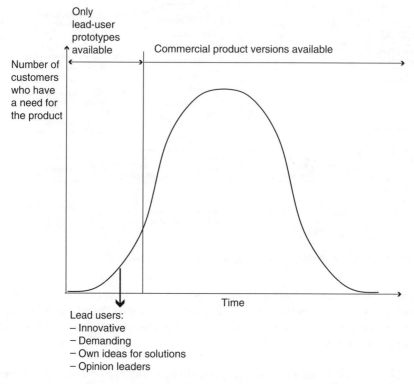

Figure 5.2 Lead-user innovations are ahead of commercial solutions[14]

Successful innovators exploit the knowledge of lead users and integrate them into the innovation process. Whilst Adidas introduced the idea of a modular sports shoe to a selected sample of runners during the idea phase, Audi involved its customers in the conception phase during the development of a new infotainment system via several Internet sites which are regularly visited by car fans. It reached over 1600 car fans who worked on the virtual development of the infotainment system. This resulted in 219 service ideas, 261 comments on the console, 728 visions of future cars, and to the optimal product configuration being selected.[15] During a design-competition phase which lasted just 4 weeks, Swarovski obtained 263 useable motifs for crystal tattoos which were produced by Internet users by means of toolkits.[16]

However, successful innovators also systematically exploit a phenomenon that has emerged in the last few years: online consumer communities,[17] which exist for almost any subject. For example, NikeTalk, which has no official connection with Nike Inc., is a community of over 45,000 basketball fans. Thousands of discussions between basketball fans take place in this virtual community every month. Basketball fanatics can be found in the community, as can sports-equipment retailers, students of industrial design, and Nike fans in general. Some of the subjects these community members deal with are "how to customize your basketball shoe," "how to distinguish a branded shoe from a fake," "design the basketball shoe for the year 2050," or there are simply discussions about Nike's latest products. Not only is an enormous amount of knowledge exchanged in these online communities, but innovations emerge there which are developed by the members themselves. Similarly too in the open source movement,[18] problems are put up for discussion and solved within the community. It is not only ideas about improving basketball shoes which are developed within the community; entirely new technologies and products are designed, such as, for example, cushioning and lacing systems. Among the members are true experts who develop products out of pure enthusiasm. For example, Jason Petrie revealed his creative and innovative potential in the community under the codename of "Alphaproject" and designed basketball shoes of astonishing quality. He was discovered by Fila and now designs for Nike. In "alt.coffee," a virtual café, coffee connoisseurs discuss how coffee machines and roasters could be improved; in the "outdoorseiten.net" online community, hikers and mountain enthusiasts develop their own equipment – for example, functional jackets and particularly light tents – and at "chefkoch.de" cooking enthusiasts consider how cooking utensils could be improved.[19]

Companies such as Hyve AG in Munich have specialized in mediating between innovation seekers and innovation providers in the role of "innomediator." They develop tools to harness the innovative power of such communities, using "netnography"[20] to identify communities, screen them for innovations, and set up a virtual dialogue with them, in order to systematically open up these sources of innovation. What is special about this undertaking is that, through methods of virtual customer integration, the entire innovation process can be opened and at the same time made more effective and more efficient in the process.

FROM SIMPLE TO COMPLEX MARKETS: UNDERSTANDING THE RULES OF THE GAME

The more networked markets are, the more difficult it will be to successfully introduce innovations and gain acceptance of them in the market.[21] In 1888, when Kodak launched the Kodak camera with the advertising slogan "You press the button, we'll do the rest," the market system was very simple. It consisted of two system partners: the customer, and the Eastman Dry Plate & Film Company, to whom the customer had to send the camera. The retail element came in 1891 when Kodak brought cameras onto the market which enabled customers to change the film themselves. When the digital camera was introduced, around 100 years later, the market system looked very different: it was heavily networked. Printer and PC manufacturers, software suppliers, broadband communications companies, mobile telephone manufacturers, specialist retailers, and so on were linked to each other in a network. The introduction of the digital camera required that all these partners believed in the new technology, invested in it, and changed over to it at the same time. Market system partners usually hold back investments if they are not sure that all the other partners who must make their contribution within the system will follow suit. It is therefore essential that a manufacturer understands the entire market system. It must be able to take the interests of the individual system partners into account, organize and coordinate them, and encourage them to change over to the new technology at the same time. This undertaking requires extensive understanding of the network.

Understanding the network structures of the market

In order to successfully accomplish this, three characteristics of networks must be taken into consideration:[22]

1. *Network externalities*: If there are network externalities (for example, size advantages through economies of scale, or increasing customer benefit due to an increasing number of users), it is particularly important to win over enough market participants who will support the new product. For example, Adobe enabled users to download Acrobat Reader from the Internet free of charge. This ensured that the program was very widely distributed and achieved enormous acceptance.
2. *Market equilibrium*: By market equilibrium, we understand a state in which each market participant aligns its behavior with that of the others. Each market participant is acting in its own interest and can rely on and predict the behavior of the other market participants. In a heavily networked market, nobody will switch to a new product on their own. In this situation, it is necessary to destroy this equilibrium and to convince a large group of network partners that the innovation is the best choice for the customer. Market participants will only switch when they believe that other network partners will also switch. It is vital to form alliances, reach agreements, or even make concessions to network partners.
3. *Power structures in the network nodes*: In order to win over the highest possible number of network partners in the shortest possible time, it is necessary to understand where the power is concentrated in the network and to use these network nodes to introduce the innovation.

The following orientations are necessary if sustained innovative success is to be achieved in networked markets:

- *System orientation*: Understanding the market as a system; that is, analysing the individual system partners, their importance, tasks, objectives, influence, and so on.

- *Problem orientation*: Understanding the key problems of the network partners that need to be solved.
- *Benefit orientation*: Continually providing benefits to the key network partners in order to win their support and cooperation.

Understanding the rules of the game

In 1976, a British wine dealer organized a blind tasting of Californian and French wine in Paris. Fifteen wine experts took part in it. When the Californian wines won, nobody really took the result seriously and some even said that the results had been manipulated. Two years later, when the Californian wines again scored highest in the blind tasting, it became clear to some traditional European wine producers that a new era in wine production had begun:[23] this was the rise of the "New World" and, above all, the triumphal march of Australian wines. In 1988, Australian wine achieved a market share of 2 percent in the British market; in 2002, it had a market share of 22 percent.[24] Considering the long European tradition of wine production and the dominance of French, Italian, and Spanish wines for centuries, one can arguably speak of a radical change in the wine market. How did the Australian producers succeed in conquering the market within such a short time?

Basically, there are two strategies for entering a new market: (1) copying the business model of the existing suppliers and optimizing it; or (2) changing the game rules in the market with a new business model and attacking the established companies head on.[25] In both cases it is necessary to look intensively at the market, the game rules, and the business models of the established companies. As a rule, the first strategy is the simpler one, but its chances of success are mostly lower, as one is going into competition with competitors who have been developing and optimizing their business model for many years. The second strategy is the riskier one, but it can bring greater success if the established companies are either unable to change their business models accordingly, or cannot or will not react in good time. IKEA pursued this second strategy, as did the low-cost airlines and the Australian wine producers, who turned the wine market on its head within a few short years.

The wine market is a market with centuries-old tradition and clear, established game rules. By adhering to a few simple principles when entering the international market, the Australian wine producers succeeded in developing a new business model, which offered customers – primarily those who bought wines in the rapidly growing $5–14 price segment – outstanding benefits. They sought answers to the following questions:

- What are the game rules in the market?
- What disadvantages do these game rules have for customers?
- How can we change these game rules in order to offer outstanding customer benefits?

The long tradition of winegrowing in Europe has generated numerous wine laws, designations of origin, and classification systems. These regulations really are a labyrinth for the consumer: their logic is often only apparent to administrative officials and statisticians.[26]

Small, narrowly defined winegrowing areas with strict designations of origin (for example, DOCG in Italy) are typical in Europe. For the designation of origin to be used (for example, Chianti, Rioja, and so on), the grapes must come from this growing area. Although this game rule gives customers certainty about the origin of the wine and guarantees them a minimum level of quality, it brings with it a few key disadvantages: (1) the wine is the product of a particular soil, therefore there is little possibility of variations in taste; (2) quality is heavily dependent on the weather and the climate; there are sometimes significant differences between years and the winegrower is at the mercy of the weather conditions in the growing area; (3) there is little opportunity to experiment with new fashionable varieties which do not thrive on the particular soil or in the respective climate of the growing area. The large Australian wine producers recognized these disadvantages and redefined the game rules. Instead of defining small growing areas and attaching designations of origin to them, the large Australian wine producers purchased grapes from different growing areas which might be up to 3000 miles apart. The wine is transported in tankers and then blended according to very exact formulae. The country of origin is then simply stated as being South Australia or even just Australia. This renders the Australian wine producers independent of the weather, climate, and soil. According to the conditions, they can buy grapes where they are good and cheap in that particular year. Consequently, the wine is not so much the product of a certain soil, but rather the product of a certain vine variety – wherever it grows.[27] Hardy also has growing areas outside Australia in Sicily and South Africa, and is therefore in an excellent position to react to fashionable varieties, since it is not dependent on a growing region.

The second important game rule in the Old World is the strict classification of wine. The distinction between quality and table wine brings with it regulations with regard to alcohol content, amelioration, deacidification, wine additives, and so on. Individual quality growing areas issue regulations regarding admitted grapes, maximum yield of grapes per hectare, minimum alcohol content and acidity, production regulations and minimum aging period, and so on. In France, the wine law is structured hierarchically according to growing area. Designations such as Vin de Table, Vin de Pays, Vin Délimité de Qualité Supérieure, Appellation d'Origine Controllé, the differentiation between Beaune Premier Cru "Les Amoureuses" and Echézeaux Grand Cru in Burgundy, Premier Cru, and Premier Grand Cru Classé may say something to a sommelier but confuse most wine drinkers. Furthermore, they entail strict regulations in wine production. The Australian wine producers are also redefining these game rules. They dispensed with a strict classification system. This gave them flexibility within the entire wine production process. Whilst, for example, a regulation stipulated that certain wines must be aged in expensive French oak barrels, the Australians achieved the same effect with a significantly less costly method. One effect of aging wine in wooden barrels is that it brings about the typical olfactory notes of sweet vanilla, roast hazelnut, cloves, and caramel. The Australian wine producers achieved the same results through the significantly less expensive method of storing the wine in steel barrels and adding wood chippings. European wine producers noted this method with some horror. The Australians also used reverse osmosis – a process in which the must, with all its natural components, is concentrated, thereby becoming richer in substances which impart taste. Finally, the Australians also dispensed with complicated wine designations and simply named the wine after the grape. Every customer could easily understand this and classify the wine without difficulty.

The third game rule related to small business sizes, through which it was not possible to achieve a critical mass in terms of production and marketing. It was not possible to achieve economies of scale, and automization methods such as mechanical harvesting were not cost-effective. In Australia, the five largest wine producers, who have largely grown through acquisitions and mergers, have a market share of about 85 percent; this compares with 8 percent in France and 4 percent in Italy.[28] Through this, they achieved a critical mass for realizing economies of scale and began to control the entire value chain, including marketing and distribution. This enabled them to develop strong bargaining power vis-à-vis the professional purchasers of the large food retail chains, which was at least as important as the economies of scale. The purchasers' main interest lay in dealing with a few reliable suppliers who could deliver large volumes at a consistently good price–quality ratio. Finally, through professional marketing and key account management, Australian wine producers are in a significantly better position to build global brands (Table 5.2).

A further example illustrates that lack of understanding of the market system can cause real innovations to fail. In the 1990s, the skiing industry found itself in a classic maturity phase. Sales figures were stagnating all over the world and the market lacked real innovations. Although most suppliers were constantly enhancing their products, this was not sufficient to boost demand. Consequently, increasing cost pressure led to heavy optimization in purchasing, production, and distribution processes.

It was in this very market phase that an Austrian ski manufacturer presented a ski at the international sports-equipment trade fairs which was dramatically different to the ski models that had been known up to that point. The ski was around 30 cm shorter and significantly wider at the tip and at the rear end than anything that had been seen before. At first glance it resembled an ugly "water ski."

Although "internal" ski tests showed that the ski represented a real revolution in performance in terms of carving feeling, retailers only ordered it with hesitation. Neither the presentation of the new skiing concept, nor the sales arguments of the sales team were sufficient to turn this different kind of ski

Table 5.2 Game rules in the wine market – the success of the Australians

Game rule in the market	Disadvantage of this game rule	New game rule	Benefit for the customer
1. Designations of origin	• Dependency on weather in the growing region (fluctuations in price and quality) • Dependency on individual grape varieties which grow in the region (no possibility of reacting to trends in grape varieties)	• Dispensing with designations of origin for small areas • Purchasing grapes from many different growing districts ("multi-district blend")	• Relatively high, consistent quality • Relatively low prices (grapes cost around one third to one half as compared with Europe) • Fashionable wines
2. Quality classifications	• Confusing wine classification • No innovation due to strict production standards	• Dispensing with complicated classification systems and designations of origin by naming the wine after the variety of grape instead • Freedom in wine production and innovations (e.g. reverse osmosis, aging in steel tanks, and adding oak chippings)	• Global brands the customer can rely on • Immediately drinkable wines with a very good price–quality ratio
3. Small company sizes	• Low economies of scale • Little possibility of automization • No control over the entire value chain	• Large growing districts covering large areas make it possible to harvest grapes mechanically; for the most part wines are also cut mechanically • Large wine producers (e.g. Hardy) control the entire value chain • Setting up own distribution and marketing	• Good price–quality ratio
4. No professional marketing and distribution	• Low chance of being listed by the large retail chains	• Professional key account management • Distribution via large food retail chains	• Good availability of the wines (advantage for end customers) • Strong brands, large volumes, and consistent quality at a very good price–quality ratio (advantage for retail)

into a big seller. Sales people could not warm to this different "water ski." This disappointment was followed by very bad retail sales figures. It seemed as though the skiing revolution would not be accepted by the market, despite the enormous product advantages.

However, meanwhile all the competitors had tested the "ugly" ski and recognized that this development had the potential to usher in a new phase in skiing history. Since the innovator could not protect its idea through a patent, these short, wide and "ugly" skis were copied by all the large manufacturers. Through a massive amount of convincing and the requisite marketing power, key individuals in retail were persuaded of the benefits of the new ski generation – the carving boom was born.

Within 2 years, the "old" ski models more or less disappeared from suppliers' ranges and retailers' shelves. Demand for the new generation skis virtually exploded – sales figures increased by around 20 percent worldwide. The only tragic thing was that the innovator was not able to benefit from its development. This manufacturer even lost market share and subsequently fought for survival while producing low volumes.

What had happened? With its radical invention, the innovator had succeeded in introducing a completely new and enjoyable carving feeling to skiers. In doing so, the company had fulfilled the basic requirement for introducing a market change. Unfortunately, though, it had not managed to also plan and implement systematic solutions for a successful market launch.

In particular, the company was denied market success because it seemingly did not realize that even a radical innovation with significant product advantages is not capable of establishing itself on the market on its own. For this, the company must succeed in identifying the game rules – or rather the strategic levers of the market system – and convincing its partners in the market system with innovative programs for the innovation. One of the key game rules in all markets is the issue of the balance of power between players in the market system; a second is the decision-making behavior of customers. Without understanding the balance of power and the decision-making behavior of customers it will be almost impossible to develop an effective strategy.

What were the most important strategic levers of the market system in the ski market at that time?

- In this system, it was not the end customer who determined success or failure; it was the retailers and, in particular, their sales staff, who guided customers' buying decisions at the point of sale (POS) with their sales arguments. The push strategy is fundamentally more important than the pull strategy in this situation.
- Any radical change initially triggers "resistance," which must be overcome. In particular, it is retailers who must overcome mental barriers with regard to the "innovation."
- Developing and preparing innovative sales tools for convincing customers at the point of sale (POS) will increase the motivation and effectiveness of the sales representatives.
- Developing a pricing concept which offers retailers the prospect of above-average earnings will increase their motivation to sell the product.

- The large retail organizations must be persuaded of the benefits of an extensive and well-supported launch of the "innovation."

If one subsequently takes a brief look at the ski market "system," one can see that consumers allow themselves to be guided in their information and decision-making process by the recommendations of sales representatives to a large degree. Over 80 percent of all buyers go into specialist sports-equipment retailers' stores with no specific brand preferences and a low level of product knowledge. Consequently, sales representatives decisively influence and steer the consumer buying process through their explanations and recommendations. Over 70 percent of customers leave the store with the product that the sales person heartily recommended to them. This shows the "power" of the sales staff, but equally that optimum market coverage is absolutely essential for market success, for if it is not possible to introduce the radical innovation to as many customers as possible within a short time, the first-mover advantage will be lost. There is the risk that the outstanding product advantages will not automatically be linked with the innovator's brand. Competitors will have enough time to themselves score on the market with the innovator's technology.

Extensive retail presence is necessary for rapid market penetration, since most customers are not prepared to look for the special products in very specific shops. This is because, for the most part, customers do not know that there is a new product with special advantages, because they rely, as shown above, on the advice they receive from well-known specialist sports–equipment retailers. If the product is not listed and appropriately promoted there, it cannot be bought.

Therefore, for the ski manufacturer it would have been important to take this innovation to the market by developing a comprehensive distribution and marketing concept together with retailers. Additionally, however, it would have been necessary to strike a new path with the launch. Instead of presenting the product innovation at the large sports-equipment trade fairs, the manu‑ facturer could have had the opinion leaders in retail experience two "launch phases" – the product experience phase and the marketing phase.

The group of sales representatives and business owners should have actually been convinced about the performance of the skis, initially at particular events to which they had been personally invited. Here, it would have been interesting to keep the ski surface at these events neutral – white – and to initially confront the "opinion leaders" only with the new shape. Following the tests, a top designer could have explained the "new" shape of the skis and presented different design proposals for "painting" the ski surface. The participants could have discussed and evaluated the proposals in small groups and subsequently been given the opportunity to discuss them with the designer. Presumably, the decision leaders would not only have experienced the special skiing feeling; through looking intensively at the appearance of the skis, they would also have gained emotional access to the products more quickly. Perhaps they would have traveled home saying: "We must have this innovation."

In parallel to this, innovative marketing concepts for the POS and an appropriate pricing concept should have been prepared. Immediately after the events, the manufacturer could have visited the individual retailers and presented the "cool" launch package for convincing the end customers to them. At the same time, it could have presented the "high-price concept" which underlines the positioning of the radical innovation, and demonstrated the very good potential the pricing concept offers to retailers for making money with this product if they keep to certain rules, for example no price reductions during end-of-season sales, and so on.

If this approach had succeeded in convincing individual retailers about the advantages of the product, its design, the sales tools, and the good prospects for individual retailers to earn money with the product, then the next phase could have followed. Together with the most important retailers, the manufacturer could have gone into negotiations with the large sports-equipment chains and presented the general concept. If this had been successful, then the actual rollout could have taken place. It would then not only have been possible to present the innovation as the highlight of the winter in each of the specialist sports-equipment retailers' stores, but also for sales staff to pitch the product to customers using the resources which had been made available.

Up to this point, the product would not have been presented at any of the large sports-equipment trade fairs, such as the ISPO in Munich, for example.

In our view, the successful launch of radical innovations calls for more than just the innovative product. A successful launch which is capable of triggering a change in the market also requires innovative marketing and distribution efforts. The basis for this is understanding the game rules in the market and the strategies that are based on them.

The success of the Australian wine producers and the failure of the Austrian ski manufacturer have one thing in common. In both cases, market orientation and exploiting the game rules were the decisive factors. The ski manufacturer failed to examine and base its market-launch strategy on the game rules of the market. The Australians did this: they developed a new business model by recognizing the weak points of the game rules and defining new ones.

The more complex market systems become, the more important it will be to understand the game rules and take them into account – especially when entering a market as a new player.

THE NEW ROLE OF MARKET RESEARCH

The approaches shown above illustrate that marketing departments must realign their roles and tasks to some extent. Peter Lorange[29] calls on marketing departments to accept the challenge of really intending to identify new market opportunities before they become obvious. This is the only way it will be possible to actively shape the market and to not always have to run behind it. However, this also requires that the marketing department in particular is shaped by visionary thinking and does not allow itself to be guided by a copycat mentality.

Here, the following aspects are of key importance:

1. It is important that companies orientate themselves toward customers' real problems and latent needs.

The difficulty of convincing customers about new solutions/developments is shown by studies which prove that less than 10 percent of all new or further developments actually win customers' favor.[30] There are doubtless complex reasons for this, but frequently the things that companies develop or communicate simply do not correspond to the real needs of the market. An important reason for this is that companies primarily orientate themselves toward the desires and needs that are articulated by customers in market research. However, frequently these statements merely reflect what is already generally known. It is not possible to derive successful developments from such results. Instead, the process must involve recognizing unconscious needs and relevant problems. The following story[31] provides a graphic example with regard to the differing quality of results produced by these two approaches.

A paint manufacturer decided to rethink its activities in the area of exterior paints. Carrying out traditional, very elaborate customer interviews brought the following desires and expectations to light:

- high durability
- good weather resistance
- good adhesion
- a cover lid that is watertight after being reclosed
- good coverage
- forms a strong surface.

In essence, nothing new. Based on these results, the paint manufacturer was not actually able to generate new knowledge from its customers and to develop an effective product strategy based on this knowledge. Consequently, it attempted, using one-to-one conversations with users, to filter out possible latent needs and all the problems that had arisen whilst the product was being used. When doing this, it did not ask about desires, but about problems. This process brought to light the following key starting points for future product developments:

- pre-treatment is laborious
- preparatory work takes a lot of time

- it is difficult to remove the old paint
- carrying out the preparatory work is tedious
- there are no practical tools for removing the old paint.

The customers saw the preparatory work as the greatest problem. Therefore, here it was important to find specific starting points. For this reason, during the brainstorming phase particular importance was attached to developing an entire system of labor-saving external paint. For example, a paint was developed which made the primer coat redundant, as it contained the primer as well as the covering coat. Another paint can be applied to surfaces that have already been painted without the necessity of tiresome preparatory work. Theodor Levitt, a marketing professor at Harvard University, always emphasized in his lectures that "Customers do not want 5 mm drills, they want 5 mm holes in the wall." In 1995, Pierre Omidyar found eBay not with the intention of creating an auction house, but rather to help people sell things over the Internet.[32] So it is less about orientating oneself toward desires identified in quantitative market research studies, than orientating oneself toward customers' real problems. Observing customers using the product works far better than interviewing them.

This is not a question of pinpointing customers' expectations of the product through unceasing market research efforts. On the contrary, numerous innovations might never have come to market had companies relied on the desires articulated by customers. Henry Ford once said: "If I had asked people what they wanted they would have said 'faster horses,'" and Akio Morita, founder and former CEO of Sony, expressed it as follows: "If you survey the public for what they think they need, you'll always be behind in this world. You'll never catch up unless you think 1–10 years in advance and create a market for the items you think the public will accept at that time."[33]

Peter Lorange sees this as a problem which affects large companies. Due to the fear of making mistakes, young brand managers – particularly in companies where employees are not encouraged to take risks – hide behind endless wide-ranging market research studies to guide their decisions. This costs time and, what is worse, it brings nothing new. This approach cannot be expected to yield groundbreaking innovations.

2. It is necessary to "interview" the right groups of customers – the innovators and "early adopters."

The basic premise of classic quantitative market research is that the group interviewed must be a representative sample of the population. This is comprehensible, since only then can the results of the sample be carried over to the population. But, when it comes to innovations, this is a problem. Not all customers are equally innovative: some react more quickly to an innovation; some need a long time until they are prepared to buy the innovative product.

The innovative ability of customers resembles a Gaussian distribution.[34] Rogers (1962) observed a curve resembling a Gaussian distribution with regard to customers' propensity to innovate (Figure 5.3).

Innovators (approximately 2.5 percent) are adventurous and prepared to take risks. Early adopters accept new ideas early but are more careful and frequently also opinion leaders. One can observe such distributions with practically all innovations. This was the case with the carving ski, just as it was with the mobile telephone or the snowboard. Not all customers react to innovation with the same speed; some need years until they take an interest in it. Therefore, quantitative, representative market research studies cannot really help in the innovation process. On the contrary, if one tries to interview a representative cross-section of customers about desires or tries to test the potential of an innovation on them, the results can be slightly misleading. Products such as the Sony Walkman, the SMS, the Blackberry, or the Pocket PC would never have come to market, if the market research studies which showed that these products had no potential were considered.

The second problem lies in the fact that customers with particularly new needs become less important in a representative sample; their opinions and ideas get lost in the crowd and are not picked up by the company.[36] Therefore, it is more meaningful to differentiate customers in market research according to their willingness to innovate.

When Audi developed a new infotainment system, it decided to integrate customers into the development process.[37] It devised a virtual lab as a web-based platform in order to generate ideas, configure a product, and test its acceptance. It attached importance to addressing customer groups with different levels of willingness to innovate and different levels of inno-

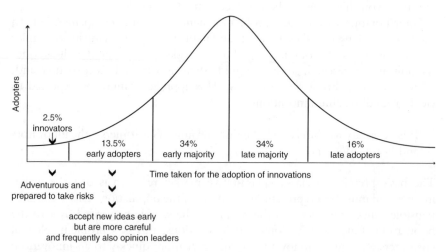

Figure 5.3 Diffusion of innovations[35]

vative ability. Lead users were to provide inspiration for future infotainment systems, early adopters were to configure aspects of functionality, such as navigation, telematics, and voice control, and heavy users in the low-end segment were to provide input as to the weaknesses of the existing system. These different customer groups were found on various portals (for example, www.autobild.de, www.tt-owners-club.de, www.automotor-und-sport.de, and so on). The results were impressive: the lead users provided vision about the infotainment of the future, the early adopters provided input about configuration, and the heavy users provided clues as to acceptance in the mass market.

3. It is important to install discussion platforms within the company in order to process and exploit the input gathered cross-functionally.

There is no doubt that it is crucial to generate the "right" information from the markets, but it is just as vital to interpret this information in terms of the company's situation as a whole and to derive effective decisions from it. This interpretation process should not take place in isolation in marketing departments. Instead, the knowledge and experience of various individuals from different functional areas must be exploited. Usually, only open and critical dialogue about the information that has been gathered will open up the chance to obtain company-specific ideas for innovative leaps. At the same time, this removes the silo thinking between the functions and creates a sense of common "importance" in terms of the matter at hand. However, a prerequisite for this is that top decision-makers themselves engage in this discussion process, because, first, this is the only way these discussions will gain vital strategic importance for the group and, secondly, this information should ultimately give rise to fundamental decisions about the company's positioning on the market.

4. The top decision-makers must themselves be market (research) experts.

In order that top decision-makers can assume their central role in the discussion platforms described above, they must themselves have an extensive understanding of the market logic and of customers' problems. This is the only way they will be able to evaluate the information under discussion effectively and drive forward the discussion process in a solution-oriented way during the phases of conflict which continually arise between the functions. Therefore, top decision-makers must invest a considerable part of their time in direct contact with customers, distribution partners, and other market players. It must be one of their key concerns to continually form a picture of the customers and the markets for themselves.

5. Top decision-makers must drive forward the propensity to experiment and take risks.

On the whole, it is fundamentally important that top decision-makers strongly support the propensity to experiment in the implementation of the solutions which have been generated. This is the only way that companies will be able to actually try out their ideas on the market in good time in order to learn important lessons from them. Or, as someone once said, to "make mistakes more often in order to learn more quickly." The key to this is the willingness to systematically learn and to view the mistakes that arise as a necessary part of this process. However, if employees are afraid of any kind of failure, then they will – as Peter Lorange put it – continually hide behind endless-data analyses and never move the market. Nestlé's experiences with the yoghurt product LC1 illustrates this approach. Nestlé initially launched LC1 in France as a new yoghurt, focusing its marketing message on a central and new product attribute – "helps the body to protect itself." However, customers did not want a "medical" product. They wanted a good and healthy product that tasted great. The "failure" in France made it necessary for the core feature of the product – being good for the health – to be marketed differently. Nestlé's top management allowed exactly the same team that had made this "mistake" to learn from it. The same team was able to launch LC1 in Germany on the basis of what had been learned in France. It became a success in Germany and subsequently also in other markets.

6 The sails determine the course, not the wind

For decades, strategy research has concerned itself with the question of where the reasons for above-average and sustained success lie.[1] Different explanations have been developed for this. The two most important approaches are the "market-based view" and the "resource-based view." These are two completely opposing viewpoints and have far-reaching consequences for the strategy process. Essentially, the issue revolves around the question of whether a company's success is determined by the structure of the market – and some key industry characteristics in particular – or whether success is more dependent on company-specific factors. Therefore, we would like to present these concepts in more detail and show why an orientation toward one's own competences should be the starting point for strategic decisions, as well as why core competences, in the form of unique skills which impart value and cannot be imitated, are considerably more decisive for the success of the company than industry characteristics.

THE MARKET-BASED VIEW VERSUS THE RESOURCE-BASED VIEW

In 1980, a book appeared which had a lasting influence on the strategy work of many companies: Michael Porter's *Competitive Strategy*.[2] In this book, Porter maintained that the success of a company was dependent on five industry forces and the way these forces act in combination. According to this view:

1. the fewer alternatives there are to the company's products;
2. the less rivalry there is among the established competitors;
3. the less pressure that can be exerted by suppliers;
4. the more difficult it is for new suppliers to enter the market; and
5. the more customers there are and the lower the extent to which they are organized, the greater the probability that the company will be successful over the long term.

Each of these points is plausible:[3] if the product or service a company is supplying can only be substituted by another at high cost, or cannot be substituted at all, the company has good potential for success. The marketing of original replacement parts is based on this principle, for example.

It is similarly understandable that a company's chances of making a profit are dependent on the intensity of the competition in the industry. Accordingly, the intensive competition between airlines has virtually destroyed profit margins in international aviation, whilst competition in other industries has remained limited.

Far-reaching measures which significantly influence a company's chances of making a profit, or often even its chances of survival, sometimes also come from suppliers. For example, Microsoft and Intel not only exploit their strong position in the PC industry in order to extract price premiums, but also put computer manufacturers under pressure in terms of the design of their products.

On the other hand, there are also such things as protected industries: cases in which only a few companies supply a product and make large profits without new suppliers being able to vie for market share. There are various reasons for this: sometimes laws protect the established suppliers or these suppliers control critical resources; sometimes the barriers to entry are so high, due to investment requirements, technologies or customer loyalty, that it is hardly economical for a competitor to enter the market.

In many industries, profit margins also suffer due to the strong position of customers. For example, concentration in food retailing has led to the food industry finding itself faced with almost monopolized demand. The fate of the manufacturers depends on a handful of large customers who can exert considerable pressure. The situation is similar for suppliers to the automotive industry.

The concept of the "five forces" is simple and logical. It is possible to derive from it clear guidelines for the strategy development process. It revolves around understanding the industry structure and identifying the driving forces in the industry. Companies which (1) position themselves in attractive industries and (2) adapt to industry structures and develop strategies accordingly will be successful. This leads to the following logic in strategy development:[4]

- In the first step, it is necessary to examine the company's environment (macro-environment, industry, competitors).
- Based on this, the company should identify industries which can be expected to yield above-average profits due to their structure.
- It should then develop strategies for these industries which are aligned with the industries' structures and game rules.
- The company then implements these strategies by procuring or developing the relevant resources, skills and technologies, and so on.

If this process works well, the company can be sure of above-average returns – according to the market-based view.

There is an entire school of thought behind this logic: the "Structure–Conduct–Performance Paradigm"[5] of industrial economics. It assumes that the success of a company depends on a few industry characteristics which determine the behavior of companies. This sounds plausible at first, but behind it lie some implicit assumptions which are difficult to support:[6]

- Above-average performance depends on how well the company manages to adapt itself to industry structures and changing basic conditions.
- The "Structure–Conduct–Performance Paradigm" assumes that companies hardly differ in terms of resources and skills.
- It assumes that all skills, technologies, and know-how, and so on are mobile and that every company can adopt or acquire these resources.

That this tends to be the exception rather than the rule in management practice should be immediately obvious to anyone. Nevertheless, this viewpoint, which established itself in strategy research back in the 1960s, has survived a long time.

It was not until 1984 that Birger Wernerfelt[7] ushered in a paradigm shift with his essay "A resource-based view of the firm" in the respected *Strategic Management Journal.* He maintained that it was not the market and the industry, but rather the strategic resources of the company that were the sources of above-average returns. This began an intense scientific debate and it took about a decade before this viewpoint also became prevalent in practice.

Jay Barney[8] identified four characteristics that resources – whether tangible or intangible – must have in order to be sources of competitive advantages: they must be (1) valuable, (2) rare, (3) inimitable, and (4) non-substitutable. If a company has such resources at its disposal, it is, to a certain extent, a monopolist. It possesses something that provides customer benefits, is rare, and cannot be imitated by competitors. This made the "resource-based view" more concrete and with Prahalad and Hamel's essay "The Core Competence of the Corporation,"[9] the term "core competences" was coined and the resource-based view made its breakthrough.

There followed numerous, wide-ranging empirical studies whose objective it was to find out what was more important for the success of the company: market characteristics or company-specific factors. Even Michael Porter, one of the most important proponents of industrial economics and the market-based view of the firm which is based on it, found in a cross-industry study of US companies that industry characteristics explained less than 20 percent of success, whereas company-specific factors explained more than 30 percent.[10] Other studies found even greater differences in favor of the resource-based view: 4 percent industry characteristics compared to 44 percent company-specific characteristics according to Rumelt;[11] 8 percent versus 36 percent according to Hawawini.[12] In other words, the sails determine the course, not the wind. The results of our study also corroborate this: core competences are decisive in determining corporate success – in two regards. They contribute to effectiveness and efficiency, as competence-based management means jettisoning ballast and concentrating on those things the company does best. This means concentrating strengths and using resources efficiently. However, core competences also increase corporate success indirectly if innovations in products and services consistently build on these unique skills and competences.

This realization has far-reaching consequences for the strategy development process: it turns it on its head. The starting point is not the environment and the industry, but rather the company's own skills and competences:

- In the first step, it is necessary to identify the particular strengths of the company.
- These strengths are then evaluated to determine whether they are unique, that is to say core competences, and could form the basis for competitive advantages.
- The next step involves finding attractive industries and markets in which these core competences can be exploited.
- Finally, strategies based on the core competences are developed for these industries and markets and then implemented.

Therefore, success is not so much a question of "adapting oneself" as a question of "shaping" (Figure 6.1).

The German PAPSTAR group is a company with over 2000 employees which operates Europe-wide and has specialized in distributing disposable bowls and plates, as well as other disposable items, packaging materials, hygiene products, decorative items, and accessories. Using its strong expertise in sourcing and logistics, it purchases over 5000 different items worldwide and bundles them into marketable ranges of goods. In doing this, it attaches particular importance to continually allowing new trends to flow into the design of its product ranges for different customer groups in order to create an optimal integrated solution for retailers.

Although through doing this PAPSTAR has succeeded in becoming a leading European supplier, the management team asked itself whether and to what extent it would be possible to enter new lines of business in order to secure and develop the company's success over the long term.

To this end, it initiated a strategy development process which involved, first and foremost, eliciting the company's fields of competence and identifying and analyzing the skills bundles that lay behind them. Based on this, it intended to find out which competences could be used to enter new areas of business.

In particular, the analysis showed that, besides its sourcing and product range expertise, PAPSTAR has at its disposal a bundle of skills, technolo-

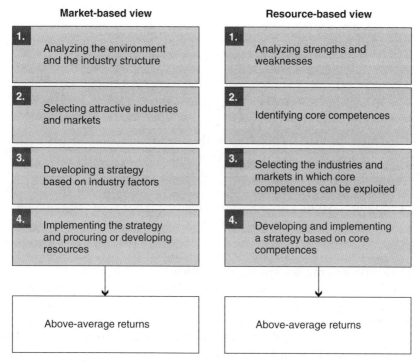

Figure 6.1 The resource-based view-turning strategy development on its head[13]

gies, and distribution structures, through which qualitatively unique logistics, service and support services, including physical shelf-space management for retailers, can be performed at optimal cost. Two central pillars account for this in particular:

First, PAPSTAR has a high-tech modular extendable logistics center, in which flows of goods from the most varied of production locations can be brought together in the most flexible way, packed, individually picked, stored, and delivered to each location on schedule.

Secondly, in the last few years PAPSTAR has succeeded in building up, training, and systematically managing a pool of over 1400 part-time staff all over the country who receive the goods at the respective locations and provide on-site professional shelf-space management services for retail customers, which range from ordering and placement to shop-refits.

Based on these insights, it was then necessary to assess the extent to which this special service expertise could also be provided to other manufacturers who supply retail customers.

It emerged from this assessment that retail companies have found themselves faced with intense cost pressure for a long time now. An increasing number of activities which were originally carried out by the retailers are now being passed on to industry or service providers and retailers are reducing their own workforces. Furthermore, the large retailers are increasingly pushing their private label businesses, for which they do not have their own distribution and merchandising systems. For this, the retail companies must have "private label" products from different manufacturing plants brought together by a service provider.

The analysis showed that many small and medium-sized companies operating in the industry are not able to serve extensive distribution channels for food retailers on their own. Many of these companies only have a regional presence or a presence in specialist retail outlets for their high-quality products. This situation is not only characteristic of medium-sized companies, it is also found in multi-national groups. Due to ongoing cost pressure and poor margins, even they are sometimes not in a position to realize processes that make logistical sense, such as bringing together products from different production locations, for example. Many of these companies have enormous difficulties visiting outlets as frequently as required and necessary, due to lack of manpower and the need to keep stocks low.

Based on these conclusions, PAPSTAR decided to offer integrated collection, storage, and delivery logistics services, coupled with extensive merchandising presence, to potential interested parties. Its success was impressive. Within a very short time, PAPSTAR was able to win customers such as 3M, Faber Castell, and Pelikan, for whom it has now taken over the entire logistics process, including retail.

PAPSTAR has thereby managed to achieve lasting success in a new area of business on the basis of its core competences. At the same time, PAPSTAR was able to bring its existing system up to full capacity through the new customers, which in turn led to higher margins in its core business.

The bundled skills which are behind this logistics competence exhibit characteristics which make them particularly interesting:

1. They are *valuable* in the market, that is, they create added value for the customer.
2. They are *rare*, that is, hardly any competitors have this bundle of special skills at their disposal.
3. They are *difficult to imitate* or to *substitute* by other skills or technologies.
4. They can be exploited in different fields of application, that is, they are *transferable* to new markets or new products.

In other words, PAPSTAR possesses core competences which render the company's services unique and provide a basis for sustained success.

This example shows how unique resources which add value can form the starting point for strategy development and for sustained competitive advantages.

THE SOURCES OF CORE COMPETENCES

Hardly any other term in strategic management has been used so frequently in the last few years as the term "core competences" – and hardly any other term is so frequently used incorrectly.

In seminars with senior executives or in MBA programs, we regularly ask the participants to take a piece of paper and write down their company's core competences. After a few minutes' thought, the result is always the same: each participant is able to name one or even several core competences. But as soon as we clearly define what core competences actually are and ask the participants to apply the four criteria (valuable in the market, rare, difficult to imitate, and non-substitutable) to the core competences they have identified, many participants do not have any core competences left. What was carelessly described as a core competence proves, upon closer inspection, to be a competence that many companies have or a competence that cannot be protected and can easily be imitated by competitors. Strengths are far from being core competences.

However, in our practical work, we often experience the opposite. Companies are often not at all aware of their core competences and by extension the sources of their competitive advantages.

A few years ago, we had the opportunity to work with a large company on its strategy process. It was about to make an important strategic decision which would bring far-reaching changes to the company: closing the company's integrated production site and relocating individual steps in the value chain. Whereas all of its competitors had already carried out this step years before, this company had always held on to its integrated site in Austria. At the end of the 1990s, the issue of closing down the site in order to generate cost advantages came up for discussion. The company considered it necessary to dismantle the value chain and relocate individual activities to countries and locations where they could be carried out more efficiently and effectively. Within the framework of the strategy process, we began by analyzing core competences and carried out a series of interviews with key customers in order to find out where the strengths and weaknesses of the company lay. This brought to light the following clear advantages in comparison to competitors:

- Immediately implementable solutions/starting points for solving customers' problems were found as early on as the sales meeting – this pleased the customers.
- The company was in a significantly better position to find solutions for problems and challenges entailing complex production processes than the competitors.
- The company regularly found innovative solutions, even finding ways to solve challenges and problems in production with the existing production facilities.

- There was fast and flexible new product development in the application technology department (no pure research) and sales quickly found solutions to problems.
- The delivery times for small batch sizes were flexible and short.
- Quality was very stable.

These were clear competitive advantages: few competitors could keep up in these areas. These advantages delivered clear customer benefits and could not be imitated. In other words, the company possessed core competences.

During the second step of our analysis, when we explored the issue of why the company had these advantages, a few interesting findings came to light:

- The company had an extremely committed, success-oriented, and technically competent sales department which cooperated closely with the application technology department.
- The employees in the sales *and* application technology departments were highly motivated to acquire new business.
- The employees in R&D, technology, and production were extremely solution-oriented, committed, and technically versed.
- The company had long-standing and fully developed skills and processes in production and logistics and in its established product areas.

In this step, we had identified the skills and processes which lay behind the company's strengths. However, we went a step further as we wanted to find out why this company was in a considerably better position to develop these skills than the competitors. We came to the same conclusion again and again: it was the integrated site which (1) made possible the pooling of knowledge and extensive sharing of common knowledge, as well as extremely fast and effective exchange of this information and knowledge; (2) led to a watertight cross-departmental network of personal relationships, which in turn led to a strong "we feeling," common goals, and commitment; and (3) rendered the company extremely flexible and powerful, due to its short information and decision-making paths.

Therefore, the decision to close the integrated site was no longer an option. This site was the basis of the core competences. If the decision had been made to close it down, the competitive advantages which had been painstakingly built up over a long time would presumably have been lost. Instead of closing down the integrated site, the company reached the decision to strengthen it in order to further develop and protect the core competences by (1) allowing more freedom for the exchange of knowledge; (2) creating the possibility at the integrated site of simulating processes ranging from the production to the customer process, independent of production capacity; and (3) creating an integrated service center to achieve the shortest possible delivery times to customers, as well as increase the level of flexibility with regard to retail deliveries.

The more difficult core competences are to imitate, the more valuable they become. So what determines whether they can be imitated or not? Core competences are primarily sources of sustained competitive advantage if they fulfill one or more of the following criteria:[14]

1. They are based on *unique historical conditions* which are connected to the first-mover advantage and path dependencies. Swarovski's development in grinding technology at the end of the 19th century and its continuous enhancement have made it possible to produce crystals which inspire customers, thanks to their diversity, shape, color, and the way they play with the light. This was and still is unique in the market. This was also the basis for Swarovski developing its own luxury brand for crystal figures in the 1970s. In turn, the brand was the basis for developing a unique international network of trend researchers, designers, and artists, in order to develop a competence in recognizing and shaping trends. These linked, historical steps (path dependency) make it extremely difficult to copy Swarovski's core competences.

2. It is not easy for competitors to establish how and why these competences emerged (*causal ambiguity*). PAPSTAR's sourcing and logistics competence developed through many years of experience. The skills of employees, individual strategic decisions, experience in the industry, the special structure of the company, and its complex product range presumably combined to play major roles in this. However, it is not possible to establish exactly when and how the individual core competences came about. Therefore, competitors have difficulty in understanding how core competences came about and imitating them.

3. They are based, among other things, on personal relationships, trust, and culture, that is, factors which are very difficult to set up and to imitate (*social complexity*). Our example of the company whose core competences were based on the integrated site shows that it is primarily personal, cross-departmental networks, corporate culture, level of motivation of employees, identification with common goals, knowledge and, above all, the willingness to share it, which are of central importance here. Creating such conditions costs time and often much painstaking detail work.

4. They are protected by *patents*, which secure at least a short-term competitive advantage.

Finally, we would like to point out an issue that we consider important. Basically, all companies are different from one another. Significant or less significant differences result from the tangible and intangible resources they have at their disposal, the special skills they have developed over the course of time, or the relationships and networks they have built up. Competitors can compensate for

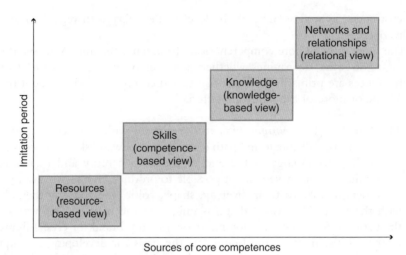

Figure 6.2 Competences and imitation periods

some of the advantages a company has due to its resources, skills, knowledge, and relationships more easily and quickly than others (Figure 6.2). Individual tangible and intangible resources can represent core competences because they lead to unique products and services or efficiency advantages.[15] Individual resources which are independent of one another are generally comparatively easy to imitate. It becomes more difficult if the company possesses skills it has developed over many years, which enable it to combine different resources with one another to form a competitive advantage. Frequently, core competences are found in unique combinations of resources and in the ability to constantly develop these further.[16] For example, the core competence of Amazon, the Internet book retailer, lies in combining logistics and distribution expertise (behind which are large investments in distribution centers and process flows), in its Internet expertise (behind which is extensive knowledge about programming the customer-oriented website), and in its enormous customer database (in which the buying histories of millions of customers are stored, making it possible to predict customer preferences by comparing their buying histories with the entire customer base and therefore make personalized offers). It is even more difficult to imitate knowledge – particularly implicit knowledge – which the company has built up over many years and which lies behind skills and innovations, and so on.[17] The highest level of non-imitability is reached if advantages have come about through combining resources, skills, and knowledge through relationships and networks, as access to such core competences, which reside in individual network partners, locks companies outside the network out and such networks can only be built up with great difficulty.[18]

So, lasting differences that are very difficult to imitate result from social and immaterial factors and not from "inventoried" factors. This means, for instance, routine processes, organizational and communication structures, or corporate culture. In particular, these factors involve what is known as implicit knowledge; that is, knowledge that cannot be articulated that has resulted from many years of experience. But networks and relationships with partner companies and stakeholders can also form the basis of long-term competitive advantages.

So how can core competences be identified? It should have become clear that core competences frequently result from very complex, non-obvious resources, skills, and so on. Nevertheless, there is a simple, pragmatic logic for analyzing core competences (Figure 6.3).

Usually, we begin with a question that at first glance seems very simple: what are the competitive advantages from the customer's point of view? In addition to this, we investigate buying criteria and find out, based on a series of customer interviews, how the company rates compared to competitors. The result is a strengths and weaknesses profile from the customer's point of view. That sounds really simple, but studying buying criteria often presents a real challenge. In most projects it emerges that customers use very different criteria and that their assessments are considerably different to what

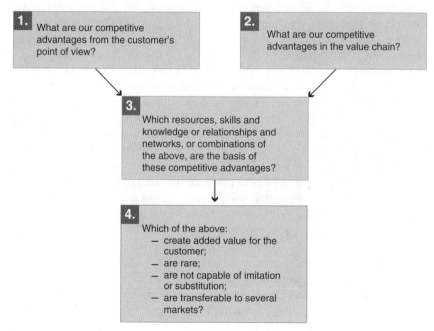

Figure 6.3 Identifying core competences

management expected. However, it also often emerges that customers are completely unaware of the advantages that companies have.

Some time ago, we were contacted by the managing director of a mechanical engineering company. He told us that he had visited some companies in China. As he was being led through the factory halls of one of the larger Chinese manufacturers, he noticed that one large machine was covered with a white cloth. When the machine was finally uncovered, he was amazed to see that it was one of his machines and realized that he could not remember having sold this machine to this company. The management team that was showing him around the company then proudly told him that they had not bought this machine from him, but had copied it, one-to-one. It was not possible to see that it was an imitation. He then asked about the price at which they sold this machine and turned pale when he heard the answer: €20,000. That was exactly one tenth of his selling price. In response to this, we said that in this case there was probably only one way to survive in the market: technological leads, innovation, and speed. The managing director said that he too had thought this until he found out how long the Chinese had needed to copy this machine. They had practically managed it overnight. Nevertheless, he was optimistic, as he knew that many customers preferred his machine because they could rely on the excellent service network. They knew that it was only a matter of hours or of 1–2 days at the most, until a broken machine could be repaired or a replacement part delivered. That was his competitive advantage. The Chinese were far from being able to guarantee this and the costs to the customer of a machine breaking down for a long period of time were so high that they could not take the risk and bought the machine from the original manufacturer. Nevertheless, he did not settle for this because he knew that it would probably be only a question of time before the Chinese competitors set up a half-decent service network. But, he continued, he did have a lead that was not so easy to close in on: he had a team of excellent production experts, as he called them. They had many years of experience in optimizing production processes – not least because the mechanical engineering company was vertically integrated and had a factory in which it manufactured using its own machines. This enabled the production experts to gain experience and build up knowledge that they could pass on to the buyers of the machines. This was valuable knowledge that sometimes brought the customer enormous increases in efficiency and productivity, since as soon as a machine was bought, the production experts went out to the customer with the assembly technicians. The production experts examined the customer's processes and advised them on how to optimize the entire production flow – this service was free of charge. None of the competitors did this, neither were they in a position to, since nobody else had these competences. Everything indicated that the machine manufacturer had a core competence here. We were commissioned to carry out customer interviews worldwide, in order to determine where the company's strengths and weaknesses lay and the direction in which the company should develop. For the most part, we interviewed the production managers and managing directors of these companies. We interviewed the production managers because they dealt with the machines on a daily basis and the managing directors because they made the buying decisions. We examined a whole range of buying criteria, weighted them, and evaluated them in comparison with competitors. On the whole, the production managers were satisfied with all aspects of the service. When we asked about the benefit provided by the production experts, many of the production managers were simply delighted. Most of them confirmed to us that the production experts were highly qualified and that they had optimized their production processes with lasting effect. This service brought significant added value to customers and they did not have to pay for it. When we interviewed the managing directors, the first thing we heard were complaints that the machines were simply too expensive. However, they also confirmed to us that the quality and the service were fine. When we finally asked the managing directors what they thought about the "additional free production-optimization service" by the production experts, the answers were surprising. Most of the managing directors said: "Additional free service!? With this company absolutely nothing is free. And I don't know anything about a production-optimization service either." The company possessed a core competence that the customer was not aware of. In this case, the problem was easy to solve: the service provided by the production optimizers was priced and appeared on the invoice, only to be immediately deducted again.

There is a principle which states: every product feature adds cost, but not every product feature delivers benefits. In this case, however, they were more than product features; they were core competences.

A thorough analysis of customer perceptions is therefore an important building block of core competence analysis. Only competences which are perceived as such by customers can be core competences.

Since customer-oriented strengths and weaknesses analyses are nothing more than snapshots and reflect past performance, in a second step we supplement them with an analysis of the value chain. To this end, we study the company's value-creation profile. We identify the individual steps in the value chain (primary activities, such as incoming logistics, production, outgoing logistics, marketing, and distribution, as well as service and support activities, such as corporate infrastructure, human resource management, technology development, and procurement).[19] We assess the strategic significance of each of these activities and compare them with the competitors. The result is a value-oriented strengths and weaknesses analysis.

This fascinating work starts with an analysis of what leads to the individual competitive advantages – from both a customer and a value-chain perspective. To do this, we ask ourselves which resources, skills, and knowledge or relationships and networks account for the fact that the company exhibits strengths compared to its competitors. Taking a step-by-step approach, we

Table 6.1 Tangible and intangible resources[20]

Resources	
Tangible resources	*Financial resources*
	Organizational resources
	• Planning systems • Control systems • Management information systems • Coordination mechanisms
	Physical resources
	• Location • Access to raw materials
Intangible resources	*Technological resources*
	• Technologies • Patents • Research establishments • Technical and scientific employees
	Reputation
	• Brands • Customer relationships • Reputation among stakeholders
	Human resources
	• Training and experience of employees • Flexibility of employees • Commitment and loyalty of employees • Trust and cooperation

try to identify the drivers for each of the identified strengths. First of all, we examine resources, then skills, using the resources listed in Table 6.1 and the skills shown in Table 6.2 as a guide. Finally, we examine the knowledge resources, relationships, and networks within the company. This item covers, for example, R&D networks, relationships with governments, relationships with stakeholders (capital markets, suppliers, and so on), and relationships with research institutions and similar organizations.

The final result is a list of resources, skills, knowledge, relationships, and networks which account for the emergence of competitive advantages. Often, competitive advantages only come about through combining individual

Table 6.2 Examples of skills[21]

Functional area	Skill
Corporate function	• Financial control • Strategic management of business units • Strategic innovation • Multi-divisional coordination • Acquisition management • International management
Management information	• Well-functioning management information system and MIS-based decision-making
Research & development	• Research capabilities • Product development competences • Process development competences
Logistics	• Logistics competence • Process control • Interface management
Production	• Exploiting economies of scale • Continuous improvement • Flexibility
Product design	• Design skills
Marketing	• Brand management • Ability to react to market requirements • Customer-relationship management
Distribution	• Efficiency in acquisition and order-processing • Speed of distribution • Quality of customer service

resources and skills, and so on. Therefore, it is also necessary at this point to study the combined effect of the individual drivers of competitive advantages, that is, the competence bundles.

In the last step, we then test whether the drivers of competitive advantages we have identified in this way are actually core competences. For this, we use a simple diagram consisting of four questions, which are shown in Figure 6.4.

MANAGING CORE COMPETENCES

Top companies have unique resources and skills bundles at their disposal. Top senior executives never settle for today's success. They constantly seek to exploit new opportunities and areas of potential. They know exactly not only

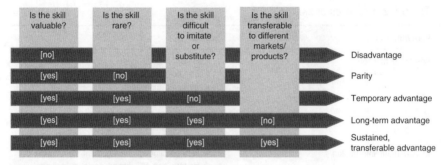

Figure 6.4 The evaluation of competences[22]

Figure 6.5 Managing core competences

what their company's core competences are, but also where their limits lie and which competences must be strengthened for the future. They are experts in the management of core competences and constantly seek answers to the following questions (Figure 6.5):

• In which new products or markets can we exploit our core competences and thereby develop new potential for success?
• Which new competences do we need in the new markets?
• How can we enhance or protect our existing core competences?
• Which new competences do we need in our existing markets?

From core competences to new areas of business

The cardinal question in competence management is this: are there any products or markets in which we can exploit our core competences? Many of the most successful companies are experts at this. They know how to leverage their core competences. There are numerous examples of market entries into new areas of business which succeeded because companies possessed core competences which were transferable. One of them is Fischer,[23] the ski manufacturer.

This Austrian ski manufacturer succeeded in firmly establishing itself as a supplier to the aviation industry, thanks to its development competence. Companies such as Boeing and Airbus are among its regular customers. Fischer Advanced Composite Components, FACC for short, has specialized in the development and manufacture of lightweight composite components and has achieved major international success in this area for over 10 years.

The starting point for this was development work for a new generation of cross-country skis. Since it was founded, Fischer had developed itself into a renowned manufacturer of alpine and cross-country skis. Superstars, such as Franz Klammer and Markus Wasmeier, placed their trust in the products from Ried im Innkreis, Austria. The company's product excellence has always been based on a revolutionary research and development spirit. Fischer succeeded in making technological leaps in both alpine and cross-country skis again and again.

Following this tradition, in the 1970s, Fischer set itself a very challenging goal. It was necessary to develop a particularly light, unbreakable cross-country ski. The developers did not attempt to optimize existing products, focusing instead on a completely new production technology which would make it possible to manufacture extremely light composite components from fiber-reinforced fiberglass. The result was impressive: it became possible to manufacture cross-country skis which had a maximum weight of 1000 g and were particularly stable. Along with this technology, Fischer had developed a clear core competence.

Nevertheless, even Fischer was affected by stagnation in the international ski market at the end of the 1970s. At that time, around 50 employees worked in its development department. Then, the financial director delivered the news that development costs would have to be reduced. Back then, Walter Stephan, who is now Managing Director and CEO of FACC, had just taken over the management of the Fischer Group's research and development department. Following a long period of deliberation, the company decided not to reduce staff numbers – as is so common – but rather to think about whether and in what form the knowledge from the new production technology could be supplied to other industries. Stephan, himself a technology freak and an enthusiastic amateur pilot, was convinced that the expertise from producing particularly light and extremely stable parts would be of particular interest to the aviation industry.

Shortly after the company had commenced activities as a development firm, Airbus Industries became the first company to order aircraft components from Fischer in 1981. In the next few years, contracts with McDonnell Douglas and Boeing, among others, were to follow. Looking back on this today, Walter Stephan says: "We were extremely motivated and began to research. However, we soon realized that nobody is interested in pure development work." Customers' needs extended far further, including into product support. Fischer took note of this: from 1985 onwards, the orders from this market grew so rapidly that Fischer created its own aviation division. Although the R&D department had continued to grow, developments in the area of sports equipment were suffering as a result of the increasing demand from the aviation industry. This finally led to a spin-off from the group in 1989 and the founding of FACC GmbH, a wholly owned subsidiary of Fischer. In the following years, FACC managed to successfully establish itself among the leading American and European aircraft component manufacturers. In 2005, FACC had 1140 employees and achieved a turnover of €150m.

FACC's first development in 1981 were structural components, and parts for aircraft interiors soon followed. Today, it produces components for engine cowls, as well as control surfaces for fuselages and tail assemblies. It also manufactures landing flaps for various types of Airbus, as well as the engine cowl and nose of the Airbus 340. Airbus's competitor Boeing also places its trust in quality parts from FACC.

Richard L. James, President of Boeing Europe, says: "FACC has always proved that it can supply its innovations at sensible market prices and also maintain that." The basis for this successful entry into the aviation industry were the core competences initially developed in the manufacture of skis.

Recognizing competence deficits in new markets

As a rule, transferring core competences to new markets and products is not sufficient: it is usually necessary to acquire new, additional competences. This requires consistent market orientation which, in turn, requires in-depth understanding of the market game rules.

In 1994, Jeff Bezos was given the task of finding attractive, promising Internet companies, in which his employer, D. E. Shaw & Company, could invest. At that time, the Internet had enormous growth rates and the number of users was rising by 2300 percent every month. Bezos began to consider which products and services could best be sold over the Internet and initially developed a list of 20 products. Two months later, he traveled across America with his wife. While she was at the wheel, Bezos drafted a business plan on his laptop and began searching for investors. Bezos chose books. There was no dominant supplier in this market. The largest was Barnes & Noble, which had a market share of 15 percent in 1994. Amazon.com was founded. The company's success – since 2003, Amazon has been one of the few dot-coms founded at that time to make a profit – rests on core competences in logistics, in customer orientation through individualizing products and services, and in the IT competences that this requires. What initially worked well with books was systematically extended to other areas. Jeff Bezos continuously searched for new products and markets in which he could exploit the company's core competences. First of all, the range was extended to include music CDs and videos. Electronic products were also added to the range, as were software, video games, electronic greeting cards, online auctions, and DVDs. Today, Amazon has over 7800 employees and sells its products in a total of 220 countries on all the continents.

However, Amazon was also to learn the hard way that its core competences were not always sufficient for successfully entering new markets. When Amazon added toys to its product range in 1999, it suffered a major setback. In the toy business, Christmas trade is of prime importance and accounts for a large part of sales. Amazon expected a multi-million-dollar business, but the company was left with vast numbers of toys and recorded losses of €39m on a turnover of €95m.[24] What was the reason for this? Its core competences were obviously not enough. It seems Amazon had overlooked a competence which is very important in this industry. Since Christmas trade accounts for a large part of sales, it is necessary to determine the product range and commence marketing activities as early as the spring or summer of that year. For this, a company must possess one of two skills: (1) it must possess the experience or intuition to predict which products will be the best-sellers in Christmas trade; or (2) it must be in a position to influence trends. Amazon lacked both of these skills. Its warehouses remained full of products that nobody wanted.

In that same year, the largest toy manufacturer, Toys'R'Us, attempted to enter the Internet business. Toys'R'Us's strength lay in its large product range and it had also mastered the game rules of the market. There is no doubt that it had the competences that Amazon lacked: core competences in purchasing and marketing. Nevertheless, even this business turned into a bitter disappointment. Thousands of customers are still waiting today for the presents they ordered for their children back then. Many of them never arrived. Toys'R'Us failed due to logistics. The Federal Trade Commission even imposed a fine of €350,000.

In both cases, the companies had clear core competences in their core markets but lacked the competences that were required in the new markets. It was obvious to Jeff Bezos as well as to John Eyler of Toys'R'Us, what had to be done. In 2000, they signed a strategic alliance in which the core competences of both companies complemented each other. Toys'R'Us assumed responsibility for purchasing management and storage risks and Amazon took on the design of the website, inventory management, and customer services. The alliance initially proved to be a success until disputes broke out in 2004 regarding obligations within the alliance.

This example illustrates how important it is to understand and master the game rules of the new market. Mergers and acquisitions or strategic alliances are possible ways of acquiring the necessary competences if these cannot be developed internally. However – as experience in practice shows – between 40 and 60 percent of these initiatives fail. A second risk lies in the difficulty of integrating the core competences and a third lies in competence drain.

Tirelessly enhancing core competences

A further characteristic of top companies is that they constantly enhance their core competences. This of course necessitates continuous investment in extending them. As learning opportunities increase, they usually leverage the enhancement of core competences. This is primarily the case if the core competences (1) are employed in different areas and (2) learning opportunities are systematically exploited. If these conditions are fulfilled, transferring core competences to different areas can contribute significantly to their further development.

Acquiring new core competences for existing markets – the risk of "core rigidities"

Oskar Barnack, an amateur photographer and head of the camera research department at the Ernst Leitz Optical Works in Wetzlar Germany, simply wanted to photograph people looking animated and true-to-life without having to carry around heavy photographic plates and tripods, just in order to take a photo. In 1925, he developed the first 35 mm camera, which soon went into series production. For professional photographers, the camera was a toy; for the photographing public it was a sensation. "Until then, the world always had to go to the camera. With the Leica, the camera went to the world," explained Hans-Peter Cohn of Leica Camera AG.[25] Legendary photographers, such as Henri Cartier-Bresson or Robert Capa, were delighted with the Leica. Famous pictures, such as the hoisting of the Russian flag on the *Reichstag* in Berlin and Korda's famous portrait of Che Guevara, were taken with the Leica. All over the world the Leica stood for leading-edge technology, German quality and consistency, and simple yet brilliant technology without bells and whistles. The company's core competence could be found in optics and mechanics. After years of declining sales, the company made a loss in 2003, as well as in 2004 and 2005. For many years, Leica resisted the trend toward digital photography, assuming that discerning Leica customers would be more interested in experiencing the joy of photography than in megapixels and seek the highest quality, in terms of both the lens system and camera mechanics, as well as the finished picture.[26] Furthermore, the management assumed that its own core competences could not be transferred to digital photography and resisted digital technology as, for a long time, the quality it produced could not come close to that of analogue technology. The company did enter the digital-camera market, although arguably too late and with little momentum.

Similarly, many television manufacturers spent years enhancing cathode ray tubes and ignored and ultimately missed out on the trend toward flat screen TVs.

Restructuring core competences for existing markets presents many companies with key and, at the same time, difficult challenges, particularly if technological changes render old competences obsolete or if new customer requirements emerge. Companies which possess strong core competences run a great risk of developing what Dorothy Leonard-Barton[27] termed "core rigidities." Strong core competences can also be core rigidities which can prevent the company from acquiring new competences.

How can companies avoid this dilemma? We put this question to Michael Mirow, who has been head of strategic planning at Siemens for many years: "Core competences can be cages when it comes to radical innovations," was his answer, and he told us of a concept used at Siemens which has proved to be of value.[28]

This concept involves distinguishing between incremental innovations and revolutionary, breakthrough innovations. Product and technology roadmaps are used for planning incremental innovations, whereas backward calculation, or retropolation, is used for radical innovations.

The product roadmap is a chronological representation of all future generations of products or product groups. The time horizon is based on the duration of product lifecycles and the estimated duration of a product development process, ranging from 2 years for PCs to 10 years for steam and gas turbines in power plant construction. In cooperation with key customers and suppliers, product managers, technologists, and industry experts work on possible future options and glean from them ideas for products and the progression of product generations. This is an extrapolative approach; that is, it is based on the existing product range.

The second type of tools are technology roadmaps, which supplement the product roadmaps. Technology roadmaps are also extrapolative. Their purpose is to identify in good time technologies which could be applied to future products. Therefore, core competences must continually be enhanced and missing competences or technologies acquired.

A comparison of the technology and product roadmaps leads to adjustments in the R&D strategy and the development of appropriate competences and technologies.

Technology and product roadmaps use "known and extrapolatable, business and technological paths."[29] Innovations are based on the company's core competences, which are also continuously being enhanced. There is therefore no deviation from "development trajectories," making radical, breakthrough innovations virtually impossible. The starting point is existing products and competences which are "extrapolated."

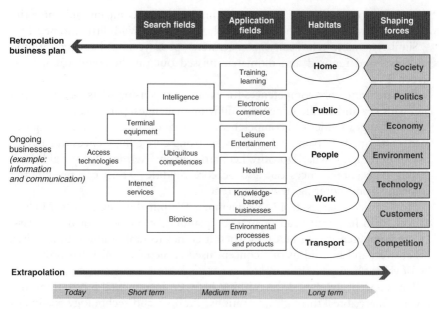

Figure 6.6 Strategic visioning at Siemens[30]

In order to achieve radical, breakthrough innovations and avoid "core rigidities," companies combine extrapolations with retropolations. This process links future visions to the current product and technology portfolio (Figure 6.6).

The starting point for retropolation is first the "shaping forces" (society, politics, economy, environment, and so on) which influence people's habitats (home, public, and so on). Derived from this are technical application fields (for example, training, health, and so on), which are carried forward into specific search fields for specific technologies. Here, the technologies derived from the roadmaps meet the "retropolated" technological developments. Comparing these two independent approaches ensures that, on the one hand, existing technologies and competences are enhanced, and that, on the other hand, new, important competence fields and competence deficits are recognized. Linking extrapolation and retropolation makes it possible to identify revolutionary breakthrough innovations, which can be traced back to discontinuities in technologies, applications, or markets.

7 Corporate culture: The latent potential

Peter Drucker, arguably one of the most important management thinkers, wrote in the *Harvard Business Review* some years ago that the only comparative competitive advantage that developed countries have today resides in their large contingent of knowledge workers. The productivity of knowledge and knowledge workers, which still receives too little attention and is alarmingly low, must be continuously and systematically increased.[1] Successful corporate management, Drucker argued, will, to an increasing extent, require knowledge about processes and conditions inside and outside the company. However, a problem resides in the fact that, to a large extent, knowledge as a resource belongs to the knowledge workers themselves. Knowledge workers carry their knowledge with them in their heads and it can be taken with them to any place of employment. Making this knowledge bear fruit requires strong orientation toward employees. Only those companies who succeed in creating value for employees will be able to tie them in and exploit their potential.

The sources of value creation have radically changed in the last few years. An analysis of the market-to-book ratio of the Standard & Poor's 500 provides clear evidence that the importance of intangible assets has increased considerably (Figure 7.1). Whereas at the beginning of the 1980s tangible assets still carried considerable weight, today the market value of companies is, on average, three to four times the book value. Even the market correction following the dot-com bubble did not change this long-term trend.

Intangible assets can be roughly divided into two groups: intellectual capital (for example, human resources, knowledge, innovative ability, and so on) and relational resources (for example, brands, reputation, stakeholder relationships, and so on). As Peter Drucker's quote at the start of this chapter points out, knowledge is one of the industrialized nations' most crucial competitive factors.

Nowadays, we speak of a "knowledge-based view of the firm"[2] in management theory. It is based on the following assumptions:[3]

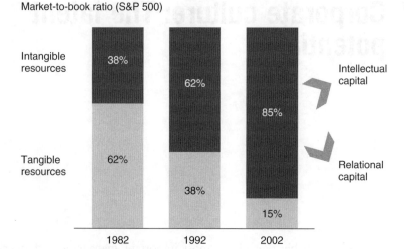

Figure 7.1 Market-to-book ratio

(*Sources*: Brooking Inst., S&P 500, Kaplan & Norton)

- Knowledge is the most important resource due to its strategic significance for increasing the value of a company.
- Unlike other resources, knowledge is inexhaustible and is not used up when it is exploited.
- Owing to its characteristic attributes, such as being highly context-specific for example, knowledge is transferable only to a limited extent.
- People are the basic building blocks of knowledge processes; knowledge is found in the heads of individual employees.

Organizing and harnessing knowledge in companies is now a key challenge, as knowledge is the basis for innovation and innovation is the basis for competitiveness. As the quote from Peter Drucker mentioned at the start of the chapter states, the only competitive advantage of the industrialized nations resides in knowledge workers, or so-called "gold-collar workers."[4] Yet even having sufficient numbers of highly qualified employees has not been a unique selling point for the industrialized nations for some time now. Germany's universities produce around 40,000 engineers a year; in India around 200,000 engineers leave university every year. These are graduates who are not only highly qualified, but also highly motivated, and who offer their services for a relatively low salary. So competition is increasing on this front too.

If companies are to develop and exploit knowledge resources, employees must be their core consideration, since only individual employees, as the carriers of knowledge, can influence knowledge processes. Therefore, the quality of the processes is determined to a significant extent by the commitment of every single employee.[5] The "productivity of knowledge and knowledge workers, which still receives too little attention and is alarmingly low, must be continuously and systematically increased":[6] a prerequisite for this is the commitment of every single employee. "Commitment," Argyris writes, "is to do with releasing human energies and activating our intellectual powers. Without commitment, the realisation of each new initiative or idea would be seriously jeopardised."[7]

Based on this insight, it is interesting to see how the top decision-makers assess the level of commitment of the employees in their companies. In top companies – we termed them as "innovators" – the senior executives work on the assumption that 70 percent of employees are committed to the company; in the average companies it was just 60 percent.

What could be the reason for this? The senior executives' answers show that the causes of a lack of commitment (Figure 7.2) are primarily seen to lie in the attitude of senior executives themselves, who are often, according to the statements of the decision-makers, not able to interest employees in their tasks, appreciate their work, formulate clear objectives, or build a culture of trust within the company.

Should one wish to consider the emergence of commitment in greater depth, in our view it is necessary to consider two dimensions. First, it is necessary to understand which basic conditions must be present in order for commitment in groups to develop at all. Based on this, it is possible to study the real triggers of goal-oriented commitment.

The work of both Stewart Wolf and Robert Putnam provides valuable insights about the basic prerequisites for creating sustained commitment. Both authors have studied certain social phenomena for many years. In particular, they succeeded in demonstrating the significance that being integrated in a

Reasons for a lack of commitment in employees

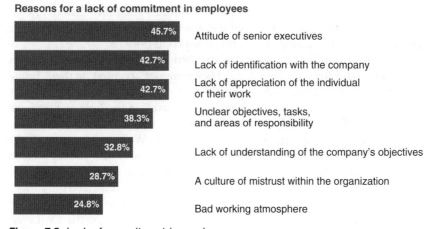

45.7%	Attitude of senior executives
42.7%	Lack of identification with the company
42.7%	Lack of appreciation of the individual or their work
38.3%	Unclear objectives, tasks, and areas of responsibility
32.8%	Lack of understanding of the company's objectives
28.7%	A culture of mistrust within the organization
24.8%	Bad working atmosphere

Figure 7.2 Lack of commitment in employees

community, finding trust within a group, and identifying with the values of the group can have for the development of each individual and the group as a whole.

The work of Viktor Frankl, a doctor and psychologist, provides useful insights with regard to triggering goal-oriented commitment. According to his findings, the approaches often used in companies for increasing the motivation of employees cannot produce a lasting effect. We will return to this subject later.

VALUES AND IDENTITY AS A BASIS FOR COMMITMENT

In the 1960s, Roseto, a small Italian-American community in Northampton County, Pennsylvania, presented medical professionals with an almost insoluble puzzle.[8] Its inhabitants were the most healthy in the whole of the US. Only one in 1000 male inhabitants died of a heart attack – the US average was 3.5; the death rate for women was even lower – 0.6 per 1000, compared to the national average of 2.09. They also had a longer life expectancy and suffered less frequently from mental illnesses and stomach ulcers.[9] The inhabitants of Roseto smoked just as much or as little as average American citizens, they had completely normal eating habits, did an average amount of sport, had similar ethnic and genetic roots, and even exhibited an above-average level of obesity. Analyses of death certificates, hospital records, autopsies, and so on provided no explanation for this phenomenon. The citizens of Roseto also used the same water as the neighboring communities and the same doctors worked there. In studies lasting many years, hoards of doctors and scientists analyzed medical histories, took blood and urine samples, measured blood pressure and carried out electrocardiograms – without result. The phenomenon could not be explained medically. When Benjamin Franklin, a local doctor in Roseto, told the health sociologist Steward Wolf that he hardly saw any patients of under 50 with heart conditions, Wolf took notice and began to take an interest in Roseto. His approach was different: it was not a medical approach. Instead, he assumed that the reasons lay in the social conditions.

Roseto was founded at the end of the 19th century by Italian emigrants. They had it hard from the very start. They were not accepted by their Anglo-Saxon neighbors and they did not have the same chance of getting good jobs. The Italians were just about good enough "to work in the hole or throw out the rubbish."[10] Presumably, it was for this very reason that the inhabitants stuck together and supported each other. Stewart Wolf and John G. Bruhn noticed that they were particularly vivacious, adventurous, and optimistic. Roseto had its own culture, shaped by old-fashioned values and customs. Family and the community were important to them, they respected old people, and they helped each other out in times of need. It was also striking that there were many clubs and organizations which were dedicated to the act of helping each other. Mutual trust and solidarity, as well as knowing they could rely on each other, shaped their social interaction. The supposition that there had to be a correlation between these social factors and health was borne out by numerous interviews and observations. A strong community, an emotionally supportive social environment, mutual trust, common values, and close relationships with each other were the reasons for the unusually good health of the inhabitants of Roseto. The connection between social relationships and health was confirmed. All the more so when, after some years, the researchers observed that the living habits of the inhabitants of Roseto were becoming "Americanized," causing the differences in health to disappear.[11]

The difference between the rich Italian North and the poor South resembles the growing difference between the First and Third World.[12] Countless initiatives by the Italian government and the EU failed in their objective of helping the economy in the South to its feet. An unemployment rate of around 20 percent, a gross national product per capita that was over 40 percent lower than that of the North, and a third less private consumption, and so on bear witness to how far behind the Mezzogiorno was. There was much speculation as to the reasons for this. The unfavorable geographical position and lack of industrialization, as well as the Mafia and often also the attitude of the population were put forward as reasons. But these explanations were not satisfactory. When Robert Putnam[13] studied the matter in depth, he found clear differences. Whereas the North Italians worked closely together within the community, had more trust in institutions and their fellow citizens, supported each other more and were also considerably more committed to their role as good citizens, the South was characterized by the principle of "never cooperate." The way of life in the South was characterized by mistrust, shirking one's responsibilities, disorder, isolation, and exploitation. The North Italians were organized into associations to a considerably greater degree, showed more interest in politics, had higher voter participation rates, read more newspapers, and had more common values within the community. Robert Putnam concluded from this that trust, norms, and social networks have very decisive influence on how efficiently a society coordinates its activities. "Social capital" explains a large part of the economic development of regions.[14]

What do the experiences in Roseto and the Mezzogiorno have in common? The role of the community, trust, the strength of relationships with others, identification with common values, and so on were decisive factors in both cases – in one case for the health of the people, in the other case for the economic development of the region.

Acquaintances and mutual recognition arise from the network of relationships. Out of gratitude, respect, and friendship grows a duty for the individual to serve the community.[15]

Norms which are recognized by all group members, mutual trust and close relationship networks – described by Robert Putnam as "social capital" – render cooperation within organizations more efficient.[16]

The idea of social capital has also been taken up in management literature, and it has been proven that more knowledge is exchanged and more intellectual capital comes into existence in companies with high social capital. In short, social capital fosters the emergence of intellectual capital. Intellectual capital is the source of innovation and competitiveness. The elements of social capital are therefore significant building blocks of a strong corporate culture which fosters efficiency and innovation (Figure 7.3).

On the whole, we may conclude from these insights that the way a group "lives together" within an organization has a decisive influence on its members' willingness to commit themselves within and to the company. However, the question inevitably arises as to how this willingness can also be aligned with the objectives of the company. It has been shown that, although mechanical approaches, such as cleverly thought-out MBO systems, are helpful in principle, they are not capable of kindling the emotional energies which are associated with "genuine" commitment. This enthusiasm can only come into existence and have long-term effect if employees can identify with the company itself, its purpose, its main objectives, and the values for which it stands in terms of content and emotion.

Now the question inevitably arises as to what conditions must be present in order that employees can identify with "their" company in terms of content and emotion. The work of Viktor Frankl on the subject of "meaning" provides

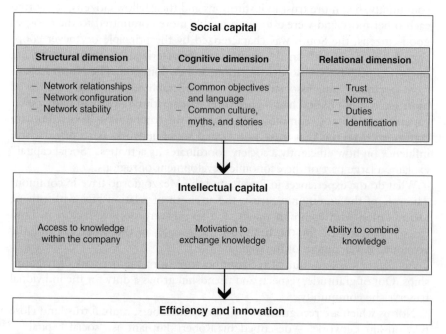

Figure 7.3 Social capital and intellectual capital[17]

important food for thought with regard to this question, among other things. The issue of creating meaning is so important in this context that we count it among those tasks of top management which should not be delegated. We will therefore discuss this topic in connection with the subject of leadership.

We have seen that a stable culture with close relationships, strong values, a high level of identification and trust, and so on is essential. Now the question arises as to how these values must be formed in order that the culture fosters the willingness to change and take risks, flexibility, and, finally, innovation orientation. In our studies, we found that a special type of culture – we call it 'entrepreneurship culture' – is a strong characteristic of top performers.

THE ENTREPRENEURSHIP CULTURE

Nicolas G. Hayek, the founder of Swatch and savior of the Swiss watch-and-clockmaking industry, has often been heard to say: "If you send a donkey to the Conservatory of Music in Salzburg, you won't make a Mozart out of him. And if you send a camel to Harvard and organize an MBA for him, you won't make a Henry Ford out of him."[18] "Where are the Bosches, Thyssens or Fords?" Hayek asks himself as he senses that nowadays there is no atmosphere of entrepreneurship anywhere. "Instead, there are a load of managers who are ripping people off and have no idea. All they do is cut jobs." Hayek's statement probably expresses the sentiments of many people. We also normally attribute the willingness to take risks, the propensity to innovate, and dynamism to entrepreneurs, rather than to managers. It is often said that entrepreneurship cannot be learned. However, in our study we found managers in the top companies who are inherently no different from entrepreneurs. They think in opportunities and are prepared to take risks. They focus on innovation and advancement and are dynamic and visionary. Above all, though, we found that the entire culture of the company was shaped by entrepreneurial values.

Such "entrepreneurial" cultures have very specific characteristics. One can characterize company cultures in a similar way to how one can describe an individual's personality. There are some companies which strongly orientate themselves toward the market and customers, and others which are more concerned with themselves and are inward-facing. Equally, there are companies in which values such as flexibility and spontaneity prevail, and some to whom order and stability are far more important. If we combine these two dimensions (inward versus outward orientation and flexibility versus stability), we obtain four types of ideals in corporate cultures (Figure 7.4).

- The *clan culture* is characterized by team spirit, loyalty, tradition, and a familiar atmosphere. Here, strategic priorities lie in the development of human resources, in the commitment of employees, and in moral principles. This internal orientation can be a contributing factor in the company not noticing changing customer needs and market factors very quickly.

- The *hierarchy culture* is characterized by the fact that clear rules, which lead to constancy, stability, and smooth-running processes, prevail. Key characteristics are standardization and formalization and, for the most part, senior executives perform the role of "custodian." Due to strong inward orientation and a low level of flexibility, changes are very difficult to implement and are often even considered disruptive.
- The *market culture* emphasizes competitiveness and achieving objectives. Market mechanisms guide the processes. Productivity, performance orientation, and achieving competitive advantages are key priorities. Although these companies have a strong outward orientation, they are also heavily oriented toward efficiency. Innovations will therefore only take place on a limited scale.
- Finally, the *culture of entrepreneurship* has a strong outward orientation and emphasizes spontaneity, flexibility, and dynamism. Innovation and growth are key strategic priorities. Therefore, this type of culture exhibits the greatest innovative ability.[19]

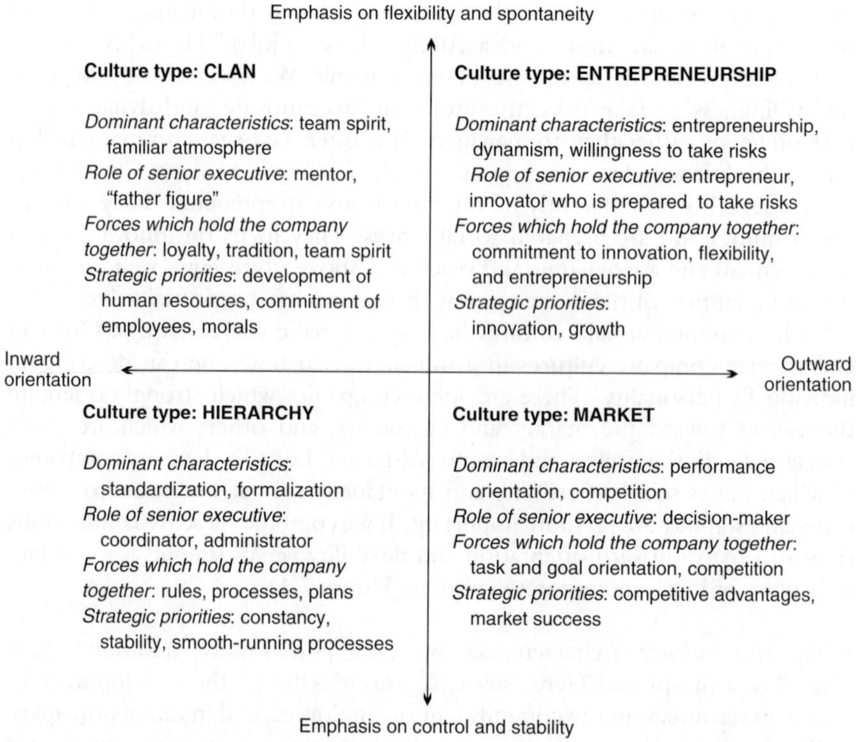

Emphasis on flexibility and spontaneity

Culture type: CLAN

Dominant characteristics: team spirit, familiar atmosphere
Role of senior executive: mentor, "father figure"
Forces which hold the company together: loyalty, tradition, team spirit
Strategic priorities: development of human resources, commitment of employees, morals

Culture type: ENTREPRENEURSHIP

Dominant characteristics: entrepreneurship, dynamism, willingness to take risks
Role of senior executive: entrepreneur, innovator who is prepared to take risks
Forces which hold the company together: commitment to innovation, flexibility, and entrepreneurship
Strategic priorities: innovation, growth

Inward orientation ← → Outward orientation

Culture type: HIERARCHY

Dominant characteristics: standardization, formalization
Role of senior executive: coordinator, administrator
Forces which hold the company together: rules, processes, plans
Strategic priorities: constancy, stability, smooth-running processes

Culture type: MARKET

Dominant characteristics: performance orientation, competition
Role of senior executive: decision-maker
Forces which hold the company together: task and goal orientation, competition
Strategic priorities: competitive advantages, market success

Emphasis on control and stability

Figure 7.4 Types of corporate culture[20]

An inwardly oriented culture which fosters stability and order may be right for companies in markets in which there is little change, where the future looks the same as the present and where innovations are not necessary or not desired. However, it is a hindrance in dynamic markets in which new opportunities are constantly emerging and change is the only thing that remains constant. Here, entrepreneurship, dynamism, the willingness to take risks, and commitment to innovation and flexibility are the required key values – values which must be shared by everybody. Only then will a climate develop in which employees will be motivated to constantly question the existing situation, think about better solutions, and seek original ways to do new things; in other words, to develop themselves and the company further.

So how is it possible to develop and embed an entrepreneurship culture in the company?

Basically, values, attitudes, and norms which shape a corporate culture have three sources:[21]

1. the beliefs, values, and premises of the person who founded the company;
2. the experiences that employees have in the course of the company's development; and
3. the beliefs, values, and premises that originate from new employees and senior executives.

They say that Albert Einstein once said: "Giving an example is not the most important way to influence others. It is the only way."[22] René Obermann, the CEO of T-Mobile and now CEO of Deutsche Telekom, is of the opinion that "People don't follow what you say, they follow what you do."

Beliefs, values, and premises can be conveyed by consciously setting an example not only through one's own behavior, but also through unconscious signals. The charisma of the senior executive is a decisive factor in this.

Mary Douglas,[23] an anthropologist, says: "Culture is all that matters" and Karolina Frenzel and her co-authors write in their book *Story-Telling*: "The things that are important to a person, a group or an organization cannot be seen at first glance. Often, one only finds this out after long periods of observation and some consideration, since what is important is not always identical to what a group says is important to it. One can only see what is really important to the group if one observes the interplay between actions, communication and rituals, and everything it does not do, although it could. It is this interplay between different factors that ultimately determines the rules according to which the group tries to obtain and achieve the things that are important to it. The group does certain things again and again and uses very specific practices and rituals to prevent certain things from happening and make it likely that certain other things will occur. This whole, sometimes simple, sometimes complex system of rules, practices, communications and objectives: that is culture."[24]

It is not just the things that are said and emphasized; it is the – often also unconscious – things that are done. And also the things that are not done. Or, as Paul Watzlawick formulates it: "One cannot not communicate."

There are a range of methods which help senior executives embed cultural values in the company. Not all of them are equally effective. Edgar Schein, a professor at the Sloan School of Management at MIT, subdivides them into embedding mechanisms and articulation and reinforcement mechanisms.[25] By doing so, he has created a useful overview of individual mechanisms in culture development (Table 7.1).

- *One of the most effective mechanisms for embedding value within the company are the signals that senior executives send by the way they allocate time and set priorities. Employees in the company are very aware of what senior executives see as priorities, as they observe what is important to them, the things they judge and how they judge them and also, above all, what they monitor.*

Across all the top performers it emerged that, when prioritizing their time, the decision-makers are very strongly oriented toward the things they want to bring into the organization. While doing this, they are conscious of their function as role models and focus everything on ensuring that employees can see, from the behavior of the most senior decision-makers in particular, the key significance of the core activities that are required of them. For instance, they do not just preach the significance of customer and market orientation for the success of the company, they also live by these principles. They spend a large proportion of their time on visiting customers, carrying out negotiations themselves, discussing potential innovations with customers, and so on. This does not only enable them to obtain unfiltered market knowledge that is

Table 7.1 Mechanisms for embedding culture[26]

Embedding mechanisms: employees orientate themselves toward...	Articulation and reinforcement mechanisms
... the things that are important to senior executives and what they pay attention to, judge and monitor	The form and structure of the company, organizational systems, and processes
... the way senior executives react to problematic events and crises	
... the way senior executives allocate scarce resources	The company's rituals and customs
... the example set by senior executives	The layout of premises, façades, and buildings
... the way incentive and reward systems are structured	Stories, legends, and myths about people and events
... the way senior executives select, recruit, promote, or exclude employees	Official statements on the philosophy, values, and doctrines of the company

important for the strategic orientation of the company; through this behavior, they also demonstrate to their employees that actively studying the market and recognizing changes as they arise is fundamental to the success of the company. They reinforce this feeling by discussing their own experiences in the market with employees. During these conversations, employees feel and see for themselves that top senior executives orientate themselves toward the market in their decision-making and are also aware of the problems and challenges in the market.

For example, René Obermann as a former CEO of T-Mobile use to 15–20 days a year in the company's shops or outside the office. It is easy to imagine how seeing their CEO in their shop, selling their products, is not merely a special experience for employees; it also draws their attention to a subject which is important within the company.

- *The way senior executives react to problems and crises clearly reveals their values and priorities.*

In particular, top performers distinguish themselves through firmly focusing on innovation. However, one of the prerequisites for innovation is that the company and its employees are prepared to take risks and possibly also accept defeats along the way, in order to be successful in the long term. In this context, Peter Brabeck-Letmathe emphasizes that, when selecting senior executives, he pays attention to whether the selected individuals also possess the necessary willingness to take risks. Therefore, only individuals who have also experienced failure in their careers are considered for management positions at Nestlé. It is also important to him to support this propensity to take risks. For him, this means always doggedly standing behind his senior executives, even if things go wrong again and again. Even and especially if the press or the capital markets exert pressure on these senior executives, he stands firmly by them and does not remove them from their respective "projects." In his view, sending these signals is the only way to keep a proactive and entrepreneurial culture alive.

Another leadership quality is mastering the balancing act between carrying on and saying "stop" in difficult situations. Particularly in difficult situations, top decision-makers distinguish themselves by not giving up at the first sign of resistance. Instead, through employing additional resources, they encourage the organization and its employees to continue to believe in the idea, to believe in it more than ever, and to fight for it. Often, they take the matter in hand themselves by working on the project and searching for solutions together with the team.

On the other hand, they are decisive enough to abandon projects they have initiated and driven forward themselves in good time if it is obvious that they are going to fail. Employees clearly recognize from this kind of behavior that even top decision-makers (must) accept defeats in order to be successful. At the same time, they also see that they have the courage to withdraw decisions they have reached and pushed through.

- *When it comes to allocating scarce resources – be they time, personnel, or financial resources – the most senior executives set priorities in line with what is important to them. These priorities are guided by their values and attitudes.*

As budgets are very important control instruments which have immediate effects on departments, projects, and employees, they are naturally of considerable importance in culture development. If support is only lent to those product-development projects which can be backed up by extensive market research studies and market tests and defended by "hard" arguments, this fosters a different innovation culture to if support is also lent to those ideas which cannot be calculated through to the last detail, for which there are only "soft" arguments, but which could "intuitively" be the right ones and also have a chance of obtaining a budget.

- *Employees also orientate themselves toward the behavior of senior executives who serve as role models to them. They adopt their behaviors, as they assume that this behavior is desired and will help them advance.*

As we have shown, top companies have a culture that we have described as an entrepreneurship culture. One of the distinguishing features of this type of culture is that employees actively exchange knowledge and work together on solutions for the company. In order for the willingness to cooperate in this way to come into existence, it is first necessary for everyone involved to realize that the team can find solutions better than an individual person. Secondly, it is necessary for the participants to treat one another with respect. Only this will bring about the kind of open exchange in team discussions which creates new knowledge.

In this context, top decision-makers must be conscious of the fact that they decisively influence this readiness to discuss things through their leadership style.

The CEO of a leading sports-equipment manufacturer continually pointed out in conversation the necessity of extensive teamwork for corporate success. He practices this himself when carrying out his managerial tasks. For example, every year over 40 individuals from different divisions of the company and from all its subsidiaries are brought together for 2 weeks to develop and adjust the corporate strategy within the framework of a 5-year rolling plan. During this time, the team members jointly develop strategic lines of attack and sign off the core initiatives that have been developed. This task would be easier to perform in a small team. However, this kind of joint planning and the inclusion of a large group of senior executives improve the quality of the ideas that are generated. This team process also increases the participants' motivation to implement the ideas and the speed at which they implement them. At the same time, it becomes evident to all the team members that the joint effort that is required of them is also actually put into practice by the CEO of the company.

- *Activities, decisions, and results which are rewarded through incentive and reward systems have as much influence on the values and attitudes of employees as behavior patterns or results which are not rewarded and therefore do not lead to any recognition.*

In the last few years, devising elaborate incentive and reward systems has developed into a discipline in itself in many companies. There is no doubt that appropriate monetary incentives can reinforce within the company the desired focus on certain areas. However, when developing these systems, companies should never forget that they only work in terms of the company as a whole if they do not put individual achievements above team achievements.

The motorcycle manufacturer KTM has a pronounced sense of team spirit within the company. Its employees help each other and produce outstanding results working together as a team. According to Stefan Pierer, the CEO of KTM, this is also reinforced by the fact that the company backs up its philosophy – that every employee makes an important contribution to the success of the company – with actions. When good results are achieved, each employee receives the same bonus; no differentiation is made between senior executives and all the other employees.

Finally, the criteria that are visible to employees with regard to selection, recruitment, promotion, and dismissal of staff members also transport the values and attitudes of the senior executives.

The role values can play in senior executive development is illustrated by Jack Welch's method of assessing senior executives at GE. In 1992, the management team of GE met in Boca Raton for a strategy meeting. Jack Welch and his top management team were able to look back on several successful years and everyone was in good spirits. Then Jack Welch said: "Look around you: five managers who sat among us last year are missing today. One went because of the figures, four went because of the core values."[27]

Jack Welch then presented the core values of GE:

- Love of acceleration
- Hatred of bureaucracy
- Willingness to change[28]

He divided all senior executives into four types (Figure 7.5).

Jack Welch said that Type 1 were absolute stars who achieved all their objectives and also lived by the values of the company. Type 2 was the opposite: "These people don't achieve their objectives and also have different values to

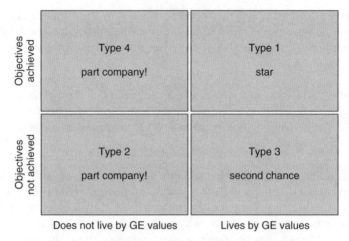

Figure 7.5 Selection and assessment of senior executives at GE[29]

us here at GE. This type won't grow old at GE." With regard to Type 3s, he said that they tried hard, achieved some of their plans and fell short of others, but worked well with other people and shared GE's values. This type deserved another chance. Although Type 4s achieved all their objectives, they did not share GE's values and demoralized their colleagues. Jack Welch said of them: "These are the typical big shots, the bullies, those people you would dearly love to get rid of – if it wasn't for the results!" Some years later, Jack Welch added: "The decision to get rid of the Type 4s was a watershed in our history, but we had to do that if we wanted GE people to talk openly, to open their mouths, and to exchange information."[30] Jack Welch introduced 360° feedback for assessing senior executives. Each employee was rated on a scale of one to five by their colleagues, superiors, and subordinates in areas such as team-building, quality focus, and vision.[31]

Edgar Schein counts the structure of the company, processes, rituals, and customs, as well as the layout of its premises and myths and stories about events and people and, finally, public statements regarding corporate philosophy among the "secondary" mechanisms for shaping culture. They are generally less effective than the primary mechanisms explained above; they are "artefacts" which result from the primary mechanisms. The messages that arise from these secondary mechanisms are more difficult to control, but they reinforce the primary ones. If they are not in alignment with them, they will be sources of internal conflict.[32]

8 Innovation: Improving existing things, creating new things

Fewer and fewer companies are succeeding in differentiating themselves in the market, either on the products and services level, or on the processes level, or on the business model level. This was shown by the results of our first survey of senior executives. Over 70 percent of the senior executives we surveyed saw little or no possibility of differentiation in their industry, either with respect to production or distribution, or on the products and services level. In other words, differences are disappearing and companies are becoming increasingly similar to one another. This is confirmed by research on neo-institutionalist theory, which is gaining influence in both management and organizational theory, as well as in sociology. This phenomenon – termed "isomorphism"[1] – arises due to increasing pressure in the market and in the institutional environment of the company. Conscious, as well as unconscious, norms, rules, and procedures lead companies to conform, rather than to be different.

Basically, the nature of a competitive advantage and a strategy are easy to define. Ultimately, they revolve around generating added value for the customer, that is customer value, either by bringing a product or service onto the market more cost-effectively, and therefore more cheaply, or by tying up a unique bundle of benefits for which the customer is prepared to pay a price premium. If a business model or core competences which are not easy to imitate lie behind the added value for the customer, the company will be assured of long-term revenues. Accordingly, Michael Porter said: "The core of a strategy consists of executing business activities differently to the competition."[2]

Basically, there are three levels on which a company can be "different" and differentiate itself through innovation:

1. the products and services level;
2. the processes level; and
3. the business model level.

These three levels of innovation are the subject of this chapter.

DELIGHTING CUSTOMERS WITH SOMETHING NEW

In autumn 1994, professor Hans Hinterhuber came to us – at the time we were doctoral candidates working as assistants at his institute – with a few poorly legible and incomplete photocopied pages from an essay and said: "Why don't you take a look at this? It's interesting!" The essay contained a model which explained how customer delight comes about and spoke of three different kinds of product attributes. We were unable to discern the title of the essay or the author, as the first pages were missing. The model was simple and plausible. It classified product attributes into three categories, the first category being basic requirements of a product which absolutely must be met. Secondly, it described performance requirements, which caused customer satisfaction to increase in line with how well they were met. Finally, it outlined excitement requirements, which were not explicitly demanded and expected by customers, but had the potential to delight them if they were present. We took an immediate interest in the model, as it contradicted the "the more, the better" and "twice as much is twice as good" viewpoints. However, it was almost impossible to find out the author and the title of the article and to obtain a detailed description of the model. The Internet was still in its infancy and there were hardly any online full-text databases at that time. We asked our library to research through interlending. We had almost forgotten the article when, around 3 months later, a letter arrived from Japan – with the complete article. It was, however, written in Japanese and had been published in 1984 in a Japanese quality journal. We contacted the author, Noriaki Kano, at the Tokyo Science University and he immediately faxed us a translation.

We found the model so exciting that we immediately carried out a study in order to test and apply it. Since we were all keen skiers, the decision was easy. We surveyed over 1500 skiers in Austria, Germany, Switzerland, and Italy directly on the piste regarding their skis. An analysis with the Kano Model provided exciting insights. Ease of turning and the edge grip of the skis were basic requirements for skiers. It caused great dissatisfaction if these requirements were not met. However, if skiers rated their skis highly on these two criteria, this did not lead to satisfaction. In other words, ease of turning and edge grip were absolute minimum requirements of the product. But we also ascertained that good performance in deep snow was an excitement attribute. A ski which made skiing in powder snow easier caused delight. Overall, we were able to clearly measure the value contribution of 10 product attributes and categorize them into basic, performance, and excitement attributes. We found the results so interesting that we contacted the ski industry. However, none of the ski manufacturers took an interest. Naturally we were disappointed and we decided to put the study findings to good scientific use and publish them.[3] Around 3 years later there was a revolution in the ski market: the carver ski made its breakthrough. Due to being between 30 and 50 cm shorter than conventional alpine skis and almost a third broader at the tip and tail, carver skis gave users a completely new skiing experience. Even average skiers could ski on the edge at a controlled speed and turn with far more confidence and less effort. The carver ski met the basic requirements of ease of turning and edge grip very well. Furthermore, it performed extremely well in deep snow – something which was not expected by skiers, but which delighted them.

Unfortunately, we were not instrumental in the development of the carver ski, which had already been invented by Reinhardt Fischer in the early 1980s. In 1997, Fischer, an outsider in the industry, said in an interview with the *Zeit* newspaper: "Fifteen years ago, I was rebuffed by all the ski manufacturers in Austria when I suggested constructing skis with a narrower waist."[4]

Nevertheless, the fact was that, based on the Kano Model and our studies, we were able to predict the success of the carver ski 2–3 years before the carving boom took place. We knew that ease of turning and edge grip were basic requirements that were not yet being met. A product that could achieve this was bound to be successful. The carver ski succeeded in this.

Let us now look at the Kano Model in greater depth.

In his model, Noriaki Kano distinguishes between three types of product attributes (Figure 8.1):

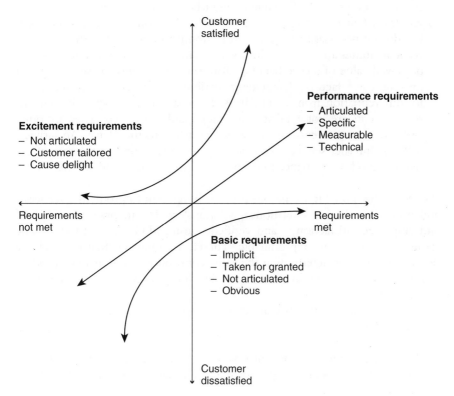

Figure 8.1 The Kano Model of customer satisfaction[5]

1. *Basic factors*: These include those product attributes which cause dissatisfaction if they are not provided in line with expectations. If these expectations are exceeded, this does not lead to satisfaction, but merely to
   "non-dissatisfaction." Basic factors are therefore minimum requirements
   which represent the core benefit of a product or service. Although meeting
   minimum requirements is necessary for bringing about customer satisfaction, this alone is not sufficient for achieving it. Basic requirements are not
   explicitly demanded by the customer; they are not articulated, but rather
   taken for granted. They are relatively unimportant if they are met, but come
   to the fore if they are not met. The proper functioning of brakes in cars,
   the correctness of a doctor's diagnosis, the punctuality of trains, and the
   reliability of bank statements are examples of this.
2. *Performance factors*: These are those product attributes which lead to both
   satisfaction if the customer's expectations are exceeded and to dissatisfaction
   if they are not met. They therefore represent a continuum without threshold
   values. Performance requirements are explicitly demanded by the customer.
   Comparisons are drawn between competitors on the basis of these product
   attributes. The fuel consumption of a car, the battery life of a laptop, or
   the resolution of a digital camera might be examples of this.
3. *Excitement factors*: These factors cause satisfaction if they are provided,
   but do not necessarily cause dissatisfaction if they are not present. Excitement attributes are not explicitly expected by the customer and increase the
   perceived value of a core benefit. However, they cannot be set off against
   missing basic factors. Excitement attributes represent a starting point
   for differentiation from competitors. Like basic requirements, excitement
   requirements are not explicitly demanded and articulated. They are often
   latent desires that customers are not even aware they have. An airline's
   in-flight Internet service, overhead displays in cars, or – in the case of the
   skiers – good performance in deep snow might be counted among them.[6]

We tested the model in numerous projects in relation to products,[7] services,[8]
and business-to-business relationships,[9] transferred it to price satisfaction[10]
and employee satisfaction,[11] and verified it using different methods.[12] The
results were stable and reproducible. Therefore, using the Kano Model is a
useful approach for determining the value contribution of individual product
attributes. It is also useful for categorizing innovations and deducing their
marketability.

We can derive several important consequences for product innovation from
the Kano Model:

1. We can classify innovations into basic innovations, differentiation innovations, and incremental innovations, and estimate what effects they might
   have in the market.
2. We can better understand the time dynamic of innovations.

3. We can determine the value contribution of the innovation for different customer segments.

The Kano Model: Three types of innovation

The Kano Model lends itself very well to distinguishing three different types of innovation (Figure 8.2):

1. *Radical innovations, which represent an entirely new solution for a basic requirement* (Figure 8.3). These innovations generally have a long-term

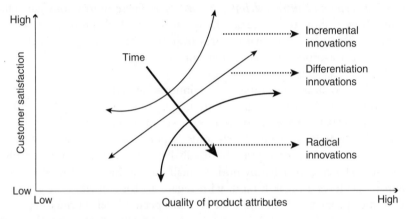

Figure 8.2 Three types of innovation

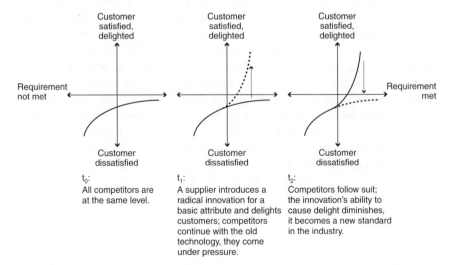

Figure 8.3 The effect of radical basic innovations

effect and give the company a competitive advantage until competitors follow suit. The question is: which basic requirements can we redefine with a radical innovation (new technology or outstanding customer value)?

2. *Differentiation innovations, which provide better solutions for explicit customer expectations (performance requirements) than the products which are currently on the market.* Generally, these innovations have a short- to medium-term effect and lead to a neck-and-neck race between suppliers. The question is: which product or service improvements could enable us to stand out from the competition in the area of explicit customer expectations?

3. *Incremental innovations, which solve small, unarticulated customer problems and surprise and thereby delight the customer.* These innovations generally only have a short-term effect. The question is: which product or service improvements or additional features over and above the core benefit will enable us to surprise and delight customers?

We speak of radical innovations when innovations affect the core benefits of a product and lead to a significantly better solution to a problem. Here, the following pattern seems to apply: if a company incrementally enhances a basic feature which, from the customer's point of view, is already being provided to a satisfactory degree, this hardly has any effect. Its marginal utility decreases. The customer hardly notices small improvements. However, if the company achieves a breakthrough with regard to basic attributes by solving a customer problem on an entirely new, unexpected level – primarily, if the basic requirement was not being met, or only being met to a low degree – the following occurs: the new technology or new product triggers delight in the customer. The innovator enjoys a unique position in the market: it has set a new standard. Competitors come under pressure and will lose market share all the time they do not adopt the innovation. In 1990, this situation could be observed in the ski industry. Some years prior to the breakthrough of the carver ski, Salomon introduced a new technology – the trapeze construction – which solved the edge grip problem significantly better than the sandwich construction which was the standard up to that point. Salomon's market entry with the new monocoque ski was so successful that it became the world market leader in the top segment within a very short time. Within 2 years, all the other ski manufacturers had to switch to the new technology. The old technology was obsolete and customers no longer wanted to buy sandwich skis. The other ski manufacturers could only prevent further loss of market share by adopting the innovation. Newcomer Salomon was able to exploit this head start to successfully position itself in the ski market.

Differentiation innovations pertain to the performance attributes of a product. There is generally intense innovation competition in this area as competitors enter into a neck-and-neck race. The objective here is to carve out competitive advantages with regard to individual product attributes and use them as a basis for differentiation.

Incremental innovations pertain to unarticulated customer expectations. They generally introduce new features which enhance a product's core benefit. These innovations tend to have a short-term effect until they are imitated by competitors. However, they are very useful for achieving a temporary competitive advantage, as they may lead to customer delight.

Figure 8.2 also contains a time dimension, which illustrates the following: excitement attributes are capable of delighting customers, but generally only in the short term. They develop into specific expectations and ultimately into basic requirements.

In order to secure competitive advantages, it is necessary for companies to perpetuate a process which is aimed at realizing innovative potential – if possible with all three types of innovation.

Gearing innovations toward segments

Basic attributes are barriers to entry: they must be met. Excitement attributes provide opportunities for differentiation. However, a cost trap may lie hidden behind these opportunities. Companies should think very carefully about whether and how incremental innovations affect a product's ability to cause delight in individual segments. The same applies to differentiation innovations. Therefore, the value contribution of innovations should be assessed according to the principle: "Every product feature adds costs, but not every product feature adds value."

What customers consider basic, performance, and excitement attributes often differs between segments.[13] Something which is an excitement attribute in one segment – and which could, for instance, be dispensed with for cost reasons – may be a basic requirement in another. Therefore, not providing it would be fatal. From the customer's point of view, the supplier would no longer be worth considering.

Let us briefly consider low-cost airlines in comparison with conventional airlines, in order to illustrate the importance of considering these factors in relation to specific segments (Table 8.1). We will consider five – somewhat simplified – customer requirements: the destination served, the service provided, the price, the possibility of making changes to bookings, and safety. Let us consider a tourist as the typical passenger on a low-cost airline and a business traveler as the typical passenger on a conventional airline.

In the case of low-cost airlines, the destination served is an excitement attribute; in the case of conventional airlines, it is a basic requirement. If a low-cost airline provides a cheap flight from Cologne/Bonn to Klagenfurt, or from Klagenfurt to London, the destination may delight the customer. Indeed, up to 50 percent of low-cost flyers only fly to a particular destination because it is served by cheap flights. This is of course different with business travelers.

Table 8.1 Market segmentation for airlines according to the Kano Model (example)

Customer requirement	Low-cost airline (tourists)	Conventional airline (business travelers)
Destination	Excitement attribute	Basic requirement
Service	Excitement attribute	Basic/performance attribute
Price	Basic requirement	Performance requirement
Possibility of making changes to a booking	Performance attribute	Basic requirement
Safety	Basic requirement	Basic requirement

The destination is a basic attribute: nobody would fly to Klagenfurt if their meeting was taking place in Vienna. For business travelers on a conventional airline, service is a basic or performance requirement; for low-cost flyers, it is an excitement attribute or even irrelevant. They want to fly for a low price and are happy to go without additional services. The low price is a basic prerequisite for low-cost flyers, whereas it is a performance attribute for business travelers on a conventional airline. Whereas the possibility of making changes to a booking is important to business travelers, as they must be flexible and able to respond to changes in their schedules, this is not so vital for low-cost customers. Finally, safety is a basic requirement for both segments.

This – somewhat simplified – illustration shows that, typically, low-cost airlines do not meet some basic requirements of business travelers and that conventional airlines rarely meet low-cost flyers' basic requirement of low prices.

Therefore, it is important to understand exactly what the basic, performance, and excitement requirements of the relevant target customer segments are. Only then is it possible to tailor products and services accordingly and effectively gear innovations toward customers' needs.

COST COMPETITION: REDESIGNING PROCESSES

Generally, process innovations have two objectives: either increasing the efficiency of the company, or increasing customer value. Our first survey of senior executives showed that overcapacity, substitutability, and market transparency are the drivers behind increasingly tough competition. This is reflected in the medium- to long-term development of price and costs (Figure 8.4):

- Over 40 percent of the companies studied have had to accept falling prices in the market over the last 3 years; over 35 percent indicated that prices were stagnating and only 20 percent of the companies were able to push through price increases on the market.

Development of sales prices and costs

	Prices have fallen	Prices have remained the same	Prices have risen
Costs have fallen	19.1%	11.8%	5.4%
Costs have remained the same	13.1%	12.4%	4.5%
Costs have risen	10.5%	12.7%	10.5%

Figure 8.4 Price and cost development in the last 3 years

- At the same time, only around a third of the companies indicated that costs had fallen in the last 3 years; a third of the companies reported rising costs.
- Almost a third of the companies found themselves in a particularly difficult situation: they either had to accept falling sales prices against a background of rising or stagnating costs, or had to contend with rising costs against a background of stagnating or falling prices.[14]

Evidently, the cost-reduction measures taken by many companies only lead to modest successes. Senior executives nevertheless attach great importance to cost-reduction programs. Seventy-five percent of the companies had carried out cost-reduction programs in the previous 3 years; 50 percent of the companies had even done this several times. However, almost a quarter of these companies did not achieve any improvement in their competitive position by doing this; a third of the companies only witnessed short-term improvements.

If one studies the main focus of the cost-reduction programs of the last 3 years (Figure 8.5), one can see that making internal processes more efficient is the most frequently employed tool. In the last 3 years, almost 60 percent of the companies focused on this measure, followed by reducing personnel (43 percent), raising cost-consciousness (40 percent), reducing purchasing costs (28 percent), and changing the value chain (30 percent).

If one compares the focal points of cost-reduction programs in the last few years with future focal points, one can see that the focus is shifting. Making internal processes more efficient as a starting point for cost reduction is gaining significance (78 percent), as is raising cost-consciousness within the company (41 percent). Whereas reducing personnel used to be the second most important cost-reduction tool, senior executives see hardly any possibility of making further savings in this area in the future (21 percent). The reason often given for this is that many companies have already reached their limit with

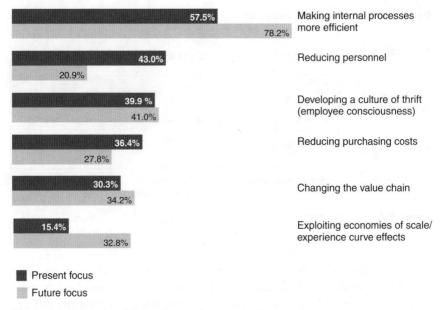

Figure 8.5 Present and future focus of cost-reduction programs

regard to reducing personnel costs, and reducing the number of employees further could jeopardize the stability of their processes.

It seems that, in the future, the most important cost-reduction lever will lie in process management. Numerous examples of companies that are run in a strictly process-oriented way show that it is very advantageous to shift organizational power from functional areas to processes: generally, costs fall, customer satisfaction increases and, as a result, profitability increases too.[15] Following its peak at the end of the 1990s and the subsequent wave of disillusionment, Business Process Reengineering (BPR), which became popular in management theory and practice at the beginning of the 1990s thanks to an essay by Michael Hammer in the *Harvard Business Review*[16] and numerous examples of success, seems to be enjoying a resurgence.[17] BPR entails a radical departure from current organizational principles and a process-oriented reorganization of the company focused on the customer through the integration of information technologies. However, experience shows that relatively few companies manage the leap from simple process changes to real process management.[18] This requires a fundamental rethink and intervention in the structures of the company. Traditional productivity measurement and assessment methods, remuneration, training, personnel development, and the physical layout of offices, workspaces, and buildings, as well as career paths, tend to be geared more toward the different hierarchical levels within companies, and less toward individual business processes or the teams that are responsible for them.[19] Successful process-oriented companies rework their principles and procedures in order to achieve long-term cost savings, reduce lead times, and increase customer satisfaction. This starts with appointing process managers and defining process-oriented performance benchmarks (for example, time targets) and initiatives range from process-oriented remuneration systems (such as bonuses linked to process-oriented objectives, cost savings, or improvements in performance, for example) and infrastructure changes (for example, physically reorganizing workspaces so that all those involved in the process sit together), through to training and development, and new career paths.[20]

As is the case with product innovation, culture, and in particular the willingness to take risks, also plays a major role in process innovation. We observed the following situation at an automobile manufacturer.

An expert in die-cast mould construction with many years of professional experience was invited by a customer, an automobile manufacturer, to visit its factory. The development and production managers at the company showed and explained the company's processes to the engineer. They asked him what he thought of the procedures and processes. Although he appeared impressed, he seemed to be preoccupied with something. When asked – mainly out of politeness – whether he had seen any means of improvement, he replied: "I think that, without any great effort, you could increase the throughput at process step X by at least 15 percent, and that this would significantly increase the productivity of the overall process." Of course, the experts at the automobile manufacturer now wanted to know more details. In the intensive discussion that followed, the production experts made clear that they valued the visitor's suggestions, but defended the current solution, pointing out that the productivity of the processes was already very good and that the main objective of the current solution was the stability of the entire process. According to the production experts, all the changes the visitor had suggested could have jeopardized this stability.

The production manager of the automobile manufacturer, who had been following the discussion intently, asked the "guest" about the reasons for the obviously defensive stance of his colleagues. In his answer, the guest praised the managers' textbook-like organization of the processes and their extraordinary production know-how, but continued by saying that the production experts did not pursue the objective of accelerating the process as a whole. "I have the impression that the process managers have a tremendous fear of doing something wrong. It seems that they put more emphasis on maintaining the process stability they have achieved than on anything else. Otherwise, there is no way of explaining why they do not schedule the tooling of machine group X differently, as they have a bottleneck in the process here which would be easy to remove," he said. When asked what else he had noticed, he referred to his previous experiences with the company: "While working with your company, one thing struck me in particular. When we receive drawings for the prototype construction from your development department, these are usually very innovative and progressive. But in virtually every project we have to fight for changes which are absolutely necessary for series production. For example, it might be that the development department requires certain very thin wall thicknesses. If we carried this out, although the prototype production would work, we would have enormous problems in series production, as we have already had on many occasions. It seems to me that the developers are very well qualified but that, due to their lack of experience in production, they have little to no access to the knowledge of experienced production people." The production manager realized that his "young" experts simply lacked the know-how that cannot be found in documents and drawings and is tremendously difficult to pass on. Ultimately, they were insecure about disrupting a stable process without knowing exactly what could happen. At the same time, it became apparent that there was a bottleneck in the development department which had a dramatic influence on both suppliers' processes, and, as a result, on the company's own processes.

Thomas H. Davenport,[21] one of the founding fathers of BPR, recently wrote in an article for the *Harvard Business Review* that a second wave of process management supported by software and IT would lead to the complete standardization of processes and thereby also a radical reorganization of corporate structures – primarily on a cross-company basis. A study of German industry by Hess and Schuller[22] also shows that BPR is becoming increasingly useful on both a cross-departmental and a cross-company basis – witness the topics of supply-chain management and outsourcing or offshoring, for example. This is also confirmed by our study, which revealed that the senior executives surveyed saw great potential for reducing costs in changing the entire value chain (34 percent).

Developing a "culture of thrift" is in second position on the list of priorities. The central importance of cost-consciousness for the effectiveness of cost-reduction measures was also empirically confirmed in a further cross-industry study of cost management in German corporate practice.[23] This study of 116 companies clearly proved the following: the higher the cost-consciousness of employees, the easier it is to identify cost drivers. This, in turn, makes cost-reduction measures more effective and increases the level of cost reduction actually achieved. This shows that cost management and cost reduction are not just a question of processes, methods, and tools, but primarily a question of corporate culture and the attitude of management and employees. The best example of this is arguably Ingvar Kamprad, the founder of IKEA, who defined cost-consciousness as one of the core values of IKEA. He continually emphasized the issue of costs in all activities and processes and set a good example himself: first-class flights are taboo, as are expensive hotels. He also demanded this level of cost-consciousness in his employees, who make a 500-km journey by car if only a first-class flight is available. His motto – "Waste of resources is a mortal sin at IKEA. Expensive solutions are often signs of mediocrity, and an idea without a price tag is never acceptable" – clearly expresses his sense of cost-consciousness.

Our study shows that reducing personnel costs will not have high priority as a cost-reduction tool in the future. In the last few years, downsizing has become popular as a means of reducing personnel costs. Downsizing is considered by many as a particularly effective method of reducing costs and increasing shareholder value.[24] In this process, almost as much importance is attached to making an effective announcement as to the act of implementing the job cuts itself. Following developments in the US, where over ten million jobs have been cut in waves of downsizing since 1979,[25] downsizing has also become prevalent as a method of increasing competitiveness and company value in Europe in the last two decades. The following four factors have contributed to this in particular:

1. the introduction of labor-saving technologies;
2. rationalization programs aimed at reducing overhead costs;
3. deregulation and privatization; and
4. increasing pressure from shareholders and the proliferation of shareholder-value management systems.[26]

Mass redundancies were made "socially acceptable" under the label of "slimmed-down companies" or "lean management." However, numerous empirical studies show that downsizing rarely makes companies more efficient in the long term. For example, Cascio *et al*[27] studied over 5000 cases of downsizing in over 500 American companies and found that companies which had cut more than 5 percent of jobs had not succeeded in improving their performance as measured by ROA (return on assets). There was hardly a difference between these companies and companies where the workforce had remained constant. However, the stock markets reacted positively and downsizing measures led to higher profits on the stock exchange. Overall, the authors of the study concluded from the findings that the success achieved by downsizing is not commensurate with the jobs cut. Other studies show that downsizing has a negative effect on the motivation of the remaining employees, as well as on innovative ability, organizational learning, and knowledge management.[28]

GEARING PROCESSES TOWARD THE CUSTOMER

The success of customer orientation depends on whether structures within the company can be changed and processes oriented toward the customer with lasting effect.[29] In other words, market and customer orientation must go hand in hand with customer-oriented process management and control.[30] A study on Customer-Relationship Management undertaken by the Gartner Group shows that this is not so simple: 55 percent of all CRM projects come to nothing.[31] One of the main reasons for this is that organizational structures and above all processes are left untouched when CRM is introduced and are not geared toward the requirements of customers.[32]

In many companies, after the initial euphoria has subsided "customer orientation" comes to nothing more than customer satisfaction statistics that disappear into drawers. Even companies in which customer orientation is a strategic priority establish after a certain period of time that satisfaction and word of month are not improving, with the result that customer satisfaction data is no longer taken seriously. The reason for this is that these companies are only superficially customer-oriented. Customer orientation is not reflected in their structures and processes.

Furthermore, under the premise of cost reduction, companies frequently invest large amounts in process optimization, without giving careful thought to how processes can be oriented toward customers. Some companies set themselves the challenge of finding an approach for reducing process costs, allocating a large amount of resources to this task. Activity-based costing is intended to reveal potential cost-saving areas. However, controlling processes and costs is not sufficient when it comes to making long-term profits. Revenues must be secured for the long term. Long-term revenues only materialize when customers are satisfied and subsequently make follow-up purchases. In addition, a company can save a considerable proportion of costs in the areas of sales and advertising through positive word of mouth.

However, often, the left hand does not know what the right hand is doing. Many companies develop long lists of criteria and benchmarks for measuring business processes that turn out to be unsuitable for this purpose on closer inspection. Many process parameters merely reflect internal benchmarks that bear little relation to one of the most important objectives of process management – increasing customer satisfaction.[33] For example, certain design guidelines and technical criteria serve as benchmarks and companies use statistical process controls to ensure that they are adhered to. Customers' opinions are barely taken into account in this process at all. Companies start with the question, "How exactly does the process/product comply with the technical guidelines?" rather than with an analysis of the extent to which the process meets the needs of customers. For this reason, it is necessary to look at individual business processes from a customer's perspective and to develop metrics based on this which are then translated into internal benchmarks.[34] This means rethinking conventional methods of measuring performance and controlling processes. Whereas many companies know their production costs – and frequently even their process costs – exactly, they do not know what percentage of their orders are processed without error, or how quickly customer requests are processed on average.

Customer-oriented companies endeavor to achieve two things simultaneously through process innovation: higher process efficiency and better orientation toward customers' needs. The following example shows how this can work.[35]

A bank set itself the objective of both making processes more efficient and managing them according to customer-oriented metrics. In order to achieve this, it decided to proceed in three steps:

1. In the first step, it analyzed customer processes by visualizing them and eliciting positive and negative critical incidents for each step by means of customer interviews.[36]
2. In the second step, it reworked the processes with the aim of simultaneously achieving both higher efficiency and greater customer orientation.
3. In the third step, it defined metrics which took customer requirements into account.

The customer-process analysis and the analysis of critical incidents revealed that the quality of the services provided, employees' attitudes, and response times frequently led to negative experiences. These were basic requirements, since they did not seem to be mentioned as positive critical incidents by customers at all, even if performance with regard to these aspects of the service was good. Individual consultation, individual service, and quality of information were excitement factors, as they led to positive reactions from customers. However, hardly any customers complained if there was a low level of performance in these areas.

This had established customers' key requirements of the service. In order to ensure that customers' expectations would continue to be met over the long term, in the second step it developed metrics which were to form the basis for process control. The objective here was to reconcile customer requirements with the strategy of the company.[37]

To this end, the bank compared the customer requirements it had ascertained in the previous step with its strategic objectives. Its strategy consisted of increasing customer satisfaction whilst simultaneously increasing efficiency. From this strategy, the bank derived strategic objectives, such as:

1. Increasing efficiency across the entire value-creation process.
2. Increasing and assuring quality in order to increase customer satisfaction.
3. Optimizing processes and releasing resources.
4. Agreeing clear time and quality standards.
5. Standardizing processes, and so on.

On closer examination of individual customer requirements, it quickly became clear that some of them conflicted with the bank's strategic objectives. It was then necessary to examine how many and which customer requirements supported a strategic objective and how many and which of them actually counteracted a strategic objective. To this end, the bank produced a matrix

	Customer requirements											
Strategic objectives · Strategy supports customer requirements (↑) · Strategy conflicts with customer requirements (◀)	Processing period	Quality of decisions	Product design	Quality of services provided	Response time	Number of employees	Individual services	Quality of information	Price	Availability of services	Individual consultation	Attitude of employees
Increasing efficiency across the entire value-creation process	↑		↑	↑	↑	↑				↑	↑	
Increasing quality in order to increase customer satisfaction	↑	↑	↑	↑	↑	↑				↑	↑	↑	↑
Optimizing processes and releasing resources	↑			↑	↑	↑	↑	↑	↑	↑		
Agreeing clear time and quality standards	↑	↑	↑	↑	↑	↑	↑	↑	↑	↑	↑	↑
Standardizing production processes	↑	↑	↑	↑	↑		◀	↑	↑	↑	◀	
...	↑	↑	↑	↑	↑	↑		↑	↑			

Figure 8.6 Requirements/strategy matrix

of customer requirements and strategic objectives. In the individual cells, the white arrows indicated that a strategy was supported by a customer requirement. A black arrow showed where a strategy conflicted with a customer requirement (Figure 8.6).

The bank therefore needed to give priority to those requirements which were important to customers, since they frequently led to positive or negative experiences, and also best supported the strategy.

The customer requirements of "individual services" and "individual consultation" conflicted with the strategic objective of "standardizing processes." However, individual services were not basic requirements for customers – they were excitement requirements. But since its strategic priority was increasing efficiency, the bank abstained from individualizing services further. Although it forewent the opportunity of creating "customer delight" in doing so, it may otherwise have fallen into a cost trap. Its next task was to find excitement attributes which did *not* conflict with key strategic objectives.

The shaded criteria in the requirements/strategy matrix – "processing period," "quality of services provided," "quality of information," and "availability of services" – were key expectations on the part of the customer. They were in line with the objective of increasing efficiency and formed the basis for reorganizing processes.

In the next step, the bank defined performance metrics for customer requirements. This involved translating individual customer requirements into "internal criteria" before establishing metrics for these internal criteria. This was necessary so that the bank could formulate specific process requirements from the still relatively abstract customer requirements. For example, the criterion of "quality of service" was translated into the question of "How frequently do performance shortfalls occur in each process step?"

Some examples of the ratios for aligning market and internal processes obtained in this way were:

- lead time (level of flow): measured in units of time;
- adherence to delivery dates: number of missed deadlines per 100 orders;
- quality of service: number of service shortfalls per 100 orders; and
- quality of information: number of information deficiencies per 100 orders.

All the ratios were formed into customer contact points based on customer requirements. This project resulted in process innovations which could simultaneously increase efficiency and customer satisfaction.

In this project, it was fundamental to compare strategic objectives with customer requirements, since this made it possible to remove conflicts which arose between the process and the customer perspective.

DEVELOPING NEW BUSINESS MODELS

Sometime between 1888 and 1890, J.C. Fargo, the head of a regional freight company in the US, traveled to Europe. He returned frustrated. Although he was head of American Express and carried letters of credit with him, he found it very difficult to obtain cash anywhere: "As soon as I strayed off the beaten path, letters of credit were about as much use to me as wet wrapping paper. If the head of American Express has such difficulties, what must a normal traveler go through? Something must be done!"[38] J.C. Fargo turned to Marcellus Flemming Berry and asked him to find a better solution than letters of credit. Berry came up with the traveler's check in denominations of $10, $20, $50, and $100.[39] The business model was simple: for a low fee, the customer has the security of knowing that the checks are insured against loss and theft, as well as the knowledge that he can change them into cash without fuss. Businesses and hotels were pleased to accept traveler's checks because they could trust the name "American Express" and made more sales. For American Express, the idea was brilliant. The business was completely risk-free, since customers paid for their checks in advance. Furthermore, American Express obtained an interest-free loan, and some checks were never cashed in at all. The idea for this business model came about through chance – an unsolved customer problem was the catalyst. The principle of the model is often still copied today. Many retailers not only increase sales through issuing gift vouchers, but also earn interest in the process.

The business model of the low-cost airlines enables them to charge considerably less for flights than conventional airlines. Dell's business model enables customers to configure exactly the product they require – at a reasonable price, since there is no middleman. eBay brings millions of sellers and buyers together in cyberspace and is highly efficient as a virtual marketplace. Its business model is based on a network effect; the more customers who participate in online auctions, the higher eBay's value as a marketplace and the more difficult it is to copy it.

In principle, the formula for achieving above-average success is simple: it is about "being different." Being different means offering higher customer value than the competition by being either better, faster, or less expensive. In order to be better, faster, or less expensive, a company must organize its value-added activities differently. In other words, it needs a better business model. Initially, business models are nothing more than assumptions about how a company can operate and how it can combine individual activities in order to bring a unique product or service to the market.

Three points are decisive when it comes to being successful with new business models:

1. They must solve a customer problem that had not been solved up to that point or had only been solved very unsatisfactorily.
2. They must change the game rules according to which a product or service is brought to the market.
3. They must change the game rules so radically that it is almost impossible to copy the business model.

At the end of the 1960s, Herber Kelleher and Rolling King drafted a business plan on a serviette. Their idea was simple: "If you get your passengers to their destinations when they want to get there, on time, at the lowest possible fares, and make darn sure they have a good time doing it, people will fly your airline."[40] Kelleher and King worked on the assumption that the market for US domestic flights was far larger than was generally assumed, and that there had to be millions of customers for whom flying was too expensive. If they could develop a business model which enabled people to fly cheaply, it would certainly be possible to access this market. They were right. Southwest Airlines was founded in 1971 and is one of the world's most successful airlines.

Its success can be attributed to a unique business model which completely redefined the game rules of the industry. Southwest Airlines is now much imitated.

The imitators succeed in keeping variable costs between 40 and 60 percent beneath those of conventional airlines and achieving around 40 percent more flying hours per aircraft per day. A low-cost airline aircraft is in the air for an average of 10.5 hours per day, compared to 7.5 hours for a conventional airline. It is on the ground for a maximum of 20 to 25 minutes between flights; other airlines' turnaround times are twice that. The low-cost airlines make profits despite charging lower prices – at Ryan Air an average ticket costs €45.[41]

Low-cost airlines operate in a fundamentally different way. Their business model is geared toward low costs (Figure 8.7).

Low-cost airlines generally only provide direct flights between medium-sized cities and small airports without turnstiles and transfers. Airport fees are considerably lower there and the airspace is rarely overcrowded. There are no connecting flights, which saves the laborious task of coordinating flight schedules and the costs of baggage transfer. Low-cost airlines use standardized fleets, such as Boeing 737s for example. Pilots and mechanics only have to be trained for this type of aircraft and can therefore be deployed flexibly. The cost of maintenance work and spare parts is reduced. There are no meals on board and no seat reservations. For the most part, tickets are sold over the Internet; whereas booking through a travel agency costs an average of $10, an online booking only costs an average of $1. Overall, low-cost airlines not only achieve significantly lower costs through this business model, but are also more punctual on average.

But what makes this business model so valuable is that it cannot be imitated by the conventional airlines.

A company can only achieve long-term, above-average success if it succeeds in standing out from its competitors on a sustained basis, that is, bringing a product or service to the market which either delivers more value to the customer or costs less. Assuring this on a sustained basis requires executing processes or activities differently – that is, better, faster, or less expensively – which means having a better business model.

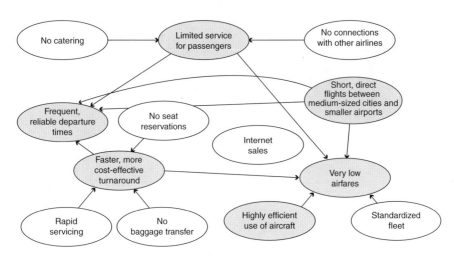

Figure 8.7 Business model of the low-cost airlines[42]

9 Top management: The architects of success

According to one of the theses we put forward in Chapter 3: "It is not individual management methods and tools, but ultimately the top management team's attitudes, values, thought patterns and approach which form the basis for sustained success." If we look at the results of our empirical analyses using the PLS model, this thesis does not seem tenable, at least at first glance, since the data from over 700 strategic business units show that there is no direct statistically significant relationship between the innovation orientation of top management and corporate success. However, if we leave culture, market orientation, core competences, and innovation in products and services to one side and only calculate a very simplified model that only takes the relationship between the innovation orientation of top management and corporate success into account, something interesting happens: the relationship suddenly becomes highly significant and strong $(\beta = 0.47***)$. How can this be explained? Expressed in scientific language, the result means that culture, market orientation, core competences, and innovative success have a strong mediator effect.[1] In other words, there is a relationship between the innovation orientation of top management and corporate success. However, this is not a direct relationship; it only comes about via the other success drivers in our model. Put simply, this means that the innovation orientation of top management alone is not sufficient. It will only create a basis for sustained success if:

- it finds expression in a strong, entrepreneurial culture;
- it leads to strong market orientation;
- the company reflects on its core competences and jettisons ballast;
- the company is able to exploit core competences; and
- innovations emerge from this.

What does this mean?

Through its innovation orientation and willingness to take risks, top management must:

- create a strong corporate culture comprised of values with which employees can identify and within which they can find meaning;
- create a culture in which employees are stimulated to strike new paths and in which creative solutions are rewarded and recognized;
- make available resources dedicated to the development of unusual competences, skills, knowledge, and relationship networks (in other words, core competences); and
- understand markets and recognize or even anticipate developments in good time.

These are the key levers of success. Ensuring that the mechanisms – as shown in our model – actually achieve their ends is the task of top management and should not be delegated.

In the previous chapters, we discussed the individual success drivers in our model and also presented some working hypotheses and tools. We would now like to address the skills, attitudes, and values which should characterize the top management of a forward-looking and innovation-oriented company.

LEADERSHIP, INNOVATION, AND CHANGE

What approaches can senior executives take to enable them to implement innovation and creative destruction – in the sense that Schumpeter meant it – on a sustained basis? Ultimately, leadership is about bringing about events, changing market situations, and introducing into the proceedings new moments which it was not necessarily possible to derive from the given premises and which potentially move everything in an entirely new direction.

What specific duties for senior executives is it possible to derive from this?

- If innovation and creative destruction are essential for creating value, then senior executives must ensure that innovation occurs. They may not restrict themselves to preserving and managing existing processes.
- If senior executives are to ensure that innovation occurs, they must endeavor to do creative work on a daily basis. They may not restrict themselves to copying or imitating the things that made others successful (in the past), or which make or appear to make them successful now.
- If senior executives are to do creative work, they must constantly question the status quo. At no time should they accept the current situation as final.
- If senior executives are to question the status quo on a daily basis, they must concern themselves with the people in their company and raise their enthusiasm for change, for it is these people who ultimately determine the status quo and possess the knowledge and power to change it. Concentrating on management systems and structures obscures one's view of the driving forces behind change – that is, people.

- If senior executives are to raise enthusiasm for new things – that is, change – among the people in their company, they must engender trust in these people. In their efforts to "enthuse" people, they may not rely on merely monitoring the situation.

Only when senior executives – be they entrepreneurs or managers – fulfill all these requirements can they do justice to their management tasks.

Developing a visionary picture of the future for the company that can bring the company's main objectives closer to employees and inspire them to fight to achieve these objectives entails:

- embedding processes which spur employees on to analyze the existing situation and to look at it from different viewpoints so that they are able to openly discuss changes which increase value;
- initiating processes which guarantee that core competences are established and developed and which constitute the basis for the uniqueness of the company in the future;
- systematically carrying out analyses to establish which core products and services the company should concentrate on in the future;
- systematically analyzing the extent to which the company is capable of differentiating itself from the competition on a sustained basis and achieving meaningful competitive advantages over competitors in order to win customer loyalty;
- developing and initiating processes which ensure that knowledge about the market and the knowledge of employees can be exploited to optimum effect; and
- ensuring that the key fundamental structures which have a sustained influence on the company's ability to exploit its own potential are forward-looking.

These are, of course, important tasks which demand a great deal from leaders. Not everyone can master them. The historian Thomas Carlyle wrote: "Universal history, the history of what man has accomplished in this world, is at bottom the history of great men[2] who have worked here."[3] According to Jack Welch,[4] "Great people built great companies." It generally holds – as leadership research shows – that the more difficult the economic and industry-specific conditions a company faces are, the more important the performance of leaders at the top of the company becomes for ensuring success.[6] Above all, leadership is important if radical changes must be implemented in order to achieve sustained and significant improvements.[7]

But what is leadership? Being a good manager is far from being a good "leader." It is necessary to possess management skills, but they are not of themselves sufficient for successful leadership. Leadership and management

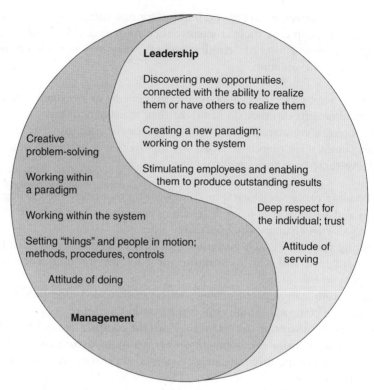

Figure 9.1 Management versus leadership[5]

are two different – but mutually dependent – competences which are possessed by successful leaders (Figure 9.1).[8]

"Leadership," Hans Hinterhuber writes, "means discovering and exploiting new opportunities, as well as shaping corporate change processes in such a way that value is created for all 'stakeholders'. . . and the value of the company is increased at the same time.[9] Leadership creates new paradigms and works on the system. Management means solving problems in a creative way. Management works within a paradigm or within the system. There are a multitude of tools, methods and approaches the company can use to achieve competitive advantages."[10] Further, leadership is ". . . the natural and spontaneous ability to stimulate employees, to inspire them and to enable them to discover new opportunities, to solve problems independently and creatively and to voluntarily and enthusiastically do what they can to support the realization of common goals. This requires not only a great amount of energy, but also respect and reverence for people on the part of the entrepreneur or the most senior executive. Leadership and a sincere interest in people go hand in hand. The natural authority and credibility of entrepreneurs and senior executives depend on whether or not the vision they are living out and their strategies and attitudes are accepted by employees. The real roots of leadership lie in ideals and values, as well as in selfless service and in dedication which extends beyond one's personal interests[11] and is directed at satisfying all 'stakeholders.' "[12]

In a conversation with Ischomachus, Socrates said: "If a master who can sorely punish bad workers and generously reward good workers visits them while they are working, and if the workers do no more than is necessary, then I do not wish to admire him. But if they set themselves in motion at the sight of him, if his presence alone provokes in every worker courage, competitiveness with others and the ambition to prove himself, then I would say that this master has something of the character of a king. And that, it seems to me, is the most important of all human activities... Yet, in the case of Zeus, I say not that one can learn this by merely watching it or by having heard it once, but I do say that he who wishes to succeed at this needs education and a good physical constitution at his disposal, and, what is most important of all, a divine spark must be inherent in him. For, to me, this fortune, leading people who gladly obey, is not of a human, but of a divine kind; it is seemingly granted to those who are truly of perfect wisdom."[13]

Leadership can be most easily compared with the role of a conductor,[14] a charismatic leader who can focus the attention of an entire orchestra on himself through the movement of the baton and lead the individual members of the orchestra to join with others to give an outstanding performance.

According to Hans Hinterhuber,[15] in addition to this, a senior executive must:

- be visionary, which entails encouraging a will to win by raising employees' enthusiasm for ideas, pointing the way, conveying meaning, and focusing the company's attention on results;
- create values, which means achieving positive results over the short term, but also adopting a long-term perspective in order to create "prosperity" for all stakeholders; and
- set an example and show courage, which means stimulating employees, setting them in motion in a positive way, and communicating effectively, which will only work if the senior executives set an example themselves and are prepared to take risks.

"If any one idea about leadership," Peter Senge wrote in his book *The Fifth Discipline*, "has inspired organizations for thousands of years, it's the capacity to hold a shared picture of the future we seek to create. One is hardpressed to think of any organization that has sustained some measure of greatness in the absence of goals, values, and missions... IBM had 'service'; Polaroid had instant photography; Ford had public transportation for the masses and Apple had 'computers for the rest of us.' Though radically different in content and kind, all these organizations managed to bind people together around a common identity and sense of destiny."[16]

When there is a genuine vision, people excel and learn, not because they are told to, but because they want to. But many leaders have personal visions that never get translated into shared visions that galvanize an organization. The practice of shared vision involves the skills of unearthing shared "pictures of the future" that foster genuine commitment and enrollment rather than compliance.

Therefore, if increasing value essentially requires innovation and "creative destruction," companies need a spirit and an environment that inspire employees to concern themselves with new things, that is, with change. If we then ask ourselves what the prerequisite for this kind of enthusiasm is, we have to conclude that this enthusiasm can only come into existence and have long-term effect if employees can identify with the company itself, its purpose, its main objectives, and the values for which it stands in terms of content and emotion.

Now the question inevitably arises as to what conditions must be present in order that employees can identify with "their" company in terms of content and emotion.

Viktor Frankl[17] provides us with a possible answer to this question: every healthy person strives explicitly or implicitly for fulfillment in life. However, according to Frankl, neither satisfying their own needs, nor concentrating exclusively on egoistic objectives guarantees an individual the fulfillment they are striving for. Instead, he concludes, each of us finds again and again that we can only find personal fulfillment by fulfilling a purpose that extends beyond our own interests. But how can we achieve this fulfillment? Frankl assumes that an individual can only achieve this fulfillment by making a contribution to a meaningful cause, a meaningful community, or a meaningful task, or through devotion to other people. Such readiness to be of service in the pursuit of something meaningful implies the highest degree of motivation and commitment.

Being able to make a contribution to something meaningful then triggers the very primary motivation that is capable of releasing unimagined power. In contrast, a lack of meaning and purpose results in indifference and apathy and to the burnout syndrome in day-to-day working life.

But what do the insights provided by Victor Frankl mean for a company? In the context of leadership, finding meaning means constantly examining the question of which visions, objectives, and values the company wants to create for and with its stakeholders. Accordingly, corporate success, in the sense of a long-term and sustained increase in value, is only ever the result of meaningful actions. Therefore, leaders in companies must invariably concern themselves with "creating and developing meaning" within and throughout the company.

The reason for this is that one can only identify with a thing, an idea, or a company, in terms of both content and emotion, if one can see for oneself a purpose in the thing, idea, company, or even the community within the company.

- The greater the sense of purpose or meaning, the more valuable the whole thing will be to us.
- The more valuable something is to us, the more important it will become to us.
- The more important something is to us, the more we will concern ourselves with the matter in terms of both emotion and content.
- The more we concern ourselves with something in terms of emotion and content, the more we will excel and be capable of achieving something special.

However, this also means that if leaders do not succeed in raising the enthusiasm of as many employees as possible for something very purposeful, it will be very difficult to ignite the spark for innovation, change, and uniqueness.

THE ABILITY TO BE LUCKY

Finally, we come to the last characteristic that we believe successful senior executives have in common: they possess the ability to be lucky. They possess the talent of exploiting chance situations. However, chance is not always something that lies completely outside of one's sphere of influence. There are people who are more capable than others of recognizing "chance" opportunities and seizing them at the right moment. Hence, what appeared to most outsiders to be chance was really intuition and the ability to do the right things at the right time. These senior executives detect weak signals that others are oblivious to,[18] they recognize patterns before others see them.[19] They are able to filter out from the "many ambiguous, contradictory and frequently deceptive pieces of information those pieces of information which are required for strategic decisions."[20] Above all, though, they have one skill in particular: intuitively making the right decisions.

If they are asked what that means, the answers they give are incredibly similar. They always have the main objective in mind and ask themselves almost every day how they could actually move closer to this objective. They have analyses carried out and hold discussions with senior executives, customers, employees, and consultants. They constantly agonize about how, why, and when, and then it is very frequently the case that a plausible idea or solution simply "comes" in a quiet moment when they are not really thinking about the company. All at once, everything becomes clear and logical and it is obvious how it could all work. They experience a certain feeling of happiness and what they would most like to do is tell as many people about it as possible. Subsequently, though, doubt often returns and they begin to think rationally about the idea and look at the analyses, and so on, but they do not receive the final reassurance they are hoping for. They then reach a decision based on whether the risk to the company is justifiable.

Professor Zeilinger, an internationally renowned scientist in the field of experimental physics, expresses this in even more drastic terms. Zeilinger's name has been known throughout the world since 1997, when his research group carried out the world's first quantum teleportation, whereby a light particle was directly transported through time and space without having traveled the path from A to B. Another world first followed in 1999: a secret message was encoded through quantum cryptography for the first time. According to Zeilinger, the security of this system, which would be ready to go into production in the foreseeable future, was ensured by the laws of nature. When Zeilinger was invited to the Siemens Academy of Life, he caused surprise with comments he made during an interview with regard to his criteria for planning projects: "At the start, there is the feeling that something is worth doing. Then there are preliminary experiments, which show everything increasingly clearly and lead to an ever more specific schedule. The research is then carried out. Very generally, if I have two or more research paths before me, I always choose the more radical one. I certainly don't take the one about which the majority of my colleagues say: 'Yes, that's OK, we'll do that.' In that situation, I always take the other one . . . When doing this, I have always been lucky in that the objectives I have set myself, although difficult, have always been just about achievable. My primary motive in choosing a certain goal was ultimately always my own intuition. I believe the most important thing is that you should not just trust your own thinking, but above all your own feeling and your own intuition, and then act accordingly . . . I haven't thought about my intuition; I simply accept it. It is part of my make-up. Intuition guides me, gives me a feeling about which direction I should continue in. You can never know for sure if it is actually the right way. At the very least it has brought me luck, in science, as well as in my personal life. Everything has worked up to now. Perhaps it will go wrong one day, I don't know . . . "[21] In an interview with the *Harvard Business Review*, Garry Kasparov said: "After just three opening moves by a chess player, more than 9 million positions are possible . . . Intuition is the defining quality of a great chess player. That's because chess is a mathematically infinite game. The total number of possible different moves in a single game of chess is more than the number of seconds that have elapsed since the big bang created the universe . . . even at the highest levels it is impossible to calculate very far out. I can think maybe 15 moves in advance, and that's about as far as any human has gone."[22]

Chess is perhaps the best example of intuitive decision-making. It is generally agreed that the game of chess requires a high degree of cognitive skill, since the player systematically analyses all moves and countermoves and does not make a move without thinking about it intensively first. However, chess masters are actually able to play several games at the same time – even against 50 opponents – and exhibit a relatively low level of cognitive activation. After all, in such competitions they hardly have time – perhaps one minute or maybe just a few seconds – to think through the moves. Even in tournaments, chess masters normally make a decision on a move within a few seconds. The rest of the time is spent thinking the move through and considering whether it is the right one, before it is actually made.[23]

In such a complex game, how is it possible to make the right decision within seconds? An experiment provides a good answer to this:[24] a non-player is shown the positions of around 25 chess pieces for a few seconds. If he is then asked to put the pieces back in the correct positions, he manages no more than an average of six correct positions. A chess master would be able to correctly position all the pieces. This could, of course, be attributed to an extraordinary ability to absorb and store visual information. However, if the experiment is repeated and the pieces are positioned on the board completely randomly – without meaning – the non-player will again position around six pieces correctly, and so will the chess master. Why? The chess master sees a pattern behind every configuration. If the pieces are positioned without meaning, then he cannot detect a pattern. It is estimated that a professional chess player can recognize around 50,000 familiar configurations altogether. What is described as intuitive decision-making is, in reality, an ability to recognize patterns at lightning speed – a process that sometimes happens completely unconsciously.[25]

Professor Gerald Hüther, a renowned brain researcher who heads a neurobiological research institute at the University of Göttingen, among other things, said in a conversation with us that the human brain only functions like a computer when making very trivial decisions, when all the advantages and disadvantages are seemingly weighed up rationally, thus leading it to a decision. With complex decisions, there is a complex process of linking knowledge, experiences, and emotions, which leads to a completely different kind of rationality than is the case with trivial decisions. He indicated that there is no such thing as intuition in the commonly appreciated sense, but that these very linked processes, which harness the most diverse types of know-how and stored theoretical knowledge in a particular way, lie behind these "instinctive" decisions. Research findings prove that people who have acquired a very large amount of knowledge through their curiosity, openness, and opportunity orientation are significantly more frequently able to reach good "intuitive" decisions than people who only possess a relatively limited sphere of experience.

Accordingly, intuition is neither a magical sixth sense nor a paranormal process. It is neither the opposite of rationality nor deciding at random. Intuition is a highly complex and highly developed form of reasoning that is based on many years of experience and learning, and on facts, patterns, concepts, procedures, abstractions, and everything we have stored in our heads as what we would call "formal knowledge."[26]

Intuition is unconscious; it is based on countless stored experiences. It is fast, and processes years of experience within seconds. It is complex, and processes information holistically and not according to linear, rational-analytical decision processes. Intuition is based on expertise, which filters down into unconscious decision-making heuristics, and on emotions, which go hand in hand with a certain situation or stimulus.[27]

The conditions necessary for the "coming about" of intuition and its benefits are still a relatively new and unexplored area of management science.[28] Nevertheless, the following initial insights can be drawn from the available studies:

- *Intuition needs experience.* Intuition has nothing to do with either instinct or clairvoyance. Intuition is "automized expertise."[29] The more complex and extensive a decision-maker's experience, the more patterns he will be familiar with. The more patterns he is familiar with, the better his intuition will be. Know-how is often stored as implicit knowledge. It cannot be articulated. Therefore, when an experienced senior executive decides "on gut instinct" because it intuitively seems right to them, this is, in truth, recognizing patterns from experience. If this senior executive is subsequently not able to clearly articulate why he considers this decision to be correct, this does not necessarily mean that the intuitive decision was bad. Studies show that senior executives at the highest level make more intuitive decisions than senior executives at the middle and lower levels, and that owners of small businesses make around the same proportion of intuitive decisions as the most senior executives of top companies.[30]
- *Senior executives need networks.* They need networks in order to share experiences and obtain a good level of feedback for their decisions. A climate of learning which supports the development of know-how can only be brought about through good feedback. Top senior executives should surround themselves with people who are their equals and with whom they can maintain an open climate of discussion. The opposite often occurs in leadership practice: "Many managers surround themselves with yes-men and people who always nod their heads in approval. This is the most disastrous thing that can happen and will sooner or later end in them collectively losing their sense of reality."[31]
- *Senior executives need emotional intelligence.* Intuition usually goes hand in hand with emotion. The neuroscientist Joseph LeDoux[32] has proven that the amygdala – our emotional memory – categorizes stimuli and triggers behavior faster than cognitive processes by means of a "quick and dirty" process. In other words, emotion takes precedence over cognition. "Gut instinct" can both protect us from incorrect decisions and draw our attention to opportunities. Thus Goleman also said that listening to feelings can lead to better decisions.[33] Furthermore, Goleman found that 90 percent of differences between top performers and averagely successful senior executives at the highest level can be explained by emotional intelligence.[34] And this primarily means being conscious of and knowing one's own feelings;

that is, being able to recognize one's own emotions, to understand them, and to interpret them correctly.

- *Learning through mistakes.* Since intuition needs experience, it is necessary to have an environment in which experiences – both positive and negative – can be had. This also requires a certain amount of willingness to take risks and tolerance of mistakes. Senior executives can create such cultures by publicly and continuously supporting senior executives who take risks and also make mistakes, and by supporting these senior executives' careers.[35]
- *Being curious and seeing opportunities rather than risks.* Senior executives must give their curiosity freedom, despite the pressures of their career. This curiosity is the prerequisite for discovering new opportunities. However, this, in turn, can only occur if they process the impressions they have gained in an "opportunity-oriented" way and do not always look everywhere for reasons why an idea might fail. In an essay in the *Harvard Business Review*, Peter Drucker wrote: "A good manager always focuses his attention more strongly on opportunities than on risks . . . constantly worrying about problems does not really move things forward. Doing this merely averts damage to the company. Positive results can only come about if senior executives consistently exploit opportunities."[36] Thinking and acting in an opportunity-oriented way is a prerequisite for striking new paths. Striking new paths is a prerequisite for gathering experiences. And intuition needs experience.
- *Intuition must not be given free rein.* No wise senior executive would make decisions that are so serious that they could destroy the company based on intuition. A wise senior executive will instead try to supplement intuition with knowledge and facts. Or, as Peter Drucker puts it: "I believe in intuition only if you discipline it. The 'hunch' artists, the ones who make a diagnosis but don't check it out with facts, with what they observe, are the ones . . . who kill businesses."[37]

10 What do top companies do differently

What do top companies do differently? After 4 years of research, we have come a significant step closer to answering this question. We were able to identify important success factors and show the roles they play. We have attempted to demonstrate the challenges that companies should concern themselves with and what we see as the levers of success.

Innovative ability, core competences, and market orientation are key drivers. Ultimately, though, we pinpoint the innovation orientation of top management and its leadership skills as the true sources of competitive advantages and above-average success. These factors have a number of effects on:

- the character of corporate culture or rather entrepreneurship culture, which we understand as a culture that is characterized by values such as dynamism, entrepreneurship, and the willingness to take risks, in which senior executives see themselves as entrepreneurs and innovators who are prepared to take risks, and where growth and innovation are key priorities;
- the strength of corporate culture; that is, the identity it creates and the values it conveys to employees;
- the innovative ability of the company in terms of its products, processes and business model; and
- the investment in and development of unique resources and skills which constitute core competences and as such guide key strategic decisions and form the basis for innovations.

These success drivers are not independent of one another; they can only deliver their effect in combination with one another. We have shown that culture and its strength have a complex effect on market orientation, innovative ability, and core competences. We have also shown that market orientation directly influences innovative ability, core competences, and success. We have discussed the characteristics of these factors and the relationships between them in depth.

At this point, we would like to highlight once more what we consider to be the key levers. This much seems clear: without the appropriate attitudes, values,

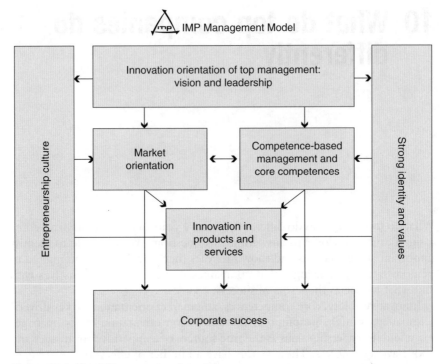

Figure 10.1 The IMP management model

norms, and orientation on the part of top management, it is very difficult for a culture which fosters innovation to develop. However, this culture alone is most certainly not sufficient. Methods and processes must be employed to ensure that the company is managed in a market-oriented way and strength must be concentrated in the areas where the company is unique and among the best in class.

Our studies were also able to show that the likelihood of success increases significantly if these factors are sufficiently well developed within companies and interact with one another. This enables us to derive a general management model from our findings (Figure 10.1).

There are methods and tools for each building block in this model. Presenting these in detail was not the objective of this book; its objective was to provide starting points. At this point, we would once more like to outline the key questions that senior executives should ask themselves on behalf of their companies.

Innovation orientation of top management

- Are we aware of the company's actual core task and have we really derived visionary objectives for the next 10 years from this?

- Are we at the top decision-making level actually prepared to shape tomorrow and to think beyond known paradigms when doing so?
- Do we at the top decision-making level have access to knowledge networks inside and outside the company and do we exploit these in order to get a firm idea of changes within the market system, customer problems, and technological developments?
- Do our top senior executives constantly look for unusual and different approaches so as to be able to develop really innovative solutions to the company's core challenges?
- Are we actually prepared to think entrepreneurially, in the sense that we invest in the development and strengthening of new core competences?
- Does the leadership work of our top decision-makers put employees in a position to appreciate the unusual qualities of the company and to experience them on an emotional level?
- Do the leaders in our company possess sufficient skills to embed the spirit of change throughout the entire company?

Entrepreneurship culture

- Is the company's culture characterized by entrepreneurship, dynamism, and the willingness to take risks, rather than standardization, formalization, and risk minimization?
- Are a propensity to innovate, flexibility, and a will to change the dominant forces that hold the company together and give it direction, rather than rules, procedures, and plans?

Strong identity and values

- Are our employees proud to work for the company and for the realization of its objectives?
- Do employees trust in the competence of management and their colleagues?
- Do employees feel and sense that they are an important part of the overall process and that their individual contribution to the achievement of objectives is important?
- Do the company's culture, the values it lives by, and its employees' daily interaction with one another promote a feeling of well-being for the individual?
- Are errors tolerated, provided employees abide by the core values of the company?

Market orientation

- Do employees at all levels within the company exploit the opportunity to generate future-related knowledge about markets and their game rules, as well as customer problems, to pass it on and to discuss it?

- Do we have access to a network of experts, institutions, partner companies, and lead users in order to be able to bring new knowledge into the company?
- Do we have discussion platforms within the company where the market knowledge that has been generated is discussed with the top decision-makers?
- Are we able to transfer this knowledge into forward-looking strategies, products, and processes, as well as new business models?

Competence-based management

- Do we in top management focus strategically on the enhancement and development of new core competences?
- Do we have a suitable plan for enhancing and systematically developing core competences?
- Do we have a process aimed at finding new markets/opportunities for our existing core competences?
- Do we specifically aim employee training at current or desired future competences?

Core competences

- Do we possess skills, technologies, resources, processes, know-how, and so on, which:

  - are valuable in the market, since they deliver a particular benefit to the customer;
  - are unique, that is, no other competitor possesses them;
  - cannot easily be imitated; and
  - also cannot be substituted by other skills, technologies, and so on?

- Are we able to systematically exploit these core competences for the purposes of innovation and opening up new markets?

Innovative ability

- Do innovative products and services form a greater proportion of total turnover than that in competitors' companies?
- When launching new products, do we pay particular attention to ensuring that product launches are based on innovative launch concepts?
- Do constant process innovations enable us to achieve higher customer value and better-cost structures?
- Do we have an innovative business model that is very difficult for competitors to imitate?

The data gathered from over 700 strategic business units from 10 European countries did not only provide the scientific basis for our management model; this research project also enabled us to compile a database which should help senior executives to identify specific fields of action for improving the performance of their own companies. From there, we developed an evaluation model that enables senior executives to compare the performance of their own companies as regards the building blocks of success with the results of the top performers and the average companies, and to derive from this appropriate courses of action.

We do not intend to assert that consistently applying our management model will guarantee success in every situation – that would be presumptuous. The markets and problems with which senior executives are confronted on a daily basis are too diverse and too complex for this to be possible. However, we firmly believe that the likelihood of success will increase if the insights from this book find application within companies.

We intended to "identify those few key levers that are decisive for the success of a company, and to increase top executives' awareness of the things that are strategically significant and therefore require their full attention." We can only hope that we have succeeded in this.

We would like to end the book with views from "architects of success." To this end, we held conversations with some of the most successful managers in the German-speaking world.

11 The insights of great leaders

PETER BRABECK-LETMATHE, CHAIRMAN AND CEO, NESTLÉ SA, VEVEY, SWITZERLAND

Nestlé sells a billion products a day, has over 130,000 different products, over 250,000 employees, production plants or branches in almost every country on earth, an annual turnover of SF91bn, and an EBITDA of over $11bn (2005) – dimensions that impressed us when we were preparing for our conversation with Peter Brabeck-Letmathe, CEO of Nestlé since 1997. The conversation itself would turn out to be at least as impressive.

It was just before 9 a.m. Mr Brabeck-Letmathe received us in a friendly manner, took the documents he had prepared from his desk and opened the conversation. We briefly presented the design and key findings of our research project to him. He was interested, wanted to know more about the individual components of the model, and made one or two notes. He indicated that he could fully corroborate the content of the findings and our model based on his own experiences and was impressed at how we had succeeded in grasping and presenting the core knowledge that one otherwise only acquires from many years of practical leadership.

We naturally then wanted to find out what Mr Brabeck-Letmathe sees as the principal reasons for Nestlé's sustained success. His answer was indicative of what was to follow: "It is not a question of thinking about what has made us successful in the past; the question is primarily what we must do so that we will be successful in the future. I'll perhaps think about the reasons for the success we've achieved when I'm retired. At first that sounds very simple, but it is perhaps the most difficult task for companies, particularly if they are already very successful, because if they are already successful the organization continually attempts to draw on past success patterns. This seems logical at first and above all gives those involved a feeling of efficiency and security. That is exactly what you must resist using all means available. In my experience, real learning can only come about through crises, or if we seriously feel challenged to reshape tomorrow. When I think I can feel rigidity developing, I have been known to consciously throw 'stones' into the water now and then, so that the 'waves' they cause spur our senior executives and employees on to start thinking about radical solutions."

We wanted to know what he considered to be the "levers" which are necessary for maintaining the desired dynamics in a company of this size on a sustained basis.

"First of all, allow me to go back in time a little. When I took up my post, I was familiar with the enormous complexity of brands, products, processes, and markets due to my previous history at Nestlé. Back then I believed – and I have been further confirmed in this view over the years – that, despite this enormous variety, it was essential to achieve the highest possible level of decentralization at Nestlé. We must comprehend the diversity of the markets, understand them, and, above all, also develop them in this way. This posed and poses an enormous organizational challenge for the company, particularly with respect to its leadership processes.

Against this background, I believe that three pillars in particular determine success: the basic attitude of senior executives, the strategic positioning of the company and the innovation that lies behind it, and the type of corporate culture at the company.

These elements require senior executives who, besides being 100 percent professional and having the necessary commitment to the company's objectives and rules, also possess a reasonable amount of willingness to take risks." As Mr Brabeck-Letmathe began to speak about this topic, he took a brochure entitled "The Nestlé Management and Leadership Principles" from his pile of documents. "Immediately after taking up my post, I devised management and leadership principles that I considered important for positioning the company. Among other things, the willingness of senior executives to take risks plays a key role in this. If they want to make a difference, senior executives must, in particular, be prepared to take risks and that is exactly what I demand of our senior executives. To illustrate what I mean by this, I would briefly like to make you aware of the things we attach particular importance to when selecting our senior executives. We naturally look at their performance and professionalism in detail. However, in my opinion, it is just as important to investigate these senior executives' failures or defeats. In my view, only someone who has some failures to show in their history can carry out a leadership role in a forward-looking way, because only then is it clear that the person was willing to take risks. If someone was only ever successful, it usually means that they didn't change very much. Consequently, only those individuals who have experienced failure in their careers are given top leadership roles at Nestlé. At selection interviews, which I carry out myself, the individuals are often visibly amazed when I mainly talk to them about this topic."

Aside from the orientation set out in the management and leadership principles, Mr Brabeck-Letmathe also pointed out the key significance of innovation for corporate success.

"When we at Nestlé talk about innovations, we distinguish between three fundamentally different innovation levels with different innovation processes. First, I believe we must rework and improve all the Nestlé products introduced within a 5-year period. To this end, we worked out a detailed schedule which 'forces' employees to examine and change around 26,000 individual products yearly in terms of their value, quality, and so on, regardless of the products' track records. We call this process 'renovation.' Since it requires, among other things, working with the knowledge of employees in the markets and specific competitive comparisons, this process is very heavily decentralized.

The second innovation level pertains to technological innovations. These are primarily driven forward in the strategic business units. In particular, this process involves developing new product and production technologies for the individual product categories.

The third innovation level pertains to pure research. It is significantly determined by the strategic positioning of the company and its output has a decisive influence on future corporate success. Accordingly, it is absolutely essential that company management actively guides this process, makes available the necessary resources, and creates a structure conducive to successful development work.

For some time now, Nestlé has faced massive challenges in this very area. We have introduced a transformation process aimed at turning Nestlé from the world's largest food company into the world's leading food, nutrition, health, and wellness company. This means, among other things, that we must produce outstanding innovations in the areas of health and wellness, as well as in our current core business. This poses enormous challenges, even to a company such as Nestlé.

For this reason, we have set up our own Corporate Wellness Unit for this transformation process at the highest level and equipped it with the necessary resources. Essentially, this unit must drive forward change in the internal and external mindset. This task involves, in particular, developing scientifically sound competitive advantages with regard to wellness and health in the product portfolio. In addition to carrying out research and development work internally, Nestlé has also founded two funds.

One is a venture fund, in which a group of specialists pursues the objective of seeking out interesting developments in the areas of health and wellness from all over the world and participating in them. In particular, the specialists look into the development work of small research groups or small companies. Should something appear promising, they try to participate in it and to support the research and development work with resources. Those developments which actually produce interesting products are subsequently transferred into the second fund. This fund has the task of developing the product idea into a successful business. Those companies whose products realize a certain volume of business are then taken into the Nestlé organization. This enables Nestlé to first track down and test ideas in the market very quickly and flexibly and subsequently to market only those products with the best prospects of success in the most global roll-out possible."

As Mr Brabeck-Letmathe reflected on the transformation process that the company had introduced, we could sense the particular strategic significance that he attaches to it. The way he gave us an understanding of developments in the markets with such conviction was impressive and, at the same time, illustrated how intensively he concerns himself with market developments. When asked how much time he himself spends in the markets, he answered:

"I spend around 70 percent of all my time in the markets with customers and employees. I need this time in order to be able to gain an understanding of and get a feeling about where we stand and which direction we must develop in. One cannot glean this understanding of markets from reports alone, or would not be able to interpret the reports correctly without spending this time in the market."

This emphasis on strategic positioning and the focus on fundamental innovation that this entails led us to ask Mr Brabeck-Letmathe's opinion about the influence of the capital markets on strategic decisions. Mr Brabeck-Letmathe leant back and we could see that we had touched upon a very sensitive subject. "If you want to position a company for the long term and make it successful on a sustained basis, you must take your leave of classic shareholder-value thinking. I refuse to consider the opinion of 'finance fundamentalists' in my decisions. Although they frequently 'punish' me for it, I must and will not follow the rules of short-term thinking. In my view, a company should strive for long-term shared value. For this very reason we developed the shared-value concept for Nestlé, together with Michael Porter. Essentially, we tried to work out how Nestlé can ensure that it creates 'long-term shareholder value.' While doing this, we came to the conclusion that it is necessary to build up a company that maintains the trust of the public on a long-term basis. In order to really be able to win this trust, it is also necessary for the company to fulfill its social responsibilities. It will only be able to do this if it integrates this key aspect into corporate strategy and follows this strategy over a long period."

Meanwhile, our time was running short and we were still eager to find out something about the significance of corporate culture that Mr Brabeck-Letmathe had mentioned.

"Ultimately, the type of culture a company has is a decisive factor in whether it is capable of delivering outstanding performance. At the same time, it is tremendously difficult to make corporate culture tangible, so as to be able to control it. Nowadays, I am of the opinion that the culture within a company is decisively shaped by the observations of its employees. Employees look very closely at what strategic decisions are made, who within the company is doing what in connection with them, and, in particular, what is not being done.

Accordingly, active culture creation naturally necessitates defining core values for the company and for cooperation between all stakeholders. It is important to continually present these core values. But the most important thing is for senior executives on all levels to actually live by these values.

For example, if I demand a willingness to take risks from my senior executives, I must personally protect them in the event of failures and encourage them to take risks again. If I do not do this, I need no longer concern myself with fostering a willingness to change within the company.

Something similar can be said of demanding that as many employees as possible think and act entrepreneurially. If I want to achieve this, I really must involve employees in major strategic decisions. When I first began to think about the subject of health and wellness, based on discussions with my colleagues, the first thing I did was to write an essay on the subject of wellness and distribute it to some of the people within the company with whom I had discussed the subject, asking for feedback or specific opinions.

Within about a year, we were able to define the initial cornerstones of the vision in relatively clear terms, based on this constructive and diverse feedback. Within a further year, we had consulted more and more employees in order to fill out the details. And this is how the current version of the 'Blueprints for the Future' – which are discussed at workshops at annual meetings involving over 400 Nestlé senior executives from all over the world and reworked every 18 months – came about. Following the workshops, these strategic blueprints are handed out to all Nestlé employees. At the same time, I myself intensively use the time I spend visiting the countries to discuss these strategic subjects with employees out in the markets."

We had come to the end of a highly interesting conversation. It goes without saying that we would have had many more questions to ask, but Mr Brabeck-Letmathe had already given us considerably more of his time than had been agreed. As we were leaving, he asked us if we had just a little more time. There was something he really wanted to show us.

During our conversation, Mr Brabeck-Letmathe had pointed out that it is extremely important to him that the people in the headquarters never forget that Nestlé's success is primarily based on its products. The systems are merely tools for safeguarding the necessary processes. For this very reason he decided that the highest floor of the exclusive headquarters should not accommodate the top management. Instead, Nestlé's products should be displayed there, there should be the opportunity to taste them, and pleasant rest areas should be set up for employees so that they come into contact with the products. We went via a wide staircase directly from the main nerve centre of Nestlé Plc into the "Nestlé exhibition." The CEO of a company that sells a billion products worldwide each day then personally presented his products to us.

MARKUS LANGES-SWAROVSKI, MEMBER OF THE EXECUTIVE BOARD, SWAROVSKI

Markus Langes-Swarovski is 32 years young and has been a member of the executive board in the Crystal division of Swarovski, a family business which employs over 16,000 employees, for 4 years. Acquaintances and employees characterize him as a visionary and a lateral thinker who possesses the talent of being able to approach people and raise their enthusiasm for new things. It is characteristic of him that one of his guiding principles is: "Ultimately, it is about taking viewpoints which reach beyond the parameters of the moment." His approach to doing this is shaped by discourse – "only open and critical dialogue about tomorrow leads to a change of perspective"; his understanding of leadership is demanding – "I set myself the task of constantly disturbing the core of the company through discourse, as only willingness to break with the status quo opens up opportunities for development"; and his "sources of inspiration" are a network of mentors and lateral thinkers from philosophy, art, design, and business.

Markus Langes-Swarovski on innovative ability and history

According to Markus Langes-Swarovski, "The future always needs an origin – not in a nostalgic, but in a forward-looking sense." In Swarovski's opinion, a company's own history is an important basis for its future actions. A study of the history of one's own company should not focus on merely continuing tried and tested and old-established patterns; it should open up opportunities and possibilities for the future. "When we hold a discourse about elements of our own history, it becomes clear that Daniel Swarovski, the founder of the company, was a progressive avant-gardist and a courageous entrepreneur. Even back then, recognizing and exploiting opportunities was an important element in his corporate philosophy: 'Every era offers possibilities for development. It is important to constantly stay awake and to exploit the opportunities that present themselves in the right way.'

With regard to this way of thinking, one can refer to the company's own history while being open to the future. Looking back therefore also enables us to look forwards, to 'attempt' to continue to write and actively shape one's own history by following Swarovski's key 'success principles' – change and avant-gardism. What emerges from this is a future orientation based on one's own past. Reflecting on this should bring about a way of thinking within the company based on a spirit of 'let's risk it again.'

The task of company management is to keep alive and foster this will to change within the company. In this process, it is important for every senior executive to start to think about new things and to discuss them within the company. The starting point of every creative process is dissatisfaction with the current situation. Communicating new approaches and ideas internally through open dialogue/discourse is an important leadership tool in this context. This kind of communication causes confusion within our organization time and again. In a company the size of Swarovski, it is almost 'disruptive.' Constantly disturbing the core of the company – continually questioning existing ways of thinking and behaving – is the only way to ensure that Swarovski remains flexible and is an important management task. However, above all, it should encourage employees on all levels to continually go a step further. Great success can only come about if people within the company itself are ready for new things and want to go this one step further.

Senior executives must assume the role of a cultural 'engine for change' within the company. They must, as already mentioned, continually disturb the core of the company in order to stimulate change. To a certain extent, employees must be permanently confused, and this applies in all areas, including after sales. My father continually challenged the employees in our company in his time too.

It is essential to remain agile in one's thinking, continually change one's viewpoint and constantly intervene with small disturbances. However, these disturbances should come in small doses so that they do not cause too much movement within the company, since it is also necessary, of course, to develop the existing basis further.

However, aside from this task of constantly 'disturbing,' it is important that senior executives also recognize that they must assume a leadership role within the company, since change in particular is also associated with constant difficulties and problems. In this regard, I see dialogue and discussion within a company as factors which contribute to an organization's maneuverability. In this context, it is important to also allow different directions of thought within a company. Change only comes about through discussion. Existing elements must remain flexible and new things must be allowed to develop in small steps. Studying the future of the company in this way is more important than simply thinking about operational excellence.

In this regard, it is important that company management creates or allows platforms that facilitate discourse within the company. Of course, we also take a large risk in doing so, since change can also lead us in the wrong direction. Let us take as an example our crystal figures, which were dismissed as 'kitsch' in some divisions of our company. It is necessary to take countermeasures when faced with such developments. This thinking merely triggered a 'now-more-than-ever' reaction in me. We subsequently dedicated an entire issue of our employee magazine to the subject of kitsch to stimulate a new discussion about 'substance beyond fashion.' However, I am not talking here about an employee magazine in the conventional sense. In our company, this tool must have a completely different quality and move employees to think about the company. Giving this communication instrument a professional and elaborate form is therefore an important prerequisite for the success of the initiative."

Markus Langes-Swarovski on culture and branding from the inside

"For us, the company's culture, which is based on open and authentic communication with employees, is an important key to our corporate success. About 3 years ago, when the new generation took over the management of the company and we initiated an integrated strategy process, it was important to us to develop challenging objectives and ideals for the future of the company. When doing so, it was essential to penetrate into the company as deeply as possible and to trigger emotional commitment with regard to actively planning for the company's future, since it is always dangerous to formulate guiding principles within the framework of normative management and to present these to employees in the form of a few lines. It is important to embed these values and ideas in employees' heads on an emotional level.

We began – initially in a small group – to describe challenging ideals for the company. Right from the start, we attached great importance to the process of implementing these basic ideas. In our opinion, dialogue and discourse were the only factors that could trigger change, because change only comes about through discussion. Looking at the company's future can trigger an important emotional bond in employees and thereby promotes the development of a suitable corporate culture and Swarovski's branding.

At Swarovski, branding starts from the inside. The brand is the 'hook' for our identity and culture. In this regard, we are certainly fortunate in that our product, crystal, inhabits a space between technology and lyricism and is therefore capable of touching everybody. From this, we formulated the principle of 'poetry of precision,' which is applied at all levels within Swarovski from technology through to management.

In order to stimulate this process of internal branding, we developed a series of tools, which, among other things, used 'euphoric TV pictures' from staged events to show future opportunities for the company. For me, the success of this exercise can partly be seen in the fact that these pictures emotionally moved our employees to the point of being touched. This approach even resulted in a very special vocabulary developing within our company.

In the centre of this was always the 'brand romance' we had developed in collaboration with artists, which was to transport our brand values by means of poetry and art (explosion of expression). Professionally designing these communication instruments is a key prerequisite for success. During brand-romance events at Swarovski, we had various pictures of the Swarovski company professionally filmed by directors from Los Angeles. That is, good realization of the ideas was always of great importance to us.

However, it is not sufficient to hire professional scriptwriters if these values and the possible future of the company are not shared honestly and emotionally. It is important to keep in mind that we only developed these very elaborate tools for the purposes of internal communication with our employees. But when content and form come together and 16,000 employees feel the Swarovski brand, you can save a great deal on traditional advertising.

Nevertheless, crystal also represents the perfect medium for telling stories. However, crystal is not a detached medium; that is, people can or must finish these stories off themselves. Therefore, the employee does not get a finished answer, but he does have a good basis from which to think about the future of the company.

Of course, such activities must run parallel to the 'classic' strategy process. Furthermore, it is important to create an open platform for discussion and discourse without changing all the main features of the brand. The brand should provide us with the direction for growth and thereby keep its validity, since collective ownership can come about through repetition."

What role do customers play if one wishes to shape the future?

"One should not listen too much to what the customer wants. You can't learn everything you need to know about the market from customers. Doing exactly what the customer wants hinders innovation and results in mediocrity. For example, a focus group raised the problem that our products were too expensive in customers' eyes. When interpreting the data one must of course be aware that every individual seeks advantages for themselves, and such a result could almost have been expected. But testing every product and every detail in a host of pre-tests is not our way.

We do, of course, carry out a large amount of market research. However, in my opinion, there are two dimensions to proximity to the market and good market research: one ear listens to the consumer, but the other listens to sources outside our target group.

In this regard, I advocate what one might call a 'transcultural' approach to market orientation. It is very important to also look outside the relevant target groups of the moment in one's market orientation.

But gathering information is far from sufficient. The real art form in marketing is the correct, or rather 'a' correct, interpretation of the information. At Swarovski, we continually seek discourse with expert groups and reference groups in order to illuminate key themes from different points of view. In this context, it is important to think of the future as complex, rather than one-dimensional. For this reason, we try to integrate different individuals and opinion leaders into our reference groups. These are people who are used to studying trends and developments. The interpretation of information in particular depends significantly on the individual. Therefore, in my view, it is important to allow different individuals to look at the data. This is the only way it will be possible to identify different approaches to 'planning the future.' A stable foundation in the form of an up-to-date and extensive database is, of course, an important prerequisite for this.

With this in mind, we also established a series of events entitled 'thinking from the outside' at Swarovski, in which we illuminate certain themes from a philosophical perspective, for example. Here, the skill is spotting the opportunities within a company that offer the greatest potential across a worldwide organization. The question we must address in the future is how we can exploit and implement this information to the greatest extent possible."

Markus Langes-Swarovski on core competences

"Ultimately, our success is based entirely on unique skills we have built up, enhanced or created from scratch over the years. These competences have a decisive influence on our strategy development. At the same time, we know that we face the challenge of building up new fields of competence around the 'Swarovski' brand.

From today's standpoint, I would say that our core competences lie in the following areas: an important core competence is certainly our basic production, in which we have made substantial investments. We will continue to do so in the future too. We are not purely a marketing organization which outsources production and everything else.

These days, we can certainly say that application technology is also a core competence. Behind this lies the ability to learn about all the applications of our basic production. A further strength of Swarovski is certainly our inward and outward branding, in which we invest a lot of resources, although I'm not entirely sure that we can speak of a core competence in this area as yet. We certainly can in comparison with our direct competitors, but I'm not entirely sure if this would also be the case in a cross-industry comparison.

Our fully integrated value chain offers us great potential for optimization, since the processes are simple and there are no difficult interfaces with external partners. This ensures that we gain a high level of market expertise through our retail shops and the proximity to customers that they give us."

PROF. DR MICHAEL POPP AND DR UWE BAUMANN, BIONORICA AG

For over 70 years, Bionorica has been deciphering the secrets of nature in order to develop highly effective pharmaceuticals from plants. Today, the company is among the world's leading suppliers of phytopharmaceuticals. In 2005, its almost 600 employees produced 1.7 million litres of liquid pharmaceuticals and around 700 million pills, capsules, and tablets. The products are sold in all continents.

Early in the summer of 2006, we met the owner and CEO, Prof. Dr Michael A. Popp, as well as his fellow board member Dr Uwe Baumann, for a conversation at the company's head office in Neumarkt, Upper Palatinate

(Germany). We wanted to find out the "success formulae" of this owner-managed, medium-sized company.

Prof. Dr Popp on developing and positioning the company

"In 1987, I took over the company my grandfather founded over 70 years ago. Since then, Bionorica has been through a dramatic transformation process. Based on my faith in nature and the possibilities it offers, I knew early on which direction I wanted to take the company in. My objective was to turn Bionorica into a 'phytoneering company' whose pharmaceuticals were available in all the important markets in the world. However, at the time I joined the company, the efficacy of plant-based pharmaceuticals was still heavily debated among medical experts and only a few competitors focused on this field. I was therefore aware that we had to do many things completely differently, not to say radically change and restructure them, in order to better understand the opportunities afforded by nature and our knowledge of them, and to market them accordingly. And this process is far from complete."

The two gentlemen proudly tell us that they have now succeeded in establishing a real "phytoneering company." Prof. Dr Popp: "Phytoneering is easy to explain: the term stands on the one hand for discovering and further developing plant-based active ingredients into special extracts, and on the other hand for developing and manufacturing modern pharmaceuticals with new dimensions in quality and efficacy. In addition, we use the most innovative pharmaceutical processes, hence the term 'engineering.'"

Furthermore, Dr Baumann points out that the term "phytoneering" also stands for Bionorica's unique and unmistakable approach. "Phytoneering has become a state-of-mind and the formula for our success. This spirit inspires our senior executives and employees and is also sensed by our customers and partners."

Prof. Dr Popp describes to us the often difficult path to success

"On the one hand, it is of course possible to structure an owner-managed family business any way you wish. It is possible to drive forward projects and ideas which at first glance are difficult to support with arguments, but where feeling and experience tell the decision-maker that the project or idea could be a success. Despite my vision, for a long time we only came closer to my objectives with great difficulty. Of course, at our company, just as at any other, things do not always go as planned and when this happens it is particularly important that the entire management team believes in the idea and does everything in its power to realize it.

During a critical phase for Bionorica, although the then management team always gave the chosen path their nod of approval, they never really put their heart, soul, and commitment into actually implementing it. When I became fully aware of this I put new senior executives, who wanted to go down this path with me and implement my ideas, into critical positions. On the one hand, the new management crew had a considerably more critical approach during discussions than the managers I had replaced. They called far more into question and long discussions were necessary for a common agreement to be reached as to which opportunities Bionorica should concentrate on. But within a short time, one could sense that something was changing within the company. Then the success came too."

Dr Baumann confirms this: "You simply must have good senior executives. They are the pillars of success and decisively determine what the company stands for internally and externally."

Decision-making in an owner-managed company is not always easy

"Of course, I fundamentally determine the direction we go in. That is my task and my duty. Nevertheless, I try to find a common direction with my management team when it comes to principal issues. I have been known to simply rethink certain things when my senior executives' arguments have convinced me. This is the corrective that owner-managed companies need in order to be successful. And, despite this, it is often the case that I have to push through decisions on my own. Often, these are 'radical' decisions. There have been times when the team has not shared my convictions and, in spite of this, I still held on to them. Somehow, I just had the feeling that it was right. Often, I also found it difficult to describe. Call it feeling, intuition, or whatever. The remarkable thing was that the team did not leave me in the lurch following these 'radical' decisions, but instead used all their ability and put 100 percent commitment into actually implementing my visions and ideas. The success that materialized was only possible due to the quality and commitment of these employees. Today, we are even more radical in our approach than we were back then and it works unbelievably well.

Let us take, for example, our involvement in Eastern Europe. In these cases, we quite simply had no basis for reaching a decision. Initially, there were many arguments against getting involved, but our success has since confirmed that the right decisions were made at that time."

Prof. Dr Popp cites the reapproval of Sinupret (a pharmaceutical which reduces inflammation of the paranasal sinuses) as a further example. In the 1990s, due to legal regulations it became necessary to formally retest the pharmaceutical Sinupret, which had been tried and tested over many years. In this situation, Prof. Dr Popp decided in favor of submitting Sinupret for reapproval despite the great cost and effort involved – and this contrary to the wishes of the entire management team. However, by taking this approach, Bionorica not only obtained reapproval for Sinupret, but also obtained approval in principle for further products. Through these efforts, which went beyond what was necessary, Bionorica acquired expertise in manufacturing plant-based pharmaceuticals. Everything Bionorica learned in the course of this approval process led to the strengthening of its position as a 'plant specialist' among the pharmaceutical manufacturers. Today, Sinupret is the best-selling, plant-based pharmaceutical in Germany.

In Prof. Dr Popp's opinion, the most important building blocks for corporate success are the competences that characterize a company and make it unique. Only through having such competences can a company clearly differentiate itself from the competition. The starting point for Bionorica's competences is its knowledge about the powers of nature:

"We are a plant specialist and have studied nature in great depth for decades. Our competence in understanding nature extends across many divisions of the company, from research and development, to cultivating medicinal plants and manufacturing processes, through to marketing. Bionorica produces extracts of a quality that was barely conceivable in the past. For example, we run our own cultivation areas in Germany, Austria, Spain, and Hungary to safeguard the quality of raw materials."

According to Prof. Dr Popp, an important basis for developing these competences lies "in the company's efforts to take the leading position in a 'field' [phytopharmaceuticals]. But, in addition, you must be prepared to make the necessary investment. In an area such as this, it cannot only be about the money. We feel committed to a task."

"We also want to convey our competences to the outside world. Our neologism, phytoneering, shows that Bionorica treads a different path to its competitors," says Dr Baumann.

At Bionorica, managing customer relationships is seen as a further building block of success. Prof. Dr Popp spends around 100 days a year with his customers. On the one hand, he simply wants to listen to customers and understand their needs; on the other, he also wants to pass on the Bionorica message: "Because when customers really understand us," Prof. Dr Popp says, "they do something for us. New ideas for the future are continually emerging." For example, customers produced studies for a new preparation without the assistance of Bionorica. Its breakthrough subsequently came in 2002.

Dr Baumann confirms this too: "We can only be successful if we fully understand our customers and markets. Furthermore, a company such as Bionorica can only operate successfully if it sees itself as a partner within a network."

The network concept has gained considerably in importance, particularly with regard to research. Prof. Dr Popp adds: "Currently, around 20 universities are involved in Germany alone. In addition to this, just as many world-renowned institutes are involved on an international level (from as far and wide as Sweden, the USA and Korea)."

In the opinion of both board members, a company and its employees must be challenged constantly if it is to achieve sustained corporate success.

"Bionorica is far from the company it was in the year 2000. Constant changes are necessary if we are to stay at the top. However, these changes also mean changes for our employees. We must explain to employees how new things work. Management must carry new ideas – changes – into the company through events and idea competitions, for example. We must take the employees with us on this journey. We can only produce outstanding results in all areas with their commitment," says Dr Baumann.

Intensively carrying out research is fundamental to Bionorica's success. Its expenditure on research amounts to approximately 15 percent of its turnover. "However, only a few companies in the industry can afford to make such large investments in research. But if you don't research, you have no chance in the natural pharmaceuticals market in the long term," says Prof. Dr Popp.

Furthermore, he says, you must believe in new concepts and ideas and doggedly drive them forward. "You have to have a vision. You must stand 200 percent behind the vision or a new project. Just think about the change in thinking in medicine; such a change couldn't have been predicted on that scale. Many large manufacturers underestimated the degree to which phytopharmaceuticals would gain importance in medical treatment. We positioned ourselves in good time."

Prof. Dr Popp himself describes his behavior when pursuing new projects as follows: "The further we come, the more of a nuisance I become. For example, initially we couldn't really gain a foothold in the market for Echinacin but we stubbornly continued to strive for success. Now Bionorica manufactures Echinacin products for well-known pharmaceutical companies and we also provide the necessary studies when required."

The two board members also see generating and initiating ideas as one of their key management tasks. Subsequently, it is management's task to break these ideas down. In the pharmaceutical industry in particular, each innovation takes a very long time due to the required approval procedures, among other things. There is no success story during this "endurance phase," when everyone is alone. During this phase, it is difficult to give employees an understanding of future success – this calls for senior executives to use their personal powers of conviction." Prof. Dr Popp gives the example of the company's involvement in Russia, which began in 1992. The real breakthrough did not come until 2002.

The two board members answered our final question about future opportunities for Bionorica as follows:

> We believe that awareness about the possibilities afforded by and the acceptance of plant-based pharmaceuticals in medical treatment will continue to increase. We see great opportunities for our company in our faith in nature and its possibilities, but also challenges. In future we will

continue to investigate the resourcefulness of nature in order to make modern medicine a little more plant based every day for the good of peoples' health.

This noble objective says it all.

STEFAN PIERER, CEO, KTM SPORTMOTORCYCLE AG

"Ready to Race" is the basic philosophy behind all KTM's product developments. All KTM vehicles have high-performance potential combined with the lowest possible weight – an everyday requirement in racing which flows unchanged into KTM's production motorcycles. However, "Ready to Race" is not only characteristic of KTM's products. According to employees and colleagues, "Ready to Race" also characterizes Stefan Pierer, the CEO of the company. A KTM employee described it as follows: "You can call him at three in the morning and he will give you an answer or a suggestion for a problem you have described with a speed and an accuracy that will always amaze you. If you travel abroad with him on business, he climbs out of the aeroplane after ten or more hours and starts working as though he had just driven from home to the factory in Mattighofen. And you can be certain that he's been working during the flight. It can be really quite exhausting."

We met Stefan Pierer for lunch, along with Gerald Kiska from KISKA, KTM's design company. Scheduling according to Mr Pierer: "Just as long as we need."

In 1992, Stefan Pierer bought the motorcycle division from the bankrupt's estate of the former KTM Motorfahrzeugbau AG. Within a few years, he and his team managed to not only develop the newly founded KTM Sportmotorcycle GmbH into a profitable company, but also into one of the largest motorcycle manufacturers in Europe.

At the start of the conversation, we wanted to find out what he considered to be the defining characteristics of good senior executives.

In Pierer's view, one of the most important prerequisites for being a good manager is to possess a certain personal drive. "Sometimes I think you can't learn it. You have to carry around this internal drive to want to successfully solve a really big challenge. You also need a certain ability to endure hard times. In my opinion, you can't be really successful if you're not also prepared and able to deal with failures. It's not by chance that many successful people say that they have benefited most of all from failures. I am of the firm opinion that an opportunity lies in every failure – but you have to want to see it."

According to Pierer, these qualities are often lost in large, established, and successful companies. These companies are prosperous and are no longer used to living with failures and fighting for success. This often leads to successful companies sliding into crisis extremely quickly.

"At the same time, you need something which is seldom talked about – and that is industriousness. You can't solve a really big challenge if you're not also prepared to put all your commitment behind the thing. I often draw an analogy between this and our involvement in motorsport. If you come into contact with professional riders, you see that the best ones don't just have extraordinary driving skills; they are also the ones who work the hardest."

Besides his personal commitment and the speed at which he operates, Pierer is also known for continually challenging his team with his strategic decisions. We wanted to know which patterns he follows in his decision-making.

"Possessing the personal drive mentioned before far from ensures that you make the right decisions. The number of correct decisions a manager makes increases with their experience. Using this wealth of experience as a basis, I branch off into a certain decision corridor, within which I then move. The risk of making wrong decisions therefore decreases as one's experience increases.

Although, now I come to think of it, I have to say that when it comes to really serious business decisions I ultimately rely on my intuition. It's sometimes the case that rational arguments speak for or against something, but then somehow the decision still won't leave me in peace. I wake up in the night and have the feeling that I should do it differently after all.

However, this intuition or 'gut instinct' is not a purely emotional decision based on one's current emotional state; I believe that experience ultimately plays a key role here too. Because so many thoughts go through your head, which can perhaps only be really properly processed during quiet periods.

As a rule, what is difficult when making strategic decisions is getting the timing right. That is, finding out or predicting when the market and the company will be ready for a particular thing. This requires senior executives to constantly study the market and the processes within the company intensively and to also be prepared to take a business risk.

"We bought the motorcycle division of KTM. Behind it lay the know-how for manufacturing excellent off-road motorcycles. Initially, we focussed on setting up the business anew and soon saw that we were already well on the way to achieving this. There then followed 10 intensive years, during which we conquered the individual segments in the off-road market one by one. Once we had secured our success in the off-road market, I reached the decision to enter the street-motorcycle-business. This was a completely different business, and at the time we at KTM didn't really know how it actually worked. Many people more or less said I was crazy. We lacked know-how, we had no access to the market, and so on, but it was clear to me that the growth potential that KTM needed could only lie in the street-motorcycle sector. We took a different path to our established competitors: we decided to build a new category of street motorcycles using unusual technology and with an unusual design, and it worked."

The success story up to now is impressive. The strategic outlook that Stefan Pierer was sharing with us seemed to us radical and fraught with risk.

"Today, we face a new challenge. In the future the motorcycle market is unlikely to continue to experience the growth rates we would hope for. We need only observe that nowadays many 18-year-olds no longer take their motorcycle test because they're told from all sides – and rightly so, unfortunately – how dangerous riding motorcycles is, so we at KTM have to ask ourselves how we're going to deal with this. We're going to build a car. Again, it will be a completely new concept and, again, everyone is saying I'm crazy. I realize that this is a risky undertaking too. Therefore, we must take all the necessary measures to minimize the risk, without letting that slow us down."

We wanted to know how he deals with the uncertainty that his radical decisions bring with them.

"If I see at any point that we're not going to manage it, I'll stop the process before it destroys us. But from today's standpoint it would be at least as risky in the long term not to try it. I am absolutely convinced that it is necessary to take a certain amount of entrepreneurial risk. Otherwise, it is incredibly difficult to be one of the winners. However, it can happen that, despite intensive preparation, one misjudges the situation at the time of making the decision. But you must then also have the single-mindedness and courage to reverse a decision that has been reached so as not to put the company at risk. Daring to say 'Stop!' usually requires more courage than standing by a decision.

For example, 4 years ago we decided to enter the top class of motorcycle road racing. We began to put all our effort into building a Moto GP engine – this cost us €3–4m. However, I subsequently stopped the project, as it became clear that, despite all our efforts, we were not ready. With the resources we had at our disposal, we were not able to drive the project forward to the point where we would also become one of the winners in the shortest possible time in that sector too. Everyone said we couldn't stop the project because we would ruin our image. But at that point that didn't matter to me, because I was sure that the project had nevertheless helped us, as developing this engine had significantly strengthened our core competence in the area of engine construction and brought good employees to KTM. So, in this way, the Moto GP initiative was a further step toward extending our core competences in engine construction.

I am absolutely convinced that you need long-term strategic positioning to achieve corporate success on a sustained basis. However, in my opinion, on the way to achieving a goal you have set your sights on, you must be prepared to move closer to this goal using the logic of calculated 'trial and error.' If you really want to make great strides, you simply can't analyze and back everything up."

We then wanted to go a step further in the model and find out what significance building and developing core competences has in KTM's success.

"Possessing, managing, and developing new core competences are fundamental requirements if the company intends to plan market-changing strategies at all. Therefore, we also invest constantly in enhancing our core competences. You have to be aware that certain investments in future core competences may only pay off in 5 years' time. It is almost impossible to argue the case for this with an anonymous shareholder structure on the stock market. For this reason, a personified owner is an important basis for our long-term strategy."

Where do KTM's core competences lie?

"Ultimately, they are all the skills that enable us to bring the 'Ready to Race' philosophy to life. Back when we took over the motorcycle division, we were in agreement that we wanted to position the KTM brand in the market in connection with the racing theme. Since then, we have been doing everything we can to remain true to this positioning strategy. The knowledge and experience from our racing department is directly transferred to our production models, starting with engine construction, through to chassis development and suspension systems.

The racing department itself faces the challenge of being among the winners in all the areas KTM is involved in. We can only succeed at this because we were able to bring the best and most experienced insiders from the most varied of areas to KTM. Nowadays, we don't just dominate the Motocross and Enduro scene; we have won Paris-Dakar seven times in succession and won all the important desert rallies in the past few years. The road that led us there was hard but tremendously important for our market successes. We only managed our first victory in the Paris-Dakar after five defeats. Since then, we have dominated this series. Entering this field has not only enabled us to acquire completely new competences in the manufacture of motorcycles; it has also enabled us, in particular, to appeal to new target groups by presenting our brand in a different way. A motorcycle crossing the desert at sunset evokes emotions and life-long dreams. We now had an additional, emotional competence.

In road racing we are just at the beginning. Nevertheless, in 2005 we won the Manufacturers' World Championship title in the 125cc series 2 years after entering the field. In 2006, we won the first race in the 250cc series and achieved several places on the podium.

At the same time, we focused on design competence right from the start. We wanted our products to function in a unique way but we also wanted to build motorcycles with a unique design. Our collaboration with KISKA had a decisive influence on our success. Their integrated design development process enabled us to develop a unique brand identity. Since then, the originality of the KTM brand has been a 'leitmotif' that runs through everything from our product design and trade show appearances to our POS design.

But, besides product and design competence, we now also possess a unique competence in sales. We currently have our own sales companies in 18 countries. Even automotive manufacturers envy us in that. In North America we are already selling 23,000 motorcycles, which puts us ahead of BMW as the largest European motorcycle brand. That proves us right."

How does KTM succeed in generating the right ideas for its innovation process?

"In my view, two conditions are essential for this. First, we must study the market intensively, particularly at top management level. Only then is it possible to anticipate those trends that we must focus on strategically in the future. I myself spend around 50 percent of my time in the market because I'm aware of the importance of unfiltered information, particularly in this field.

Secondly, you need 'obsessive' developers who do everything in their power to bring the ideas to fruition. I determine our strategic direction to a significant degree. Ideas for specific new products then develop out of numerous conversations with product experts. In this regard, we at KTM have the advantage that 250 of these 'obsessive' developers work for us. These people live for racing and motorcycling and everything that is connected with it. Therefore, I'm constantly confronted with new ideas for products. We then develop a feasible plan out of these ideas.

New products or product ideas must consequently meet four criteria: conformity with the strategic positioning of KTM – 'Ready to Race'; differentiation from the competition; the potential to give customers something that distinguishes them from others and fills them with pride; and meeting the highest quality requirements.

When launching new products, we choose a radical path wherever possible. For example, following our decision to branch out into the street-motorcycle segment, we chose a very forward-looking market strategy. Worldwide PR coverage was very important to us. For this reason, we traveled to Tokyo to 'beard the lion in his den' and presented our first concept study. And this despite the fact that it would still be some time until the product would be completely ready for market. However, this caused an enormous stir and led to good coverage. Early PR work is also crucial in terms of our decision to go onto four wheels, because by the time the product arrives everyone is already familiar with the product or with the idea."

The descriptions given of Mr Pierer give a clear picture of the dynamism that lies behind KTM's success. We therefore wanted to know which elements decisively shape the culture at KTM.

"I believe that racing is a particularly important element of our culture. It is a strong glue, which binds the 'KTM family' together. The racing teams are based in Mattighofen and come into contact with the employees. Even the top stars in our teams regularly come by the factory. This is important and also conveys the feeling of 'I screwed that together for this or that star.'

However, at the same time, racing also illustrates the high level of commitment that is necessary in order to achieve success. You have to be finished by a certain time, otherwise you can't go with the team. It's certainly not a nine-to-five job.

In my opinion, however, this team spirit at KTM is also reinforced by the fact that we back up our philosophy – that every employee makes an important contribution to the success of the company – with actions. When good results are achieved, each employee receives the same bonus; we don't differentiate between senior executives and all the other employees. I am against hierarchical thinking on principle.

In general, we face the challenge of further developing the flexibility we have built up within the company. However, this is not for everyone, because people also seek stability and security. This is also shown by the fact that new strategies and ideas always meet with great resistance within the company at first. This could also be felt when KTM went onto the street. The further away you went from the company, the easier it was to persuade people about the idea. I'm aware that, to a significant degree, I myself must drive forward this willingness to change in the future too. Mind you, nowadays the employees at KTM are used to things changing constantly. Furthermore, with an average age of just 32, we are a young team, although, ideally, the team is made complete by 'old hands.' "

RENÉ OBERMANN, CEO, DEUTSCHE TELEKOM

René Obermann has always stood out for his entrepreneurial thinking. He founded ABC Telekom in Münster immediately after completing his commercial training as an industrial clerk at BMW AG in Munich. "I started off selling fax machines, but even back then I was fascinated by digital communications technology. I made great efforts to acquire the necessary knowledge and was determined to make something of it." His dedication and entrepreneurial spirit paid off. ABC Telekom became Hutchinson Mobilfunk GmbH, where René Obermann was managing partner from 1994 to 1998. He moved to T-Mobile in 1998 and in 2002 he became CEO of T-Mobile international AG & Co and in 2006 he became CEO of Deutsche Telekom AG. At the time of our conversation in August 2006 he was still CEO of T-Mobile.

René Obermann has lost nothing of his curiosity, his commitment, or his entrepreneurial spirit. His knowledge is impressive, as is the intensity with which he speaks of the changes that the company must inevitably carry out in order to be successful in the future.

Our meeting took place in Bonn at T-Mobile's headquarters. We waited for René Obermann to arrive. He entered the office five minutes before the meeting was due to start dressed elegantly yet informally. Within a few moments we struck up an animated conversation with a tremendously likeable person.

He is currently dealing with some of the components examined in our model, such as corporate culture for example, in his day-to-day management of the company. He therefore wanted to know, for instance, exactly what we understood by corporate culture, and whether or not one should also take this or that factor into account in order to bring about developments within the company.

Our main question concerned how a company in a market as dynamic and competitive as telecommunications can succeed in being an innovation leader, while at the same time providing the highest quality of service in the industry and also possessing a competitive costs structure.

"This market is extremely dynamic and competition is fierce. You can't afford to be caught napping. Our success is largely based on the fact that since the company was founded we have never rested or settled for today's success. Not everything has gone according to plan but, on the whole, we have always backed the right horse. When our first international successes began to materialize we initiated a rigorous integration program with a focus on Europe. We focused all our energy on merging our subsidiaries, which had largely been operating independently until that point, into one company. We were aware that we could only really develop our strengths if we were able to fully exploit synergies. Worldwide, this has enabled us to achieve €1.3bn in measurable cost savings annually since 2003, while significantly improving the quality of our service at the same time."

The most recent major initiative at T-Mobile was launched in 2004. "Developments in the market showed us that we had to optimize our costs structures following the end of the first growth phase in our industry and at the same time keep pace with increasing innovation dynamics. We could see that competition would increase dramatically and that aggressive price competition would intensify, primarily as a result of overcapacity in the market."

The company initiated a project involving the 40 most important senior executives of T-Mobile under the title of "Save4Growth." "It was particularly important to me that efficiency and growth potential should be identified and exploited from our own ranks, as this is the only way to exploit our knowledge and experience, and it also enables us to engender the commitment necessary for implementing our ideas. We decided that these 40 top managers should work closely together every day from 8 o'clock in the morning until 4 o'clock in the afternoon for 6 weeks in order to share experiences on this subject, to analyze and discuss, and of course to formulate ideas and suggestions for meaningful cost savings. From 4 p.m. to 7 p.m. – and sometimes it was, of course, far later – each team member carried out his or her 'actual' management tasks. It was a radical project which helped us make tremendous progress on two levels in particular.

After 6 weeks, we had formulated over 120 individual building blocks; many of these offered huge savings potential, others less so. For example, it became clear to us that we should radically reduce our range of mobile phone models. We decided to only continue to subsidize 40 models, instead of the previous 80. Our aim was to be able to counter suppliers' bargaining power more effectively, as well as to move suppliers to push through for us certain technological developments that we considered essential for successfully marketing our innovations.

Through innovative thinking, the team had come up with some impressive ideas for taking T-Mobile forward, including where costs were concerned. At the same time, something had come to life within this team that was of tremendous importance for realizing the more than 120 projects. We were all proud of the results and realized that we had to carry this very emotive topic into the company together. It was clear to us that the workforce would not welcome us with open arms and that for this very reason we would have to do everything in our power to convince them of the benefits of 'Save4Growth.'

When we presented our program to employees and other stakeholders, the what were in some cases radical changes – of course – came up against criticism and resistance. But the team was undeterred. We remained very consistent in our implementation and communication of the program and the employees began to come to terms with it and understand its purpose. However, just 'coming to terms with it' was not enough for us and we stepped up our personal commitment. After about a year, the success we had been striving for started to come. An increasing number of employees recognized the opportunities behind the program and one could feel the growing emotional commitment. Our internal opinion barometer, which is fed by all our employees on a monthly basis, shows higher readings now than before 'Save4Growth.' Today, I venture to say that the employees in the company are, for the most part, proud of what we have achieved and feel well equipped to deal with the challenges of the future, thanks to our 'thrift.' I believe this is due in particular to the fact that some of the resources we save are invested in new developments and growth. Here's just one example: we are the innovation leader in the industry with our open mobile Internet access service, 'Web'n'walk', which is part of 'Save4Growth.'

Today, I would venture to say that our cost structures are 'best in class,' without us having put our innovation and quality leadership at risk. For example, in 2005 we reinvested €424m of the €686m we saved in distribution, marketing, networks, and services. In 2006, we will save considerably more than €1bn and operate according to the same principle."

We wanted to know how T-Mobile will pursue this project in the future. "Continuing the 'Save4Growth' program is of course one of the key prerequisites for assuring future success. This is not a question of us temporarily 'tightening our belt,' but rather of changing our corporate culture, which in the past was strongly influenced by the phase of unbridled growth experienced during the period when mobile telecommunications were just taking off. At the same time, however, we are conscious that we are not able and do not intend to differentiate ourselves in the market through our costs structure. Therefore, in the next few years we will place an even greater strategic focus on customer orientation than we have done already. In the last year, we have focussed strategy on developing T-Mobile into the 'most highly regarded service company.' We want to provide customers with a level of added value that no other telecommunications company is capable of providing and that cannot easily be copied. We must not only succeed in developing innovative products and services, but also provide a quality of service that impresses customers at every point of customer contact. We have launched a Europe-wide service-culture program, primarily based on impulses picked up from our American subsidiary – TM US has been known for the best service in the industry for many years – which must again be carried down through the company by the top senior executives. They – and I naturally include myself in this – must convey the basic philosophy that lies behind the program in just the same way that we would carry out specific sales training courses, for example. For me, it goes without saying that I also spend days working in our shops. Here, I rigorously follow the motto of: 'People don't follow what you say, they follow what you do.'

Our strategic positioning as a leading service company is also reflected in our variable salary system. This affects the most senior executives in just the same way as all the other employees in the company. The net promotor score, which is measured on a monthly basis through customer and employee surveys, provides us with our control factor. In this regard, we are less interested in the level of customer satisfaction we have achieved, since satisfying customers far from guarantees that we will be able to keep them or win new customers. In my view, it is far more meaningful to measure how many customers intend to recommend us. This does not only show that customers are satisfied; it also shows the actual strength of the brand compared to competitors. Customers really have to be sure about your services in order to recommend them."

In this context, we of course also wanted to know what was happening in the area of direct product innovations. "It is logical that innovation is of key importance in a market such as ours. However, we have also recognized that bombarding the market with new, innovative bundles of products and services every month cannot be a successful strategy, since customers are no longer able to process this enormous amount of information. Therefore, in our view, innovation is also about identifying a few main themes and pushing them through over the long term.

However, in our industry, besides developing innovative prices or bundles of products and services, innovation especially means developing completely new services. In this context, I believe that we cannot ascertain the potential of the products of tomorrow from quantitative market research. For example, classic market research predicted that the SMS had no future in the market. We all know the success story. There was a similar situation with the Blackberry e-mail service: market research predicted that the product would only have limited appeal. The pocket PC is a further example of this. The general consensus was that there was no market for these products. Within 6 months, over 250,000 of these products had been sold in Germany. Based on these experiences, we rely very heavily on the results of qualitative research and on our own intuition in our new product development process. The entire management and development team has extensive experience in the market and I believe it is able to very accurately assess what areas we should pursue."

Right from the very start of the conversation we could see how much importance René Obermann attaches to corporate culture. He indicated that, in his opinion, besides key values, a company needs additional core strategic themes that ultimately move the entire organization on an emotional level, since this is the only way to align the company's culture with its strategies. This requires 'culture development' work, which must be profoundly shaped by the decisions and approaches of the most senior executives. René Obermann's motto – "People don't follow what you say, they follow what you do" – illustrates his point perfectly. But how does this viewpoint manifest itself in his day-to-day work?

"On the one hand, we think very carefully about how we can succeed in carrying the core strategic themes into the company. We invest a great deal of our management capacity in these transfer processes. At the same time, I try to maintain very close contact with employees from different hierarchy levels and functions. I spend 10 to 15 percent of my time moving around the company on a very informal basis. I talk to many employees about the most varied of issues in corridors and offices, and so on. I spend 15–20 days a year working directly in field sales or helping out in the shops. A further 15 days are taken up with internal presentations. Last but not least, I regularly visit our subsidiaries inside and outside Germany together with my fellow board members. During these visits we discuss the most varied of subjects in depth with the senior executives and employees out in the markets."

Finally, Mr René Obermann took another look at our success model, with which we are able to explain the around 50 percent of corporate success that we believe can be directly influenced. "At the start of my management career, I believed that it was possible to directly influence 80 percent of success. Today, based on my experience, I would put this at 50 percent at the most. The remaining 50 percent is accounted for by developments in the environment that you yourself have no direct influence on. However, you must be capable of recognizing the opportunities that could arise from these developments and of focussing all your energy on exploiting them for the benefit of the company."

PROF. DR MICHAEL MIROW, FORMER HEAD OF STRATEGIC PLANNING, SIEMENS AG

Professor Michael Mirow was head of the strategy department at Siemens for over 10 years prior to leaving the company in 2001. He is now an Honorary Professor of Strategic Management at the Technical University of Berlin. We met Michael Mirow in a café in Munich.

Michael Mirow on leadership

"During my professional career, I had the good fortune to be able to continually engage in an intensive exchange of ideas with a large number of different senior executives from top companies. Based on my experiences, I can only confirm the results of the research project. Top senior executives have a decisive influence on companies' success. They do not only influence the strategic positioning of a company through their decisions, the way they communicate and their behavior; they also influence the culture of the company through these factors in a conscious, and especially in an unconscious, way.

If one has had the opportunity, as I did, to really look behind the scenes at various companies, one is in a good position to observe how poor appointments to top management have virtually led some successful companies to ruin. In other cases, one doubted certain companies' chances of survival and, within a short time, the appointment of the right manager triggered a transformation that nobody believed these companies were capable of."

Michael Mirow on the key strategic challenges of today

"The strategic challenge of today can be seen in the necessity for companies to strive for a combination of cost, performance, and technology leadership. The key to this is innovation. Innovation can lead to time advantages, price premiums, and cost advantages. Innovative companies secure a price premium for themselves, thanks to their differentiated value proposition to customers. They can be the first to exploit the experience curve effect and achieve cost advantages from this leadership position. Highly innovative companies enter attractive markets early and secure their head start in innovation by continually producing new or enhanced products based on their lead in experience. Firms such as Intel, Cisco, and also – in many areas – Siemens provide good examples of such strategies. In my opinion, especially nowadays, managing innovations is one of every company's core tasks. Top decision-makers have to recognize that innovations are basic prerequisites for safeguarding a company's earning power and value creation over the long term. Ultimately, innovation is the only guarantor of long-term survival. However, we must be clear that an innovation can only be a success if it offers the customer a solution that is better than the one currently available on the market. The impetus for an innovation may come from technological developments, but it may also originate from the market, or from a customer requirement itself. In any case, consistent orientation toward customer value is the decisive success factor."

Michael Mirow on the risk posed by success

"In my experience, today's success represents one of the greatest dangers for established companies. Companies should not allow themselves to become frozen in today's success and no longer agonize about what they need to do for tomorrow's success. I am convinced, and my experience tells me this, that tomorrow always works differently to today. But in order to master tomorrow, companies must do everything they can to prepare themselves today. By that I mean that the entire management team must also think radically now, for who can really guarantee that the company will continue to be successful for the next 10–20 years with today's products and technologies. Even at Siemens, it has occasionally been the case that very successful business units have been the ones to miss radical leaps in technology. They were so enthusiastic about the here and now that they could always produce reasons which argued against a change. But at some point the market and requirements did actually change and there was in fact no more time available to act in a meaningful way."

Michael Mirow on planning innovations

"New ideas need space to develop and they spring from an act of creativity. They generally tend to grow in places where nothing or only very little is planned. On the other hand, in extreme cases, total freedom can lead to unfocussed chaos. In my experience, what is required is a new understanding of innovation planning that can span the divide between freedom and control. Such planning must be restricted to establishing basic parameters. The units are then still able to move freely, which also provides the creative space that is so important for innovation. Uncertainty and complexity are therefore not only tolerated, but are even encouraged within the company, and no attempt should be made to absorb them into cleverly thought-out classical planning systems. At the same time, the definition of basic parameters must provide directions or possible development paths. This reduces risk, thereby increasing the hit rate of innovations. If one takes this viewpoint, it is entirely possible to plan innovation within a company, if not with regard to results, then certainly with regard to direction.

In this context, I consider it essential that, in addition to the incremental approach to innovation, space is also created for breakthrough innovations.

Incremental innovations are generally generated from the bottom-up on the basis of existing products and technologies. In addition, companies frequently develop what are known as product and technology roadmaps, with which they primarily move within existing technological paradigms. However, in my view, a different approach to innovation is required when it comes to creating a basis for so-called breakthrough innovations. Siemens employs the tool of strategic visioning, for example. This involves studying the shaping forces within society and first trying to generate 'pictures of the future' which are 10 or more years away from now. Ultimately, the aim is to predict which direction society as a whole, our way of life, the world of work, and so on, could develop in. New or changed technical application fields are subsequently derived from this and described in pictures. The next step is to compare these application fields with existing product and technology roadmaps. This process of comparing, in which R&D experts, among others, are confronted with sometimes radical 'pictures of the future,' opens up the opportunity to generate ideas for radical breakthrough innovations on the product and system level. I believe this approach is particularly important in technology-driven companies. A company can only gain the time necessary for proactively dealing with new things if it is able to recognize emerging or required technological breakthroughs in good time."

Michael Mirow on core competence management

"In 2004, Heinrich von Pierer and I pointed out in an essay in the German version of the *Harvard Business Review* that, in our view, the conditions in which companies have to create value have changed dramatically. Creating value has less and less to do with an integrated and sequential process that begins with procuring raw materials and ends with producing the finished product. Today, it often takes place in complex networks. Conventional-style companies – diversified, closed, heavily integrated, and with highly hierarchical structures – are increasingly being replaced by focussed, open, and networked high-performance organizations. In these circumstances, decision-makers can no longer formulate and pursue their strategies independently. The company must think, plan, and operate beyond its own borders on many different levels. Strategies must be coordinated, capacity must be planned jointly, technological developments must be agreed upon, and risks must be shared. All this extends way beyond the conventional customer–supplier relationship. Every company must ask itself more urgently than before which real core competences behind its success must be developed further within a network. In my view, this also brings us back to innovation management. A company can only operate successfully within such networks if it is capable of offering new solutions within its fields of activity which create value for the network."

PETER LORANGE, PRESIDENT OF IMD BUSINESS SCHOOL, LAUSANNE

Peter Lorange is among the world's most respected experts in both management theory and management practice. He researched and taught at the most renowned universities for over 20 years. Among other things, he was Director of the Joseph H. Lauder Institute of Management and International Studies at the Wharton School of the University of Pennsylvania for many years. He taught at the Sloan School of Management (MIT) for 8 years. He has written 15 books and published over 110 articles in the most prestigious management journals. Since 1993, he has been head of the IMD Business School in Lausanne. IMD has ranked among the world's most distinguished management training centers for many years. Every year, around 5500 managers from over 70 different countries take advantage of the training programs on offer at IMD.

It seemed only logical to us that we should also discuss our research findings with Peter Lorange. When we visited him in Lausanne, he had already worked through all the documents we had sent him prior to the meeting and made some notes. The conversation started – as was to be expected – with a discussion about the research design we had chosen and the type of statistical analysis. "I am impressed by the methodology chosen and the results, as, in my opinion, the second generation of multivariate methods of path modeling provide a sound basis for analysing, evaluating, and illustrating complex relationships. Showing the relationships between the building blocks of success that had been identified delivers the very knowledge that is essential for successfully positioning companies." These words of encouragement were followed by an intensive discussion about the individual building blocks in the model, during which Peter Lorange first underlined the relationship between market orientation and innovation, which he considers to be of key importance.

"Companies can only work on future-oriented innovations if they succeed in anticipating the challenges in the markets. In this context, it is especially important to review the role of marketing departments within companies. Marketing departments must take on the challenge of really intending to identify new market opportunities before they become obvious. This is the only way it will be possible to actively shape the market and to not always have to chase the market. This requires that marketing departments in particular are shaped by visionary thinking and are not just guided by a copycat mentality. However, today it is often the case that vast amounts of quantitative market research data are evaluated and processed in marketing departments by young and sometimes very inexperienced marketing people. There is no doubt that this is of considerable help to companies in developing low-risk innovation strategies. Frequently, though, this conceals the danger that endless statistical analyses obscure one's view of what is really important, that is, the future. This makes it impossible for the marketing department to perform its proper role – that of an innovation driver.

Marketing departments must be hauled out of their 'silos' and integrated into the strategic decision-making process at the top level to a significantly larger degree than in the past. Only with this kind of integration it is possible to encourage cross-company thinking in the marketing department and oblige it to constantly maintain strategic dialogue with other functions while carrying out its work. Nowadays, much data is evaluated and interpreted by marketing departments behind closed doors, which allows no opportunity for also taking the know-how of internal and external experts into account.

However, in order that the marketing department can actually perform the task I am describing here, it must take a considerably broader and more open approach with regard to market research activities. For example, this involves intensifying qualitative market research activities, carrying out active market observations on the ground, obtaining the opinions of internal decision-makers who actually operate within the market, or searching for information sources which lie completely outside the company's own market.

At the same time, the most senior decision-makers must ensure that the information that has been gathered is not evaluated by the marketing department in isolation, but discussed and processed in conjunction with many different decision-makers within the company. The most senior executives must themselves assume a central role in these discussion sessions; only then will they be able to provide research and development departments with a clear development brief with regard to these opportunities. Elaborating and signing off such briefs is the task of top management. Strategic positioning strategies and their implementation in the market can only really work within the framework of concerted actions on the part of the whole company."

Developing new products is one issue; marketing them successfully is another. We wanted to know what Peter Lorange considers essential for marketing "new" products successfully.

In Peter Lorange's view, there are three fundamental points when it comes to successfully launching innovations:

The market must be prepared for the innovation before it is actually launched. This is because each new development also leads to uncertainties in the markets, as innovations are always associated with risks. It is important to take all the necessary communicative measures to ensure that the market is open to the innovations and starts to become interested in them at an early stage. This can be done by involving key customers in the process as early on as the development phase, for example, or by arousing the curiosity of end customers with innovative advertising campaigns some time before the product is launched.

The value of the innovation must be clearly worked out and presented to the market through very focused communication work. According to Peter Lorange, this poses a particular challenge nowadays, since "customers are bombarded with large amounts of information every single day. For this reason, it is often difficult to get information about the new product through to customers. Due to information overload, today's customers are no longer prepared to read "long" lists. In my view, this situation requires that companies radically reduce their message down to what is really important. This must have such an active effect on customers that they subsequently turn to the new product with the necessary level of interest."

However, according to Peter Lorange, it is fundamentally important that top decision-makers strongly support the propensity to experiment in the implementation of the solutions that have been generated. This is the only way that companies will be able to actually try out their ideas on the market in good time. Or, as someone once said, to "make mistakes more often in order to learn more quickly." The key to this is the willingness to systematically learn and to view the mistakes that arise as a necessary part of this process. However, if employees are afraid of any kind of failure, they will continually hide behind endless-data analyses and never move the market.

"Nestlé's experiences with the yoghurt product LC1 illustrate this approach. Nestlé initially launched LC1 in France, focusing its marketing message on a central and new product attribute – 'helps the body to protect itself.' A unique product and a short key message. However, customers did not want a 'medical' product. They wanted a good and healthy product that tasted great. The 'failure' in France made it necessary for the core feature of the product – being good for the health – to be marketed differently. Nestlé's management allowed exactly the same team that had made this 'mistake' to learn from it. The same team was able to launch LC1 in Germany on the basis of what had been learned in France. It became a success in Germany and subsequently also in other markets."

The conversation then naturally turned to the topic of competence management. "Core competences are the real assets of a company, and by that I do not mean a company's strengths, but rather the bundle of characteristics, skills, and resources that enables it to produce unique products and services. The key challenge is to constantly invest in these assets. Unfortunately, I see that in Europe short-term thinking and thinking in terms of costs are currently standing in the way of this view. But if companies are not prepared to constantly invest in strengthening and enhancing competences, they will come to be among the main losers in the global competitive environment in the near future. I consider continuity to be particularly important in this area. Knowledge and skills can only be developed if there is constant dialogue and the requisite strategic importance is attached to this dialogue. In my opinion, this also brings us back to what I said regarding the 'new' form of market orientation. Ultimately, companies can only develop their competences in line with their objectives if they concern themselves with the market of tomorrow. Forward-looking core competence management requires discourse with the market of tomorrow.

However, this approach requires top decision-makers to understand the strategic relationship between market orientation, core competence management, and innovation as a whole and to also manage these factors collectively."

Next, we wanted to know what was required for the "internal growth" Peter Lorange was calling for.

"Growth through mergers and acquisitions was and is important in many sectors. On the whole, though, I believe that this 'growth strategy' will become less important in the future. In my opinion, companies should once again aim more strongly at organic growth in the future. This kind of growth requires an appropriate level of innovation, which is essentially founded on the interaction between market orientation and competence management we have talked about. What is decisive, however, is the most senior executives' basic understanding of strategy, as their decisions significantly determine the direction the company takes. If companies focus on internal growth, they must also invest the necessary financial resources and, in particular, think in different time dimensions. This calls for a return to the original form of entrepreneurial thinking: we want to be the best in the market and not to become the largest at all costs. Because sustainable size is essentially brought about through the ability to continually develop unique products and services for the markets.

In my experience, decision-makers who move their companies in this direction do not delegate the search for future growth potential to their employees. They study the markets intensively themselves and know exactly which people inside and outside the company can help them to pinpoint these opportunities. At the same time, besides the requisite willingness to take risks, they also possess a sure instinct and tend to focus on really promising opportunities. Sometimes it may almost seem as if they only make their decisions based on their intuition. Once the decision is made, they drive the development process forward themselves and provide the relevant teams with both the necessary resources and the right support inside and outside the company."

HANS-JOACHIM RECK, PARTNER, HEIDRICK & STRUGGLES, GERMANY

Hans-Joachim Reck is a partner at Heidrick & Struggles, one of the world's leading executive search and leadership consulting firms. He can look back on an impressive career in the public sector, politics, and private industry: General Secretary of the Christian Democratic Party, Germany; Senior Executive Vice President, Human Resources with Deutsche Telekom, where he was responsible for top management personnel at the company's headquarters; head of the central office for sales personnel at Deutsche Telekom; member of the State Parliament of North Rhine-Westphalia, Germany, and so on. We took the opportunity to discuss the subject of leadership with him.

Hans-Joachim Reck knows a number of top managers in many areas, in both business and politics. He has come into contact with many stars, but has also seen some fail. In his view, what characterizes a successful leader?

"There are of course many factors, many of which are self-evident. I do not intend to discuss those factors now. However, I have noticed again and again that great leaders have a few things in common, including the following: they have mastered their craft, they are balanced individuals, they have emotional intelligence, they can take an interest in almost anything, and they speak the language of all those they deal with."

Is management a craft?

"Yes and no. A senior executive must of course master the craft of management. Managers are doers. One cannot be an efficient and effective leader without mastering certain methods and techniques. But there is more to it than that. Tools and methods are there for the purpose of implementing things efficiently. However, top managers are also constantly searching for new opportunities and are seldom satisfied with the current situation. As Peter Drucker once put it, top managers always focus their attention more strongly on opportunities than on risks. Constantly worrying about problems does not move things forward. Top senior executives first see an opportunity in every change. The balanced scorecard is a good analogy for the attitude and skills a top manager must possess. Top managers must have internalized the concept of the BSC. They must be able to recognize opportunities. They must then also be able to turn visions into strategies and to convert strategies into actions – or have others do this. This means senior executives must be leaders and managers at the same time. They must have great objectives and visions, but they must also have the skills to implement them. If they are not able to 'break down' strategies, to flesh them out with ratios, and effectively communicate them, they will fail, even if the vision and strategy were sound. There are three explanations for this: they do not understand the strategy themselves, the strategy is not well thought out and cannot be communicated or implemented, or they are not capable of making things concrete.

Finally, top managers must possess the ability to create new paradigms, as well as to implement them. They must do more than just continuously improve things. They must be able to constantly question the status quo and to radically change it if necessary. This is the only way to safeguard the company's innovative ability on a sustained basis."

What is meant by "balanced" individuals?

"Top managers are constantly under pressure, but they do not show it. Even when they are anxious and stressed on the inside, they exude calmness and give the impression that they have everything under control – as they usually do, in fact. This ability to be calm and composed is important. This is the only way it is possible to stand back and see things from a bird's eye perspective. Poor decisions are often made because the decision-maker identifies too strongly with things and is no longer able to view them objectively. Secondly, it is important to be calm and composed in order to exude an air of competence. A hectic approach is usually a sign of poor personal organization. People who cannot organize themselves will not be able to successfully lead others.

A person who is not perceived as competent and organized will find it difficult to earn the trust of employees.

Top senior executives are balanced individuals and draw their calmness from their families and friends, and so on. Often, they will pursue a hobby to the point of perfection. They may play an instrument, run marathons, or take up an artistic hobby. Two things lie behind this: versatility and the pursuit of excellence. Both are qualities that I consider very important. Top people are interested in many things – including things outside their career – and are curious. Taking an interest in everything and insatiable curiosity seem to be two basic characteristics."

What role does emotional intelligence play?

"Top senior executives can deal with emotions. They are able to pick up on the emotional state of the person they are dealing with and to tune in to it. But they also know themselves and know how to interpret and control their own feelings. This is more important than is generally believed. The higher the level of management, the more important instinct – feeling, intuition, or whatever you wish to call it – is. Intuition always goes hand in hand with 'gut instinct.' Good managers know whether or not they can trust their intuition, because they know when and how much they can rely on their feeling.

I also consider it very important for senior executives to possess a capacity for empathy. They are able to understand other people's feelings in delicate situations, even if these people do not show them. They can pick up emotional signals from other people, interpret them, and react to them. This is not only important in negotiations, it is also important for managing employees. Only people who have this skill can be good leaders and build up a loyal team around them. Top managers know that they need their teams. Daniel Goleman put his finger on it when he said: 'A person who wishes to attract and hold onto good employees must mature into an emotionally intelligent manager. Because employees do not leave companies, they leave bad managers.' A senior executive must first earn the trust of employees and appear credible to them, as well as to the broad public. This will only be possible if they are full of integrity and absolutely genuine."

What role does language play?

"One can recognize top senior executives by the language they use. They have mastered the language of their industry, their customers, their business partners, and their employees. They are able to communicate with them effectively. One can recognize three things in the language they use. First, whether or not they have expertise in their field. Top managers stand no chance if they do not speak the language of their business. They will never be able to gain credibility. Secondly, one can tell from the language a person chooses whether or not they have an in-depth understanding of the problems of the person they are dealing with and whether they are able to rapidly tune into them. Thirdly, one can recognize top managers by whether or not they can communicate with other people 'as an equal,' regardless of whether they are talking to fellow board members, the doorman, or the cleaner at the company. Something very important lies behind this skill: respect for and interest in people. Because, ultimately, management is also about the desire to serve others. It is a senior executive's task to make employees successful. They must enable them to achieve outstanding results – ideally results of which even the employees would not have thought themselves capable at all. A senior executive who does not master this will be average at best."

Notes

1. IN SEARCH OF THE SECRETS OF SUCCESS

1 Peters & Waterman, 1982
2 Ibid.
3 Simon, 1996
4 Buzzell & Gale, 1987; Nohria, Joyce & Roberson, 2003
5 Collins & Porras, 1998
6 Kirby, 2005
7 Nicolai & Kieser, 2002
8 Denrell, 2005
9 D'Aveni, 1994; 1995
10 Pfeffer & Sutton, 2006

2. THE CUSTOMER-VALUE COMPETITION IS PUSHING MANY COMPANIES TO THE LIMIT OF THEIR POSSIBILITIES

1 D'Aveni, 1994; 1995
2 Gale, 1994; Matzler, 2000; Matzler, Stahl & Hinterhuber, 2006
3 Adapted from D'Aveni, 1994
4 Matzler, Bailom, Tschemernjak, Anschober & Hinterhuber, 2005
5 Schumpeter, 1987
6 Kieser, 2002
7 Hinterhuber, 2003a
8 Ibid.
9 Ibid.
10 Grötker, 2003
11 Ibid.
12 Rappaport, 1981; 1986
13 Schredelseker, 2003
14 Matzler, Rier, Hinterhuber, Renzl & Stadler, 2005
15 Malik, 2002
16 Coenenberg & Salfeld, 2003
17 Achleitner & Bassen, 2002
18 Mintzberg, Simons & Basul, 2002
19 Author unknown, 2002
20 McCarthy, 2000
21 Koen, 2005
22 Malik, 2002

23 Ibid.
24 Coenenberg & Salfeld, 2003
25 Adapted from Coenenberg & Salfeld, 2003, pp. 104 and 105
26 Christensen & Raynor, 2003

3. THE IMP MODEL: THE STRATEGIES OF WINNERS

1 We chose the PLS approach as three of our constructs had a formative character (corporate culture, market orientation and core competences). The items of these constructs each cover different facets of the construct, therefore the direction of causality should be understood as being from indicator to construct; the individual indicators are not interchangeable, do not necessarily correlate with one another, and do not necessarily have the same antecedents and consequences. Multi-collinearity was tested, as recommended in literature, and did not present a problem (see: Jarvis, MackKenzie & Podsakoff, 2003; Diamantopoulos & Winkelhofer, 2001).

2 Hansmann & Ringle, 2004

3 For interested readers we recommend: Bliemel, Eggert & Fassot, 2005. In order to ensure that only reliable and valid scales are used before the structure model is assessed, we followed the analysis process proposed by Hulland (see Hulland, 1999).

4 The internal consistency of each reflective construct is greater than 0.80; the average variance is greater than 0.50 in each case (with the exception of corporate success, where the average variance extracted equals 0.48); the discriminant validity was assessed using the Fornell-Larcker Ratio (square root of the average variance extracted/intercorrelations among the factors) and is far below 1 in each case. The individual scales used therefore exhibit good reliability and validity (see Fornell & Larcker, 1981).

5 Kohli, Jaworksi & Kumar, 1993; Kohli & Jaworski, 1990. Here, senior executives indicated whether their companies performed better, the same or worse than their strongest competitors with regard to generating market knowledge, sharing market knowledge internally and using market knowledge as a basis for decision-making.

6 Wang & Ahmed, 2004. They measure statements regarding whether (1) products and services are often considered novel by customers; (2) the products and services help the company to advance in relation to competitors; (3) the company has a higher success rate than the competition with regard to launching new products and services; and (4) the company often has revolutionary marketing programs compared to its competitors.

7 Tallman & Fladmore-Lindquist, 2002. This factor was measured using the following questions: (1) We have a clear plan for systematically strengthening core competences, that is, we analyse, plan and develop them over the long term. (2) We have a systematic process for identifying new markets/opportunities for existing core competences. (3) Employees are trained specifically with present or desired future competences in mind.

8 Barney, 1991; Hinterhuber, 2004a

9 Desphandé, Farley & Webster, 1993

10 Based on: Collins & Porras, 1998

11 Wang & Ahmed, 2004

12 Prahalad & Hamel, 1990

13 Buzzell & Gale, 1987

14 Tellis & Golder, 1996

15 Ibid.
16 Ibid.
17 Ibid.

4. WHAT MAKES TOP PERFORMERS DIFFERENT

1 Hinterhuber, 2004b
2 Hinterhuber, 2000; Hinterhuber, 2003; Hinterhuber & Krauthammer, 2002
3 Willenbrock, 2005
4 Siemens, 1966
5 Hamel & Getz, 2004
6 Matzler, Bailom, Tschemernjak, Anschober & Hinterhuber, 2005
7 Sirisha & Dutta, 2002
8 Some years later, this concept was extended into a three-circle model incorporating core business ("reinvesting in productivity and quality"), high-technology ("stay on the leading edge") and services ("add outstanding people and make contiguous acquisitions"). (Bartlett & Wozny, 1999)
9 PIMS = Profit Impact of Market Strategies, (Buzzell & Gale, 1987)
10 Christensen, 1997
11 Farhoomand & Tao, 2005
12 Malik, 2005
13 Christensen, 1997
14 Hutzschenreuter, 2005
15 Douglas, 1991
16 Frenzel, Müller & Sottong, 2004
17 Desphandé, Farley & Webster, 1993; Ernst, 2004; Matzler, Renzl & Rothenberger, 2004

5. MARKET ORIENTATION: UNDERSTANDING MARKETS, SHAPING THE FUTURE

1 Chesbrough, 2003a
2 Adapted from Chesbrough, 2003b
3 Chesbrough, 2003a; Huston & Sakkab, 2006
4 von Hippel, 1988
5 Wesselhöft, 2006
6 Chesbrough, 2003b
7 Chesbrough, 2003a
8 Sawhney, Prandelli & Verona, 2003
9 Sawhney *et al.*, 2003
10 Huston & Sakkab, 2006
11 Herstatt, Lüthje & Lettl, 2002
12 Adapted from Herstatt *et al.*, 2002
13 von Hippel, 2005
14 Adapted from von Hippel, 2005
15 Füller & Matzler, 2007
16 Füller, Mühlbacher & Riedler, 2003
17 Füller, Jawecki & Mühlbacher, 2006
18 von Krogh, 2003

19 Füller, Jawecki & Bartl, 2006
20 Füller, Bartl, Ernst & Mühlbacher, 2006
21 Chakravorti, 2004
22 Ibid.
23 Rachman, 1999
24 Bartlett, Cornebise & McLean, 2002
25 Bartlett & Ghoshal, 2000
26 Priewe, 1998
27 Ibid.
28 Bartlett *et al.*, 2002
29 Lorange, 2005
30 Christensen, Cook & Hall, 2006
31 Matzler & Bailom, 2006
32 Christensen *et al.*, 2006
33 Lorange, 1998
34 Rogers, 1962
35 Adapted from Rogers, 1962
36 Reichwald & Piller, 2006
37 Füller & Matzler, 2006

6. THE SAILS DETERMINE THE COURSE, NOT THE WIND

1 See: Müller-Stewens & Lechner, 2005
2 Porter, 1980
3 See: Hinterhuber, Handlbauer & Matzler, 2003
4 Hitt, Ireland & Hoskisson, 2005
5 Bain, 1956
6 Hitt *et al.*, 2005; Hunt & Morgan, 1995
7 Wernerfelt, 1984
8 Barney, 1991
9 Prahalad & Hamel, 1990
10 McGahan & Porter, 1997
11 Rumelt, 1991
12 Hawawini, Subramanian & Verdin, 2003
13 Adapted from Hitt *et al.*, 2005
14 Dierickx & Cool, 1989; Barney & Hesterly, 2006
15 This is the assumption of the classic resource-based view, for example Wernerfelt, 1984
16 This is the perspective of the capability-based view, for example Teece, Pisano, & Shuen, 1997
17 Here, the theory refers to a knowledge-based view, for example Grant, 1996
18 This is based on a relational view of the firm, for example Dyer & Singh, 1998
19 Porter, 1985
20 Adapted from Grant, 2005
21 Ibid.
22 In reference to: Barney & Hesterly, 2006
23 http://www.hitech.at/archiv/1_00/flug1.htm
24 Hollensen, 2003
25 Ullrich, 2000

Notes 189

26 Koch, 2006
27 Leonard-Barton, 1992
28 Mirow, 1999; 2003
29 Mirow, 2003
30 Adapted from Mirow, 2003

7. CORPORATE CULTURE: THE LATENT POTENTIAL

1 Drucker, 1998
2 Grant, 1996
3 Renzl, 2003b
4 Kelley, 1990
5 Renzl, 2003a
6 Drucker, 1998
7 Argyris, 1998
8 Bruhn & Wolf, 1979
9 Greenberg, 1978
10 Bruhn & Wolf, 1979
11 Greenberg, 1978
12 Scott & Matthews, 2002
13 Putnam, 1993
14 Putnam, 2000
15 Bourdieu, 1986
16 Putnam, 2000
17 Adapted from Nahapiet & Goshal, 1998; Inkpen & Tsang, 2005
18 Fischer, 2005
19 R. Desphandè, Farley & Webster, 1993; Ernst, 2004; Matzler, Renzl & Rothenberger, 2004; Desphandè & Farley, 2004
20 Adapted from Cameron & Freeman, 1991; Desphandè, Farley & Webster, 1993; Quinn, 1988
21 Schein, 1992
22 Magretta, 2002
23 Douglas, 1991
24 Ibid.
25 Schein, 1992
26 Adapted from Schein, 1992
27 Magretta, 2002
28 Ibid.
29 Adapted from Hinterhuber, 2003a; Abfalter, Hinterhuber & Raich, 2005
30 Magretta, 2002
31 Wozny, 1999
32 Schein, 1992

8. INNOVATION: IMPROVING EXISTING THINGS, CREATING NEW THINGS

1 Hegele-Raih, 2006
2 Porter, 1997

3   Bailom, Hinterhuber, Matzler & Sauerwein, 1996; Matzler & Hinterhuber, 1998; Matzler, Hinterhuber, Bailom & Sauerwein, 1996

4   Loppow, 1997

5   Adapted from Berger, 1993; Bailom *et al.*, 1996; Kano, 1984

6   Kano, 1984; Bailom, Tschemernjak, Matzler & Hinterhuber, 1998

7   Bailom *et al.*, 1996

8   Matzler & Sauerwein, 2002; Matzler, Sauerwein & Heischmidt, 2003; Matzler, Fuchs, Binder & Leihs, 2005

9   Matzler, Bailom, Hinterhuber, Renzl & Pichler, 2004

10   Matzler, 2003

11   Matzler, Fuchs & Schubert, 2004; Matzler & Renzl, 2007

12   Matzler, Sauerwein & Stark, 2005

13   Füller & Matzler, 2006a

14   Matzler, Bailom *et al.*, 2005

15   Hess & Schuller, 2005

16   Hammer, 1990

17   Hess & Schuller, 2005

18   Ibid.

19   Hammer & Stanton, 2000

20   Hess & Schuller, 2005

21   Davenport, 2005

22   Hess & Schuller, 2005

23   Kajüter, 2005

24   Kieser, 2002

25   Budros, 1999

26   Kieser, 2002

27   Cascio, Young & Morris, 1997

28   Kieser, 2002; Dougherty & Bowman, 1995

29   Matzler & Fässler, 2004

30   Hammer & Stanton, 2000

31   Rigby, Reichheld & Schefter, 2002

32   Rigby *et al.*, 2002

33   Kordupleski, Rust & Zahorik, 1994

34   Hinterhuber, Handlbauer & Matzler, 2003a

35   Matzler & Fässler, 2004

36   Matzler, Pechlaner & Kohl, 2000

37   Hammer & Stanton, 2000; Kaplan & Norton, 1997

38   Magretta, 2002

39   http://de.wikipedia.org/wiki/Hauptseite

40   A brief profile article on Southwest, www.beysterinstitute.org

41   Heuer, 2002; Sommer, 2005

42   Adapted from M. Porter, 1999

9. TOP MANAGEMENT: THE ARCHITECTS OF SUCCESS

1   Baron & Kenny, 1986

2   Women are naturally also implied (authors' note)

3   Hinterhuber & Raich, 2006

4   Hinterhuber & Rothenberger, 2006

5 Adapted from Hinterhuber, 2003b
6 Waldman, Ramirez, House & Puranam, 2001; Hinterhuber & Stadler, 2006; Raich, 2005
7 Taylor, 1995
8 Here, we followed the many works of Hans Hinterhuber on leadership and management (Hinterhuber, 2003b; Hinterhuber, 2004b; Hinterhuber, Friedrich & Krauthammer, 2001; Hinterhuber & Krauthammer, 1998, Hinterhuber & Krauthammer, 2002; Hinterhuber & Renzl, 2004; Hinterhuber, Renzl & Matzler, 2006; Hinterhuber, 2002)
9 Kirzner, 1980
10 Hinterhuber, 2004b
11 Donnithorne, 1994
12 Hinterhuber, 2004b
13 Xenophon, 1992, cited in: Hinterhuber, 2003a
14 Abfalter & Hinterhuber, 2006
15 Hinterhuber, 2003b
16 Senge, 1996
17 Here, we follow the work of Pircher-Friedrich, 2001
18 Sadler-Smith & Shefy, 2004
19 Miller & Ireland, 2005
20 Hinterhuber & Rothenberger, 2006
21 Zeilinger, 2002
22 Coutu, 2005
23 Simon, 1987
24 Ibid.
25 Khatri & Ng, 2000
26 Barnard, cited in: Simon, 1987; Prietula & Simon, 1989; Khatri & Ng, 2000
27 Sadler-Smith & Shefy, 2004
28 Sinclair & Askhanasy, 2005
29 Miller & Ireland, 2005
30 Sadler-Smith & Shefy, 2004
31 Schmid, 2005
32 LeDoux, 1996
33 Goleman, 1996
34 Goleman, 2004
35 Sitkin, 1992
36 Drucker, 2004
37 Cited in: Miller & Ireland, 2005

Bibliography

Abfalter, D., & Hinterhuber, H. H. (2006). Was Führungskräfte von Orchesterdirigenten lernen können. In K. Götz (Ed.), *Führung und Kunst*. Mering: Hampp Verlag.

Abfalter, D., Hinterhuber, H. H., & Raich, M. (2005). Die Auswahl und Beurteilung der Mitarbeiter und Führungskräfte. In H. Pechlaner, P. Tschurtschenthaler, M. Peters & B. Pikkemaat (Eds.), *Erfolg durch Innovation. Perspektiven für den Tourismus- und Dienstleistungssektor* (pp. 137–157). Wiesbaden: DUV.

Achleitner, A.-K., & Bassen, A. (2002). Entwicklungsstand des Shareholder-Value-Ansatzes in Deutschland – Empirische Befunde. In H. Siegwart & J. Mahari (Eds.), *Meilensteine im management, Vol. XI: Corporate governance, shareholder value & finance*. Zürich Schäffer-Poeschel Verlag.

Argyris, C. (1998). Empowerment – nur eine Illusion? *Harvard Business Manager, 20* (6), 9–16.

Bailom, F., Anschober, M., Matzler, K., & Kausl, A. (2006). Preis- und Innovationswettbewerb: Ergebnisse einer Führungskräftebefragung. In H. H. Hinterhuber & K. Matzler (Eds.), *Kundenorientierte Unternehmensführung* (5th ed., pp. 523–542). Wiesbaden: Gabler Verlag.

Bailom, F., Hinterhuber, H. H., Matzler, K., & Sauerwein, E. (1996). Das Kano-Modell der Kundenzufriedenheit. *Marketing-ZFP, 18*(2), 117–126.

Bailom, F., Matzler, K., Anschober, M., & Tschemernjak, D. (2006, März). Einsatz für Innovationen. *Harvard Business Manager*, 11–13.

Bailom, F., Tschemernjak, D., Matzler, K., & Hinterhuber, H. H. (1998). Durch strikte Kundennähe die Abnehmer begeistern. *Harvard Business Manager, 20*(1), 47–56.

Bain, J. S. (1956). *Barriers to new competition*. Cambridge: Harvard University Press.

Barney, J. (1991). Firm resources and sustained competitive advantage. *Journal of Management, 17*(1), 99–120.

Barney, J. B., & Hesterly, W. S. (2006). Strategic management and competitive advantage. Upper Saddle River, NJ: Pearson Education.

Baron, R. M., & Kenny, D. A. (1986). The moderator-mediator variable distinction in social psychological research: Conceptual, strategic, and statistical considerations. *Journal of Personality and Social Psychology, 51*(6), 1173–1182.

Bartlett, C. A., Cornebise, J., & McLean, A. N. (2002). Global wine wars: New world challenges old. *Harvard Business School Case,* No 9-303-056.

Bartlett, C. A., & Ghoshal, S. (2000). Going global: Lessons from late movers. *Harvard Business Review, 78*(2), 132–142.

Bartlett, C. A., & Wozny, M. (1999). GE's two-decade transformation: Jack Welch's leadership. *Harvard Business School Case 9-399-150*.

Berger, C. (1993, Fall). Kano's methods for understanding customer defined quality. *Center for Quality Management Journal*, 3–35.

Bliemel, F., Eggert, A., & Fassot, G. (Eds.). (2005). *Handbuch PLS-Pfadmodellierung. Methoden – Anwendung – Praxisbeispiele*. Stuttgart: Schäffer-Poeschel Verlag.

Bourdieu, P . (1986). The forms of capital. In J. G. Richardson (Ed.), *Handbook of theory and research for the sociology of education* (pp. 241–258). New York: Greenwood.

Bruhn, J. G., & Wolf, S. (1979). *The Roseto story*. Norman: University of Oklahoma Press.

Budros, A. (1999). A conceptual framework for analyzing why organizations downsize. *Organization Science, 10*, 69–82.

Buzzell, R. D., & Gale, B. T. (1987). The PIMS Principles. Linking Strategy to Performance. New York: The Free Press.

Cameron, J. P., & Freeman, S. J. (1991). Cultural congruence, strength and type: Relationships of effectiveness. In R. W. Woodman & A. Passmore (Eds.), *Research in organizational change and development* (pp. 23–58). San Francisco: Joessey-Bass.

Cascio, W. F., Young, E. E., & Morris, J. R. (1997). Financial consequences of employment-change decisions in major U.S. corporations. *Academy of Management Journal, 40*, 1175–1189.

Chakravorti, B. (2004). Neue Regeln für Innovationen. *Harvard Business Manager*, Juni, 23–37.

Chesbrough, H. W. (2003a). The era of open innovation. *MIT Sloan Management Review, 44*(3), 35–41.

Chesbrough, H. W. (2003b). *Open innovation*. Boston, MA: Harvard Business School Press.

Christensen, C. M. (1997). *The innovator's dilemma*. Boston: Harvard Business Press.

Christensen, C. M., Cook, S., & Hall, T. (2006, März). Wünsche erfüllen statt Produkte verkaufen. *Harvard Business Manager, 28*, 71–86.

Christensen, C. M. & Raynor, M. E. (2003). *The innovator's solution*. Boston: Harvard Business School Press.

Coenenberg, A. G., & Salfeld, R. (2003). *Wertorientierte Unternehmensführung*. Stuttgart: Schäffer-Poeschel Verlag.

Collins, J., & Porras, J. I. (1998). *Built to last: Successful habits of visionary companies*. London: Harper Business.

Coutu, D. L. (2005, Juli). Das Ego des Gegners zerschmettern. *Harvard Business Manager, 27*, 115–119.

D'Aveni, R. A. (1994). *Hyper competition. managing the dynamics of strategic maneuvering*. New York: The Free Press.

D'Aveni, R. A. (1995). Coping with hypercompetition: Utilizing the new 7S's framework. *Academy of Management Executive, 9*(3), 45–57.

Davenport, T. H. (2005, June). The coming commoditization of processes. *Harvard Business Review*, 101–108.

Denrell, J. (2005). Selection bias and the perils of benchmarking. *Harvard Business Review, 83*(4), 114–119.

Desphandè, R., & Farley, J. U. (2004). Organizational culture, market orientation, innovativeness, and firm performance: An international research odyssey. *International Journal of Research in Marketing, 21*(1), 3–22.

Desphandè, R., Farley, J. U., & Webster, F. E. (1993, January). Corporate culture, customer orientation, and innovativeness in Japanese firms: A quadrat analysis. *Journal of Marketing, 57*, 23–27.

Diamantopoulos, A., & Winkelhofer, H. M. (2001). Index construction with formative indicators: An alternative to scale development. *Journal of Marketing Research, 38*, 269–277.

Dierickx, I., & Cool, K. (1989). Asset stock accumulation and sustainability of competitive advantage. *Management Science, 35*, 1504–1511.

Donnithorne, L. R. (1994). *The westpoint way of leadership*. New York: Currency.

Dougherty, D., & Bowman, E. H. (1995). The effects of organizational downsizing on product innovation. *California Management Review, 37*, 28–44.

Douglas, M. (1991). *Wie Institutionen denken*. Frankfurt/Main: Suhrkamp.

Drucker, P. (1998). Wissen – die Trumpfkarte der entwickelten Länder. *Harvard Business Manager, 20*(4), 9–11.

Drucker, P. (2004, August). Das Geheimnis effizienter Führung. *Harvard Business Manager, 26*, 27–35.

Dyer, J. H., & Singh, H. (1998). The relational view – cooperative strategy and sources of interorganizational competitive advantage. *Academy of Management Review, 23*(4), 660–679.

Edvinsson, L. (2004). The new knowledge landscape. In S. Crainer & D. Dearlove (Eds.), *Financial Times handbook of management* (pp. 19–23). London: McGraw Hill.

Ernst, H. (2004, Februar). Unternehmenskultur und Innovationserfolg. *Zeitschrift für betriebswirtschaftliche Forschung und Praxis, 55*, 23–44.

Farhoomand, A., & Tao, Z. (2005). Shanghai Volkswagen: Time for radical shift of gears. *Asia Case Research Center,* University of Hong Kong, No HKU373.

Fischer, G. (2005). Was ist ein Unternehmer? *Brand Eins, 8* (4), 70–75.

Fornell, C., & Larcker, D. F. (1981, February). Evaluating structural equation models with unobservable variables and measurement error. *Journal of Marketing Research, 18*, 39–50.

Frenzel, K., Müller, M., & Sottong, H. (2004). *Storytelling*. Das Harun-al-Raschid-Prinzip. Munich/Vienna: Hanser Verlag.

Füller, J., Bartl, M., Ernst, H., & Mühlbacher, H. (2006). Community based innovation: How to integrate members of virtual communities into new product development. *Electronic Commerce Research, 6*, 57–73.

Füller, J., Jawecki, G., & Bartl, M. (2006). Produkt- und Serviceentwicklung in Kooperation mit Online Communities. In H. H. Hinterhuber & K. Matzler (Eds.), *Kundenorientierte Unternehmensführung* (5th ed., pp. 435–454). Wiesbaden: Gabler Verlag.

Füller, J., Jawecki, G., & Mühlbacher, H. (2006). Equipment-Related knowledge creation in innovative online basketball communities. In B. Renzl, K. Matzler & H. H. Hinterhuber (Eds.), *The future of knowledge management* (pp. 161–183). Houndmills, Basingstoke, Hamsphire and New York: Palgrave Macmillan.

Füller, J., & Matzler, K. (2006). Customer delight and market segmentation: An application of the three-factor theory of customer satisfaction on lifestyle groups. *Tourism Management*.

Füller, J., & Matzler, K. (2007). Virtual Product Development and Customer Participation – a Chance for Customer Centred, Real New Products. *Technovation*, Vol. 27, June–July, 378–387.

Füller, J., Rieder, B., & Mühlbacher, H. (2003, August). An die Arbeit, lieber Kunde! *Harvard Business Manager*, 36–45.

Gale, B. T. (1994). Managing Customer Value. New York: Free Press.

Goleman, D. (1996). *Emotional intelligence: Why it can matter more than IQ*. London: Bloomsbury.

Goleman, D. (2004, January). What makes a leader? *Harvard Business Review*, 1–11.

Grant, R. M. (1996, Winter Special Issue). Toward a knowledge-based theory of the firm. *Strategic Management Journal, 17*, 109–122.

Grant, R. M. (2005). Contemporary strategic analysis (5th ed.). Malden, Oxford, Carlton: Blackwell Publishing.

Greenberg, J. (1978). The Americanization of Roseto. *Science News, 113*(23), 378–381.

Grötker, R. (2003). Das neue Spiel. Die Sache mit dem Shareholder Value: Wo er herkommt. Und wo er hinführt. *Brand Eins* (Nr. 3), 73–79.

Hamel, G., & Getz, G. (2004, November). Erfindungen in Zeiten der Sparsamkeit. *Harvard Business Manager*, 10–24.

Hammer, M. (1990, July–August). Reengineering: Don't Automate, Obliterate. *Harvard Business Review, 68*, 104–112.

Hammer, M., & Stanton, S. (2000). Prozessunternehmen – wie sie wirklich funktionieren. *Harvard Business Manager, 22*(3), pp. 68–81.

Hansmann, K.-W., & Ringle, C. M. (2004). *SmartPLS manual.* Hamburg: Universität Hamburg.

Hawawini, G., Subramanian, V., & Verdin, P. (2003). Is performance driven by industry – Or firm-specific factors? A new look at the evidence. *Strategic Management Journal, 24*, 1–16.

Hegele-Raih, C. (2006, August). Was ist Isomorphismus? *Harvard Business Manager, 28*, 43.

Hemetsberger, A., & Füller, J. (2006). Qual der Wahl – Welche Methode führt zu kundenorientierten Innovationen? In H. H. Hinterhuber & K. Matzler (Eds.), *Kundenorientierte Unternehmensführung* (5th ed., pp. 399–433). Wiesbaden: Gabler Verlag.

Hemetsberger, A., & Reinhardt, C. (2006). Learning and knowledge-building in open-source communities. *Management Learning, 37*(2), 187–206.

Herstatt, C., Lüthje, C., & Lettl, C. (2002). Wie fortschrittliche Kunden zu Innovationen stimulieren. *Harvard Business Manager* (1), 60–68.

Hess, T., & Schuller, D. (2005, Juni). Business Process Reengeneering als nachhaltiger Trend? Eine Analyse der Praxis in deutschen Grounternehmen nach einer Dekade. *Zeitschrift für betriebswirtschaftliche Forschung und Praxis, 57*, 355–373.

Heuer, S. (2002). Economy class. *Brand Eins* 4(1), pp28–33.

Hinterhuber, H. H. (2000). Massstäbe für die Unternehmer und Führungskräfte von morgen: Mit Leadership neue Pionierphasen einleiten. In H. H. Hinterhuber, S. A. Friedrich, A. Al-Ani & G. Handlbauer (Eds.), *Das Neue Strategische Management – Perspektiven und Elemente einer zeitgemäen Unternehmensführung* (2nd ed., pp. 33–60). Wiesbaden: Gabler Verlag.

Hinterhuber, H. H. (2002). Leadership als Dienst an der Gemeinschaft. *Zeitschrift Führung + Organisation, 71*(1), 40–52.

Hinterhuber, H. H. (2003a). Die Bedeutung von Leadership für die strategische Unternehmensführung. In M. Ringlstetter, H. Henzler & M. Mirow (Eds.), *Perspektiven der Strategischen Unternehmensführung. Theorien – Konzepte – Anwendungen* (pp. 255–276). Wiesbaden: Gabler Verlag.

Hinterhuber, H. H. (2003b). *Leadership.* Frankfurt am Main: FAZ Institut für Management.

Hinterhuber, H. H. (2004a). Strategische Unternehmensführung, Volume 1: Strategisches Denken (7th ed.). Berlin, NY: De Gruyter.

——. Strategische Unternehmensführung, Volume 2, Strategisches Handeln (7th ed.). Berlin, NY: Walter deGruyter Verlag.

Hinterhuber, H. H., Friedrich, S. A., & Krauthammer, E. (2001). Leadership als Weltanschauung? Aufgeschlossene Führungskräfte schaffen offene Unternehmen. In H. H. Hinterhuber & H. K. Stahl (Eds.), *Fallen die Unternehmensgrenzen? Beiträge zur Auenorientierung der Unternehmensführung* (Vol. 3, pp. 129–143). Renningen-Malmsheim: Expert-Verlag.

Hinterhuber, H. H., Handlbauer, G., & Matzler, K. (2003). *Kundenzufriedenheit durch Kernkompetenzen. Eigene Potentiale erkennen, entwickeln, umsetzen* (2nd ed.). Wiesbaden: Gabler Verlag.

Hinterhuber, H. H., & Krauthammer, E. (1998). The leadership wheel: The tasks entrepreneurs and senior executives cannot delegate. *Strategic Change, 7*(3), 149–162.

Hinterhuber, H. H. & Krauthammer, E. (2002). Leadership – mehr als Management (3). Wiesbaden: Gabler Verlag.

Hinterhuber, H. H., & Raich, M. (2006). Leadership als zentrale Kompetenz von und in Unternehmen. In H. Bruch, S. Krummaker & B. Vogel (Eds.), *Leadership – Best Practices und Trends* (pp. 49–56). Wiesbaden: Gabler Verlag.

Hinterhuber, H. H., & Renzl, B. (2004). Der Unternehmer als Innovator und Erkenntnistheoretiker. In E. Schwarz (Ed.), *Nachhaltiges innovations management* (pp. 3–28). Wiesbaden: Gabler Verlag.

Hinterhuber, H. H., Renzl, B., & Matzler, K. (2006). The leadership company–leadership as core competency in the firm of the future. In T. del Val (Ed.), Economy, entrepreneurship, science and society in the XXI century: Díaz de Santos, Piramide oder die Universität.

Hinterhuber, H. H., & Rothenberger, S. (2006). Führung und Strategie verbinden. *Frankfurter Allgemeine Zeitung* (06.02.2006).

Hinterhuber, H. H., & Stadler, C. (2006). Leadership and strategy as intangible assets. In B. Renzl, K. Matzler & H. H. Hinterhuber (Eds.), *The future of knowledge management* (pp. 237–253). Houndmills, Basingstoke, Hampshire, New York: Palgrave Macmillan.

Hitt, M. A., Ireland, R. D., & Hoskisson, R. E. (2005). *Strategic management. Competitiveness and globalization*. Mason, Ohio: Thompson South-Western.

Hollensen, J. (2003). *Marketing management. A relationship approach*. Edinburgh Gate: Pearson Education Limited.

Hulland, J. (1999). Use of partial least squares (PLS) in strategic management research: A review of four recent studies. *Strategic Management Journal, 20*(2), 195–204.

Hunt, S. D., & Morgan, R. M. (1995). The comparative advantage theory of competition. *Journal of Marketing, 59*(2), 1–15.

Huston, L., & Sakkab, N. (2006, August). Wie Procter & Gamble zu neuer Kreativität fand. *Harvard Business Manager*, 21–31.

Hutzschenreuter, T. (2005, November). Wachstum ist kein Allheilmittel. *Harvard Business Manager*, 104–111.

Inkpen, A., & Tsang, E. W. K. (2005). Social capital, networks, and knowledge transfer. *Academy of Management Review, 30*(1), 146–165.

Jarvis, C. B., MackKenzie, S. B., & Podsakoff, P. M. (2003, September). A critical review of construct indicators and measurement model misspecification in marketing and consumer research. *Journal of Consumer Research, 30*, 199–218.

Kajüter, P. (2005, Februar). Kostenmanagement in der deutschen Unternehmenspraxis. *Zeitschrift für betriebswirtschaftliche Forschung und Praxis, 57*, 79–100.

Kano, N. (1984). Attractive Quality and Must Be Quality. *Hinshitsu (Quality), 14*(2), 147–156 (in Japanisch).

Kaplan, R. S., & Norton, D. P. (1997). *Balanced scorecard. Strategien erfolgreich umsetzen*. Stuttgart: Schäffer-Poeschel Verlag.

Kelley, R. (1990). The gold collar worker – harnessing the brainpower of the new workforce. Reading, Mass.: Addison-Wesley.

Khatri, N., & Ng, H. A. (2000). The role of intuition in strategic decision making. *Human Relations, 53*(1), 57–86.

Kieser, A. (2002). Downsizing – eine vernünftige Strategie. *Harvard Business Manager, 24*(2), 30–39.

Kirby, J. (2005, November). Auf der Suche nach der Weltformel. *Harvard Business Manager*, 92–103.

Kirzner, I. M. (1980). The primacy of entrepreneurial discovery. In I. o. E. Affairs (Ed.), Prime Mover of Progress (Readings 23, pp. 3–30). London: I.E.A.

Koch, J. (2006). Der gefährliche Pfad des Erfolges. *Harvard Business Manager, 28*(1), 97–102.

Koen, C. I. (2005). *Comparative international management*. London: McGrawHill.

Kohli, A. K., Jaworksi, B. J., & Kumar, A. (1993, November). MARKOR: A measure of market orientation. *Journal of Marketing Research, 30*, 467–477.

Kohli, A. K., & Jaworski, B. J. (1990). Market orientation. The construct, research propositions, and managerial implications. *Journal of Marketing, 54*, 1–18.

Kordupleski, R. E., Rust, R. T., & Zahorik, A. (1994). Qualitätsmanager vergessen zu oft den Kunden. *Harvard Business Manager* (1), 65–72.

LeDoux, J. (1996). *The emotional brain: The mysterious underpinning of emotional life*. New York: Simon & Schuster.

Leonard-Barton, D. (1992, Summer). Core capabilities and core rigidities: A paradox in managing new product development. *Strategic Management Journal, 13*, 111–125.

Lev, B. (1999, February). Seeing is believing. *CFO Magazine*.

Loppow, B. (1997). Skifahren: Die neuen Carver sollen den Skifahrern völlig neue Kurvengefühle vermitteln. Der Kniff mit der Kante. *Die Zeit online*, http://www.zeit.de/archiv/1997/1907/carver.txt.19970207.xml?page=all.

Lorange, P. (1998). Strategy implementation: The new realities. *Long Range Planning, 31*(1), 18–29.

Lorange, P. (2005). Memo to marketing. *Sloan Management Review, 46*(2), 16–20.

Magretta, J. (2002). *Basic management*. Munich: dtv.

Malik, F. (2002). *Die neue Corporate Governance* (3rd ed.). Frankfurt: Frankfurter Allgemeine Buch.

Malik, F. (2005). *Management. Das A und O des Handwerks. Volume 1*. Frankfurt am Main: Frankfurter Allgemeine Buch.

Matzler, K. (2000). Customer Value Management. *Die Unternehmung, 54*(4), 289–307.

Matzler, K. (2001). Konsequente Kundenorientierung von Bankdienstleistungen durch Customer Value-Strategien. *Österreichisches BankArchiv* (4), 285–294.

Matzler, K. (2003). Preiszufriedenheit. In H. Diller & A. Herrmann (Eds.), *Handbuch Preismanagement* (pp. 303–328). Wiesbaden: Gabler Verlag.

Matzler, K., & Bailom, F. (2006). Messung von Kundenzufriedenheit. In H. H. Hinterhuber & K. Matzler (Eds.), *Kundenorientierte Unternehmensführung* (5th ed., pp. 241–270). Wiesbaden: Gabler Verlag.

Matzler, K., Bailom, F., Hinterhuber, H. H., Renzl, B., & Pichler, J. (2004). The asymmetric relationship between attribute level performance and overall customer satisfaction: A reconsideration of the importance-performance analyses. *Industrial Marketing Management, 33*(4), 271–277.

Matzler, K., Bailom, F., Tschemernjak, D., Anschober, M., & Hinterhuber, H. H. (2005). Kostensenkungsprogramme in der Praxis: Ergebnisse einer Managerbefragung. *Der Controlling-Berater, 11*(5), 723–738.

Matzler, K., & Fässler, R. (2004). Kundenorientierung: Steigerung der Kundenzufriedenheit durch Prozess-Controlling. *Der Controlling-Berater* (5), 627–649.

Matzler, K., Fuchs, M., Binder, H. J., & Leihs, H. (2005). Asymmetrische Effekte bei der Entstehung von Kundenzufriedenheit: Konsequenzen für die Importance-Performance Analyse. *Zeitschrift für Betriebswirtschaft, 75*(3), 299–317.

Matzler, K., Fuchs, M. & Schubert, A. K. (2004). Employee Satisfaction: Does Kano's Model Apply? *Total Quality Management and Business Excellence, 15*(9–10), 1179–1198.

Matzler, K., & Hinterhuber, H. H. (1998). How to make product development projects more successful by integrating Kano's model of customer satisfaction into quality function deployment. *Technovation, 18*(1), 25–38.

Matzler, K., Hinterhuber, H. H., Bailom, F., & Sauerwein, E. (1996). How to delight your customers. *Journal of Product and Band Management, 5*(2), 6–18.

Matzler, K., Pechlaner, H., & Kohl, M. (2000). Formulierung von Servicestandards für touristische Dienstleistungen und Überprüfung durch den Einsatz von "Mystery Guests". *Tourismus Journal, 4*(2), 157–176.

Matzler, K., & Renzl, B. (2007). Assessing asymmetric effects in the formation of employee satisfaction. *Tourism Management 28*(4), 1093–1103.

Matzler, K., Renzl, B., & Rothenberger, S. (2004). Unternehmenskultur und Innovationserfolg in Klein- und Mittelunternehmen: Ergebnisse einer empirischen Studie. In P. Tschurtschenthaler, H. Pechlaner, M. Peters, B. Pikkemaat & M. Fuchs (Eds.), *Erfolg durch Innovation* (pp. 277–290). Wiesbaden: Gabler Verlag.

Matzler, K., Rier, M., Hinterhuber, H. H., Renzl, B., & Stadler, C. (2005). Methods and concepts in management: Significance, satisfaction and suggestions for further research – perspective from Germany, Austria and Switzerland. *Strategic Change, 14*, 1–13.

Matzler, K., & Sauerwein, E. (2002). The factor structure of customer satisfaction: An empirical test of the importance grid and the penalty-reward-contrast analysis. *International Journal of Service Industry Management, 13*(4), 314–332.

Matzler, K., Sauerwein, E., & Heischmidt, K. A. (2003). Importance-performance analysis revisited: The role of the factor structure of customer satisfaction. *The Service Industries Journal, 23*(2), pp. 112–129.

Matzler, K., Sauerwein, E., & Stark, C. (2005). Methoden zur Identifikation von Basis-, Leistungs- und Begeisterungsfaktoren. In H. H. Hinterhuber & K. Matzler (Eds.), *Kundenorientierte Unternehmensführung* (5th ed., pp. 289–313). Wiesbaden: Gabler Verlag.

Matzler, K., Stahl, H. K., & Hinterhuber, H. H. (2006). Die Customer-based View der Unternehmung. In H. H. Hinterhuber & K. Matzler (Eds.), *Kundenorientierte Unternehmensführung: Kundenorientierung – Kundenzufriedenheit – Kundenbindung* (5th ed., pp. 3–31). Wiesbaden: Gabler Verlag.

McCarthy, D. J. (2000). View from the top: Henry Mintzberg on strategy and management. *Academy of Management Executive, 14*(3), 31–42.

McGahan, A. M., & Porter, M. (1997). How much does industry matter, really? *Strategic Management Journal, 18*(1), 15–30.

Miller, C. C., & Ireland, R. D. (2005). Intuition in strategic decision making. Friend or foe in the fast-pased 21st century? *Academy of Management Executive, 19*(1), 19–30.

Mintzberg, H., Simons, R., & Basul, K. (2002). Beyond Selfishness. *Sloan Management Review, 44*(1), 67–74.

Mirow, M. (1999). Innovation als strategische chance. In N. Franke & C.-F. von Braun (Eds.), Innovationsforschung und Technologiemanagement (pp. 481–492). Berlin/Heidelberg.

Mirow, M. (2003). Wertsteigerung durch Innovation. In H. Henzler, M. Mirow & M. Ringlstetter (Eds.), Perspektiven der strategischen Unternehmensführung – Theorien, Konzepte, Anwendungen (pp. 331–346). Wiesbaden: Gabler Verlag.

Müller-Stewens, G., & Lechner, C. (2005). *Strategisches Management – Wie strategische Initiativen zum Wandel führen* (3rd ed.). Stuttgart: Schäffer-Poeschel.

Nahapiet, J., & Goshal, S. (1998). Social Capital, Intellectual Capital and the Organizational Advantage. *Academy of Management Review, 23*(2), 242–266.

Nicolai, A., & Kieser, A. (2002). Trotz eklatanter Erfolglosigkeit: Die Erfolgsfaktorenforschung weiter auf Erfolgskurs. *Die Betriebswirtschaft, 62*, 579–596.

Nohria, N., Joyce, W. F., & Roberson, B. (2003). What really Works: The 4+2 formula for sustained business success. New York: Harper Collins Publishers.

N. N. (2002, April). Aktienoptionen werden integraler Vergütungsbestandteil. *Frankfurter Allgemeine Zeitung* (Nr. 92), p. 25.

Peters, T. J., & Waterman, R. H. J. (1982). *In search of excellence*. New York: Harper Business Essentials.

Pfeffer, J., & Sutton, R. I. (2006, April). Management by Fakten. *Harvard Business Manager*, 44–63.

Pircher-Friedrich, A. (2001). *Sinn-orientierte Führung in Dienstleistungsunternehmen*. Augsburg: Ziel Hochschulschriften.

Porter, M. (1997). Nur Strategie sichert auf Dauer hohe Erträge. *Harvard Business Manager* (3), 42–58.

Porter, M. E. (1980). Competitive strategy – techniques for analyzing industries and competitors. New York: The Free Press.

Porter, M. E. (1985). Competitive advantage – creating and sustaining superior performance. New York: Free Press.

Prahalad, C. K., & Hamel, G. (1990). The core competence of the corporation. *Harvard Business Review, 68*(3), 79–91.

Prietula, M. J., & Simon, H. A. (1989). The expert in your midst. *Harvard Business Review, 67*(1), 120–124.

Priewe, J. (1998). *Wein. Die neue groe Schule*. Munich: Verlag Zabert Sandmann.

Putnam, R. (1993). *Making democracy work: Civic traditions in modern Italy*. Princeton: Princeton University Press.

Putnam, R. (2000). *Bowling alone: The collapse and revival of the American Community*. New York: Simon & Schuster.

Quinn, R. E. (1988). *Beyond rational management*. San Francisco: Joessey-Bass.

Rachman, G. (1999, December 18). The globe in the glass. *Economist*, 91.

Raich, M. (2005). *Führungsprozesse. Eine ganzheitliche Sicht von Führung*. Wiesbaden: DUV.

Rappaport, A. (1981, May–June). Selecting strategies that create shareholder value. *Harvard Business Review*, 139–149.

Rappaport, A. (1986). *Creating shareholder value: The new standard for business performance*. New York: The Free Press.

Reichwald, R., & Piller, F. (2006). *Interaktive Wertschöpfung*. Wiesbaden: Gabler Verlag.

Renzl, B. (2003a). Mitarbeiter als Wissensressource. In K. Matzler, H. Pechlaner & B. Renzl (Eds.), *Werte schaffen – Perspektiven einer stakeholderorientierten Unternehmensführung* (pp. 319–334). Wiesbaden: Gabler Verlag.

Renzl, B. (2003b). *Wissensbasierte Interaktion – Selbst-evolvierende Wissensströme in Unternehmen*. Wiesbaden: Deutscher Universitäts-Verlag.

Rigby, D. K., Reichheld, F. F., & Schefter, P. (2002). Customer Relationship Management – Wie Sie die vier gröten Fehler vermeiden. *Harvard Business Manager, 24*(4), 55–63.

Rogers, E. M. (1962). *Diffusion of innovations*. New York: Free Press.

Rumelt, R. P. (1991). Does industry matter much? *Strategic Management Journal, 12*(1), 167–185.

Sadler-Smith, E., & Shefy, E. (2004). The intuitive executive: Understanding and applying "gut feel" in decision-making. *Academy of Management Executive, 18*(4), 76–91.

Sawhney, M., Prandelli, E., & Verona, G. (2003). The power of innomediation. *MIT Sloan Management Review, 44*(2), 77–82.

Schein, E. (1992). *Organizational culture and leadership* (2nd ed.). San Francisco: Joessey-Bass.

Schmid, F. W. (2005, April). Der Manager-Macher. *Harvard Business Manager, 27*, 101–106.

Schredelseker, K. (2003). Zwölf Missverständnisse zum Shareholder Value aus finanzwirtschaftlicher Sicht. In K. Matzler, H. Pechlaner & B. Renzl (Eds.), *Werte schaffen. Perspektiven einer stakeholderorientierten Unternehmensführung* (pp. 99–123). Wiesbaden: Gabler Verlag.

Schumpeter, J. (1987). Theorie der wirtschaftlichen Entwicklung (7th ed., unveränderter Nachdruck der 1934 erschienenen 4th ed.). Berlin: Duncker & Humblot.

Scott, B. R., & Matthews, J. L. (2002). "One country, two systems?" Italy and the Mezzogiorno (B). *Harvard Business School Case*, 9-702-097.

Senge, P. M. (1996). *Die fünfte Disziplin – Kunst und Praxis der lernenden Organisation* (3rd ed.). Stuttgart: Klett-Cotta.

Siemens, W. V. (1966). *Lebenserinnerungen*. Munich: Piper-Verlag.

Simon, H. (1996). *Die heimlichen Gewinner*. Frankfurt: Campus Verlag.

Simon, H. (1999). Hidden Champions: Lessons from over 500 world's best unknown companies. Boston: Harvard Business School Press.

Simon, H. A. (1987, February). Making management decision: The role of intuition and emotion. *Academy of Management Executive* (1), 57–64.

Sinclair, M., & Askhanasy, N. M. (2005). Intuition. Myth or decision-making tool? *Management Learning, 36*(3), 353–370.

Sirisha, D., & Dutta, S. (2002). GE and Jack Welch. *ICFAI Center for Management Research Case,* No 402-006-1.

Sitkin, S. B. (1992). Learning through failure: The strategy of small losses. *Research in organizational behavior, 14,* 231–266.

Sommer, C. (2005). Zeichen am Himmel. *Brand Eins* 7 (3), 24–36.

Stadler, C., & Hinterhuber, H. H. (2005). Shell, Siemens and DaimlerChrysler: Leading change in companies with strong value. *Long Range Planning, 38*(5), 467–484.

Tallman, S., & Fladmore-Lindquist, K. (2002). Internationalization, globalization, and capability-based strategy. *California Management Review, 45*(1), 116–135.

Taylor, B. (1995). The New Strategic Leadership – Driving Change, Getting Results. *Long Range Planning, 28*(5), 71–81.

Teece, D. J., Pisano, G., & Shuen, A. (1997). Dynamic Capabilities and Strategic Management. *Strategic Management Journal, 18*(7), 509–533.

Tellis, G. J., & Golder, P. N. (1996, Winter). First to market, first to fail? Real causes of enduring market leadership. *Sloan Management Review*, 65–75.

Ullrich, C. (2000). Objektiv betrachtet. *Brand Eins* 2 (4).

von Hippel, E. (1988). *The sources of innovation*. New York: Oxford University Press.

von Hippel, E. (2005). *Democratizing innovation*. Cambridge, London: The MIT Press.

von Krogh, G. (2003). Open-source software development. *MIT Sloan Management Review, 44*(3), 14–18.

Waldman, D. A., Ramirez, G. G., House, R., & Puranam, P. (2001). Does leadership matter? CEO leadership attributes and profitability under conditions of perceived environmental uncertainty. *Academy of Management Journal, 44*(1), 134–143.

Wang, C. L., & Ahmed, P. K. (2004). The development and validation of the organizational innovativeness construct using confirmatory factor analysis. *European Journal of Innovation Management, 7*(4), 303–313.

Wernerfelt, B. (1984). A Resource-based View of the Firm. *Strategic Management Journal, 5*(2), 171–180.

Wesselhöft, P. (2006). Achtung, Baustelle! *McK Wissen, 6*(17), 8–11.

Willenbrock, H. (2005). Die Spur der Steine. *Brand Eins, 6*(3),102–106.

Wozny, M. (1999). GE's two-decade transformation: Jack Welch's leadership. *Harvard Business School Case*, 399–150.

Xenophon. (1992). *Ökonomische Schriften*. Berlin: Akademie Verlag.

Zeilinger, A. (2002). Dinge, die ohne Grund geschehen. Protokoll der Academy of Life, published in the *Wiener Zeitung* (12./13. Juli).

Index